A Marriage WITHOUT REGRETS

KAY ARTHUR

HARVEST HOUSE™ PUBLISHERS

EUGENE, OREGON

Cover by Koechel Peterson & Associates, Inc., Minneapolis, Minnesota

A MARRIAGE WITHOUT REGRETS
Copyright © 2000 by Kay Arthur
Published by Harvest House Publishers
Eugene, Oregon, 97402

Arthur, Kay, 1933–
    Marriage without regrets / by Kay Arthur.
        p. cm.
    ISBN 1-56507-451-3 (Hardcover edition)
    ISBN 1-7369-0440-9 (Trade edition)
    1. Marraige—Religious aspects—Christianity. 2. Spouses—Religious life. I. Title.
    BV4596.M3A78   1999
    248.4—dc21   99-14080
                                                                                             CIP

02   03   04   05   06   / VP-CF /   10   9   8   7   6   5   4   3

This is dedicated to our precious family—

Our sons and their wives...
our grandchildren
and their children to come...

With the fervent prayer
that your lives and your marriages
will give a true estimate
of the One from whom every family in
heaven and on earth
derives its name.....

Remember, precious ones,
His grace is sufficient...
and
His power is perfected in our weaknesses.

May you say with Paul,
"By the grace of God, I am what I am,
and His grace was not poured out on me in vain...
but I labored more than them all—
Yet not me, but the grace of God in me."

Acknowledgments

God never intended us to do it all by ourselves, to do His work all alone.

He gives us spiritual gifts, but not all of them.

We are not complete in and of ourselves and that is why He placed us in the body, one member among many…and only One receiving the glory, our precious Lord and Savior Jesus Christ.

How thankful I am for my Harvest House family and for all each one of you do to help me produce a book and get it to the bookstore. Bob Hawkins, Jr. sets the standard as a man of integrity, a man true to his word—and his example permeates throughout the organization.

Carolyn, LaRae, dear brother Larry Libby, Stella, and my patient husband, Jack—thank you—each one of you—for your time, gifts, talents, and abilities that contributed to this book. You were with me all the way, encouraging me in my writing. My prayer is that many marriages and homes will become lighthouses of truth in these dark days as a result of your labors of love.

John 15:16

CONTENTS

A Fresh Challenge

Therefore I urge you, brethren, by the mercies of God, to present your bodies a living and holy sacrifice, acceptable to God, which is your spiritual service of worship. And do not be conformed to this world, but be transformed by the renewing of your mind, so that you may prove what the will of God is, that which is good and acceptable and perfect (Romans 12:1,2).

Have you ever driven at night across the wide prairies of the American Midwest? Maybe you're somewhere in the middle of Nebraska, or crossing the dark, lonely miles of Montana or South Dakota. Sipping black coffee from an insulated cup, you drive for what seems like hours without seeing a light. All you have is the soft glow from your dashboard, the pool of your headlights out front, and maybe the glint of stars up in that great empty sky overhead.

You feel swallowed up in the darkness, like a little rowboat out alone on the wide Atlantic. Then, way, way off to the left or right of the highway, you see something.

A tiny glimmer.

One little square of light in a sea of inky blackness.

It's so far away it may be no more than a winking pinpoint, but it attracts your attention and interest. After miles and miles of weary darkness, it draws your eyes like a magnet. *(What else is there to look at?)*

As you draw nearer, you conclude that it's coming from a little farmhouse, surrounded by acres and acres of open pastureland. Staring at that little fleck of gold on the bosom of the dark night, you find yourself wondering:

- Is someone up late, going over the farm's financial status, bills, or balancing the checkbook?

- Is the family watching an old movie on TV?

- Is there a croupy child in the home needing attention?

- Is Grampa up late, drinking a glass of warm milk because he can't sleep?

- Is there a teenager out on a late date somewhere in town, and Mom and Dad have left a light burning to guide the homeward journey?

You can't help but feel a sense of longing as you drive by. No one on that little farm realizes you exist. If they could even hear you across the miles, it would be nothing more than the faraway drone of a passing car. All too soon, you leave that welcome little light behind and the mystery remains unsolved. You'll never know who lives within the bounds of that light. The night swallows you up again in a darkness so complete you begin to wonder if the light had really been there at all.

Dear friend, I believe that happy Christian marriages and homes can be just like that farmhouse light on a midnight prairie. If you build a loving marriage and a home with light and laughter brightening everything inside its walls, there will be those who see. There will be those passing by in the darkness who will note the contrast. And they will want what you have found.

As our world grows darker every day before our Lord's return, many in our culture scorn and mock Christian family values. In 2 Timothy 3:1-5, Paul clearly warned that "difficult times" were coming in the last days. People will be "lovers of self, lovers of money, boastful, arrogant, revilers, disobedient to parents, ungrateful, unholy, unloving, irreconcilable, malicious gossips, without self-control, brutal, haters of good, treacherous, reckless, conceited, lovers of pleasure rather than lovers of God." These are people—many of them our neighbors, our associates at work, even members of our own extended family—who have no time for God and no desire to understand His commands and precepts.

Yet even so…even to these folks, the darkness can grow oppressive. And there is something wonderful about a Christian marriage, something that draws a curious eye in this cynical age. There's a radiance there…a light that shines through the hard-edged darkness of a skeptical culture. No matter how humble the Christian home, there's something about the light shining through its windows that creates a longing in weary hearts. Despite themselves, people are attracted by a home that radiates the love of Christ.

You may never know who observes the light shining from your home. The observers may seem as distant and anonymous as cars driving by on the highway at night.

Yet there are those who watch.

There are those who wonder.

There are those who catch a glimmer of the light that is Jesus Christ—and it creates a wistful, wondering hunger and yearning deep within them.

A Culture Within a Culture

Sometimes in my teaching, I describe marriage based on the precepts of God's Word as a "culture within a culture." We are living in a day and time when marriage is devalued, minimized, trivialized, and even scorned. It is an era of history when marriage vows are shallow and fragile and may be quickly abandoned for any vague, emotional reason—or for no reason at all. We are living in a world where the truths and principles of God's eternal Word are rejected, mocked, belittled, or just plain ignored.

That's the culture.

That's where you and I live today.

In years past, preachers and Bible teachers used to warn that our nation was entering twilight—that the light was beginning to fade. Now it seems more like we're in the pitch-black of midnight.

Nevertheless, a Christian marriage based on the precepts of God's Word can become a mini-culture of its own that refuses to be conformed to the larger culture. It resists being assimilated or swallowed up by the darkness, no matter how great and prevailing that blackness may be. It is so strong, so resilient, so compelling that it both impacts and influences those who observe it. Those who drive by on the dark highways see its light from afar and wonder what it's all about.

Rather than being swallowed up by the darkness, that marriage, that home, becomes a radiant, shining light.

Those who create such homes declare, "The world around us may be going in this direction, but we're going another way. It may be fashionable—even the expected thing—to have both parents bringing home income, for the woman to work outside the home from the time her child is six weeks old, but we're going to put a higher priority on the care of our little ones. We are not going to be conformed to this world. We're not going to let the world squeeze us into its mold."

Rather than listening to the counsel of talk radio, magazines, or the neighbor over the fence, these stalwarts find out what God has to say about the role of a man and the role of a woman in marriage. They discover what God has to say about communication between husband and wife, about finances, about the sexual relationship, about the raising of children. They learn and put into practice the truths from His eternal Word so that their marriages will last a lifetime.

We can become these people, Beloved of God.

And then, at the end of time when we stand before the Lord as a wife or a husband, a mother or a father, we will have no regrets. We will have done our best, and we will have done it His way. It may not come out like a Hollywood production with a couple walking into the sunset with a great orchestral theme welling up all around us. It may not boast all the thrills and chills that romance authors like to portray in their novels. But we will have the peace, contentment, and satisfaction of knowing that we did it God's way.

In the end, our standard of success has to be *His* standard of success, not the world's!

God's Standard of Success

What is God's standard of success? It is obedience to His Word.

Just hours before Joshua was to lead the nation of Israel into Canaan, a land filled with great promise and great peril, the Lord gave him the following charge. His words continue to bring strong help to you and me as well.

> Be strong and very courageous; be careful to do according to all the law which Moses My servant commanded you; do not turn from it to the right or to the left, so that you may have success wherever you go. This book of the law shall not depart from your mouth, but you shall meditate on it day and night, so that you may be careful to do according to all that is written in it; for then you will make your way prosperous, and then you will have success. Have I not commanded you? Be strong and courageous! Do not tremble or be dismayed, for the LORD your God is with you wherever you go (Joshua 1:7-9).

The Lord was saying to Joshua, "Do you want to succeed in this endeavor? Do you want to conquer territory for Me in a land filled with giants and people who hate the very mention of My name? Then you will need to invest time thinking about My Word. Don't let it go in one ear and out the other. Think about it. Ponder its logic. Consider its promises. Meditate on the One behind every word of it. Remember, it is *My* Word, not man's word. It is for all seasons, all times, all cultures, all situations, all ages, all people. It doesn't alter; it doesn't change. It is never out of date and never out of fashion. Remember that, Joshua. Meditate on these things and put them into practice. And then you will have success."

The book you hold in your hands is about success in marriage...about building a marriage without regrets. To find success, we must do precisely as the Lord told Joshua on the east side of the

Jordan: *We must meditate on God's commands and precepts concerning marriage.*

He has not left us in the dark! In His timeless Word, God has given us wonderful specifics about the role of the man and the role of the woman...about how to bring up our children...about handling finances...about responding correctly in the sexual relationship...about communication between husband and wife...and even about divorce and remarriage.

The people of Israel, remember, were about to enter a culture completely hostile to everything God had taught them in His Word. The nations in that land sacrificed their children to idols. They engaged in every imaginable sexual perversion. It was a culture ripe for the judgment of God. For families to succeed in such an oppressive environment would require two very important things: a wholehearted commitment to know and follow God's Word and courage.

Courage to go God's way when everyone else was going the other way.

Courage to believe God would provide and protect in an aggressive, intimidating culture.

Courage to do the right thing even when cutting cross-grain against outward pressures—and even inward desires.

It really comes down to a choice, doesn't it? In his final days, Joshua verbalized that choice very clearly to the people. "If it is disagreeable in your sight to serve the LORD," he told them, "choose for yourselves today whom you will serve: whether the gods which your fathers served which were beyond the River, or the gods of the Amorites in whose land you are living; but as for me and my house, we will serve the LORD" (Joshua 24:15).

It's the same for you and me in our marriages and homes. We may find it disagreeable or old-fashioned or inconvenient or financially limiting to pursue God's precepts for the home. We may find it much easier simply to conform to the world's standards and go along with the flow. But in the end, Beloved, that choice will bring regrets. When we stand before Jesus Christ, we will be compelled to look back over a lifetime of missed opportunities, needless suffering, and wasted potential.

But if we choose with Joshua—if we say, "As for me and my house, we will serve the Lord"—we will find ourselves on a pathway that invites God's richest blessings. We will enjoy His peace, His power, His presence, and His provision—even through the darkest days and deepest trials.

And when we stand before our Lord, there will be joy...with no regrets.

This book can help you start on that journey.

CHAPTER 1

A MARRIAGE
WITHOUT REGRETS

⚬❈⚬

MY PLATINUM WEDDING BAND ROLLED ROUND and round on the recreation room floor. Tom dropped to his hands and knees, looking for the diamond engagement ring I had thrown at the same time.

I watched him in the shadows, groping for the rings. *That's all he cares about?* I asked myself. *The rings? Doesn't he know what's just happened? I've taken off my wedding band! Doesn't he realize—hasn't it occurred to him—that it has never been off my hand since the day of our wedding?*

I heard him murmur from the floor, "That's a very expensive diamond."

Feeling like a detached spectator, I stood there watching him. No crying. No screaming. No hysteria. I was beyond all that. In fact, I felt nothing. I might as well have been chiseled from a block of ice. As far as I was concerned, the marriage was over.

The quarrel had begun upstairs in our bedroom. For the first time in the six years of our marriage, Tom had slapped me across the face. I had cut him down with yet another hateful remark, and he had lost control. As the warm, salty blood from my nose touched my lips, I felt strangely calm—and ice cold. "It's over, Tom. You've done it." I grabbed my pillow, tore a blanket off the bed, and headed for the rec room couch. We were now downstairs, and I didn't intend to go back up those stairs. Ever. Tom followed immediately, pleading, his eyes wide with panic. It wasn't what he wanted. He "hadn't meant to hurt me." He'd "just lost his head."

I wasn't listening. He might as well have been talking to the wall.

In Retrospect

I've had lots of time to look back on that terrible night. In later years, I wondered if Tom at that moment was reliving the horror of an incident from his boyhood—a night when his mother stormed out of his parents' bedroom never to return. Was this why my strong husband followed me downstairs, pleading? Did that explain the fear in his eyes? Was he remembering the panic and stress of his boyhood, when he sat on the stairway in the darkness listening to his parents scream bitter words at one another? Was he recalling the inevitable drinking sprees, the cold hostility of a couple who continued to live under the same roof but in separate bedrooms the rest of their lives? Was he remembering the hatred and animosity—and the humiliation—when the drunken arguments spilled out in front of friends and guests? Could he have been wondering what would become of our two precious sons he had tucked in bed that night while I was out modeling in a swank restaurant?

I don't know what Tom was thinking. At the time, I really didn't care. Nor did I stop to consider how a divorce might hurt our young boys. At the time, I was totally focused on me—too hurt, disappointed, and angry to give those things a second thought. I just wanted out of that marriage, and the quicker the better.

Tom slept alone that night. For the first time in our marriage, I willfully moved out of our bedroom. The next day we called our priest. He came over, listened to our sad tale, and told us he thought it would be best for us to separate.

That was that.

No words of counsel, no advice from Scripture, and not a single word uttered in prayer. He never talked about how to make our marriage work, never explained what God said about marriage, never mentioned the power, hope, and healing available in Jesus Christ, and never asked us to consider the effect it might have on our sons. In his mind it was cut and dried: We were unhappy and unfulfilled, so we ought to go our separate ways.

I suppose that was what I had wanted to hear, and yet...it was still a bit of a shock. Somehow, I'd never thought it would come to this.

What Happened to the Dreams?

All through my growing up years, I had wanted only one thing: to be divinely in love, happily married, raise wonderful children, and live the good life. When I was in nursing school and met Tom, I was just sure that's how it was going to be. He would succeed in his career, and I would excel as a homemaker. We would go to church, someday belong to the country club, and live just like "Father Knows Best" or "Ozzie and Harriet." I wanted a good marriage—one like my parents had.

I never once heard Mom and Dad quarrel. If they ever spoke cross words, it was never in my presence. What I do remember is hearing Mom call from the kitchen, "I love you, Jack!" And I remember Daddy walking by, patting her on the bottom and saying, "I love you, Leah."

Sometimes when a familiar tune would come on the radio, my mother would leave the kitchen, wiping her hands on her apron, and look invitingly at my father—who never needed a second invitation. Daddy would take her in his arms, and they'd dance from the kitchen to the living room. Every now and then he'd hold her at arm's length, then dramatically sweep her back into his embrace...just like Fred Astaire and Ginger Rogers in the movies. After I thought they'd had sufficient time to be mushy, I'd tap Mother on the shoulder and cut in to dance with Daddy.

It was a Pollyanna world, and I loved every moment of it. *That* was what I wanted. *That* was what I dreamed of. It was what my first-grade readers promised in their stilted words and primary colors. "Run, Jane, run. Run, Spot, run. See Daddy come. See Daddy come." And there in the picture was Daddy coming home to a hero's welcome, hat on his head, tie loosened, briefcase in his hand, a happy family waiting to greet him.

But it wasn't like that for me. It hadn't turned out that way at all—and I couldn't understand why. It had all begun with such promise.

When I first met Tom, it was as though he stepped right out of my dreams. Of all the Phi Deltas I dated while cheerleading for Case Institute of Technology in Cleveland, Ohio, I knew that this tall, handsome basketball star was "The One."

We talked about God on our very first date. Our values seemed to mesh perfectly. Here was a man with depth of character, nobility of purpose, and a firm set of principles. I knew instinctively that Tom would always be faithful to me.

He was a gentleman—polished, confident, well-dressed. He knew his way around the country clubs, cut a handsome figure in a dinner jacket on the dance floor, and never bragged about his accomplishments. He never told me he'd been offered professional baseball contracts to pitch for the Yankees, Phillies, Pirates, and Indians. Nor was I aware that Casey Stengal had personally pursued Tom with an extraordinary contract. (I discovered these things only when Tom's mother showed me a scrapbook she had kept on her son.) He never told me of his academic achievements, or that his classmates in University School had voted him "Most Likely to Succeed." Tom abhorred bragging—and visibly cringed at the way his father flashed his money, tipping all those who called out his name as he moved through the Lakewood Country Club or the Cleveland Athletic Club.

"Good evenin', Mr. Goetz."

"So good to see you, Mr. Goetz."

Dad Goetz had come up the hard way—and had made it! He was dear in his own special way, and I did love him. While he clearly relished all the attention his generosity brought, it made Tom wince.

When our engagement was announced, my picture appeared on the front page of *The Cleveland Plain Dealer*'s society section. Was I impressed! My family had never been "society." Tom and I flew off for a romantic honeymoon in Bermuda at the crown jewel of the hotels. I was ecstatic, absolutely elated. This was the honeymoon I'd dreamed of, had talked about in the nurses's dorm at Saint Luke's School of Nursing. We girls would curl up on our beds, hug our knees, and gab about marriage, and how wonderful it would be. We didn't talk about sex—although it was never far from our minds. Those things weren't openly discussed in our circles.

We simply dreamed of romance and talked about the relative merits of different negligees...red or black...slinky or sweet...satin or lace. In such a garment, we would offer to our husbands our virginity. It was a gift I vowed to keep for my husband long before I knew who he would be.

How quickly a lifetime of dreams can be deflated!

We arrived in Bermuda on the second night of our honeymoon. And there in that idyllic setting, my new husband sat me down, looked me in the eyes, and said, "Kay, you are now Mrs. Frank Thomas Goetz, Jr., and these are the things I don't like about you. I want them changed."

My bubble burst, pricked by those few devastating words. Words I could never imagine my father saying to my mother in a hundred years. Just that quickly, I wanted to run away. To erase the bad start and begin again. To reach for another chance at love. I suddenly realized the devastating truth: *I was not loved unconditionally; I was not adored. Tom wasn't even pleased with me!*

What a horrible, sinking feeling to realize I had made the biggest mistake of my life—and now I was trapped. Trapped forever because at that juncture of my life, divorce was simply not an option.

Now it was six years later and divorce definitely *was* part of my vocabulary. I wanted out of this roller-coaster marriage as quickly as possible. Oh, yes, there had been interludes of peace and a measure of happiness...interludes when Tom seemed to find himself and experience some contentment. In spite of myself, my hopes would soar again; I dared to dream that we might make a life of it after all. But then, with sickening suddenness, the roller coaster would plunge over the edge again, and Tom would plummet into depression. Again and again, I felt myself going down with him—falling, falling—with no strong arms to hold me. Was there any end to this nightmare ride? What would happen if I jumped out somewhere along the way and just brought all my disappointments to an end?

I hadn't realized Tom was manic-depressive. Even as a nurse, I'd totally missed it. All I knew was that I wanted out. Forget the girlhood dreams. Forget Pollyanna. Forget the society page. Forget "till death do us part." I would find someone else. I would have a marriage without regrets.

In spite of it all, I really had no other goal. My only ambition was to be loved and happily married.

Crucial Questions

What went wrong? What could I—we—have done differently?

As you read these words, you might find questions just like these on your mind. Maybe it's because you have a good marriage—and want to keep it that way. The dreams are still intact and you don't want anything to cast a shadow over your happiness. What can you learn from a book such as this? How can you make sure that no matter what happens, you will have no regrets when you stand before God?

Then, again, perhaps you've found yourself asking those questions about your own marriage. Life hasn't turned out the way you hoped and expected. Somewhere along the way, you came to the disconcerting realization that your "beloved" wasn't as charming or lovely as you'd once thought. Your marriage is "ho-hum," and you both know it. You exist together under the same roof and file a joint tax return, but there is precious little that is "joint" in your emotions, your dreams, your activities. For the most part, each of you goes your own separate way.

Maybe you're concerned because the passion and joy you knew at the beginning of your marriage has disappeared. The flame of love has so died that you can touch the coals without burning yourself. They're barely warm. You've fanned and fanned the fire, but to no avail. You're fanned out. You're perplexed, wondering if your marriage is salvageable or if you ought to just shovel up the embers, dump them in the garbage, and go looking for new wood.

Maybe the marriages of one of your children, some of your friends, and someone you're counseling are heading for the rocks. What do you tell them? How do you help them? How do you take what's wrong and turn it around? How do you help them work it out in a biblical way so that there are no regrets, no backlash that will bring them to their knees enslaved in regret?

How?

That, dear reader, is what this book is all about. There is one key reason why Tom and I got started off on the wrong foot in our marriage and ended up walking off the dance floor. There is a reason why divorce shattered our home and Tom ended up committing suicide. It is because each of us went into marriage with our own set of ideals and expectations without once bothering to find out what ideals, standards, and precepts *God* had set for the marriage relationship. I had my notions of what kind of a husband Tom should be, and he had some expectations about what kind of wife I should be.

But neither of us bothered to check with God.

Neither of us took the time to ask the Creator of human life and architect of marriage what *His* opinion might be.

We didn't begin our marriage by asking Him, and when things got rough and turned desperate, we didn't ask Him even then.

Tragically, it never dawned on either of us that God might have a design for husbands and wives, and a good plan to protect and bless our marriage.

The Design

These things are true for many Christian marriages today. We enter into the relationships with our own set of expectations and desires, and when our spouses don't live up to them, we find ourselves disappointed, hurt, frustrated—and maybe even looking for the back door. Sometimes it seems that the harder we try to improve our marriages, the worse matters become. And so we walk away…only to find that the nagging doubts and aching regrets are with us for the rest of our lives.

God designed marriage to be a permanent, meaningful, truly fulfilling, and—yes—*joyful* relationship. Yet if we don't know His plans, if we haven't cried out for His counsel, we're likely to miss that fulfillment.

Even if your mate insists on walking away, calling it quits, and abandoning you, you *still* need to understand God's precepts and alternatives for you. *What does the Word of God say?* That will always be a relevant question. Does the Bible guarantee that every marriage is salvageable? And if not, where does that leave you? Condemned to a lifetime of lonely singleness? Maybe yes, maybe no. It all depends on what God says. Either way, if you want peace of mind and quietness of heart which cannot be purchased by anything but obedience, you need to know how God's eternal Word speaks to your situation.

And it does. God's Word is alive and powerful, and like a powerful, radiant lamp it will roll back the shadows and show you where to turn, what to do, and how to weather any situation life may throw at you.

More than that, the Bible will show you how to live in such a way that you will one day stand before Jesus Christ as a valiant warrior with no regrets in your heart. Come what may, you will have the confidence that you have lived in obedience and have done all that could be done to make your marriage a success.

In a very real sense, this is a holy moment. If you choose to read this book and pursue the precepts of God's Word for your marriage, you're beginning down a path that will change your life and the lives of those in your family. The effects will reach into eternity.

If I were sitting beside you right now, Beloved, I would say, "Let's pray together." Can we do that right now—even through the pages of this book? Let's approach our loving Father together….

> *Father, we are about to broach a subject that is causing such distress and turmoil, such pain and disillusionment in so many lives these days. Hopes, dreams, and expectations of a good and happy marriage are being shattered daily. Marriages all around*

us seem to be failing, and we don't know what to do to help. Father, more than ever before, we need Your wisdom, Your insights, and Your counsel.

Thank You for assuring us that when we turn to You, rather than to the arm of flesh or the wisdom of man, You will guide our steps. When we trust in You, You will make us like a tree planted by streams of water, with green leaves and fruit even when drought withers all around. Your Word is truth!

Together, Father, we pray that you will lead and guide us into all truth. We want to know Your mind and Your heart. We want to be able to stand in the holy presence of our Lord Jesus Christ one day without regrets. You, Lord, are the One who created us male and female. You ordained marriage and called it a covenant relationship that must not be broken or violated. We long to love and be loved by our mates—to have wonderful, fulfilling marriages. And we are so thankful that you understand this longing, even when we can't put it into words.

Show us, Lord, what to do to make our marriages all that You intend them to be. Teach us Your timeless precepts about marriage, and we will walk in them, no matter what others may say or do. We thank You for Your assurance that "nothing is impossible with God." We cling to that assurance this day, Lord, and it is on this basis that we come to You in the name of the One who sits at Your right hand interceding on our behalf, Your Son and our own Savior, the Lord Jesus Christ. Amen.

CHAPTER 2

IS IT POSSIBLE TO LIVE HAPPILY EVER AFTER?

A<small>ND THEY ALL LIVED</small> happily ever after."

That's the way our storybooks end, isn't it? And isn't that what we all long for when we walk down the aisle, arm in arm, with our new matcs?

I certainly did, but then I've always been a romantic at heart. I grew up watching those happily-ever-after endings in the movies and on TV and reading about them in novels. Why couldn't I have one, too? *Was that too much to ask?*

What I had forgotten, until I wrote a novel of my own, is that the author can make the story turn out any way he or she chooses. Authors, after all, sit almost in the place of God, with the power of life and death in their pens, creating and designing men and women according to their desires. With a flick of the pen or a tap on the keyboard, they shape destinies, orchestrate events in characters' lives, and thread them through circumstances of their own devising.

What kind of a story was I living? What did I want out of life?

> I wanted a happy, wonderful marriage with a man who was head-over-heels in love with me…a man who adored me and intuitively knew how to meet my every need.

> I wanted a man who enjoyed the things I enjoy, longed to be with me, yet would give me space when I needed it.

> I wanted a good-looking, well-dressed man, who knew how to carry himself in every situation…a man for all occasions.

> I wanted a man who could take charge—but do it just like I would do it if I were in charge!

> I wanted a hard-working, diligent, capable man who would put me, family, and home before anything else.

> I wanted a man who was a great lover and knew how to romance me…learning my tastes, delighting me with surprises, and always telling me he loved me.

> I wanted a man that I could talk to for hours and hours—a man vitally interested in life.

After I came to Jesus Christ at the age of 29, I added to that wish list in a significant way.

> I wanted a man who loved God with a passion, a man of the Book who was totally sold out to God. I wanted a man who would give his life to be the husband God ordained him to be.

In all my dreaming and fantasizing, the emphasis was always on what *I* needed, what *I* wanted. *As my needs and wants were met,* I told myself, *I would respond to my mate accordingly.* He would love me unconditionally, and I would respond in kind.

It all sounded perfectly rational and reasonable to me.

But what would happen if he didn't respond that way? What would happen if this Prince Charming of my dreams didn't measure up to that list of cherished expectations? What would happen if *I* became a difficult person to live with? What would happen if selfishness clouded our horizons and anger and bitterness stole away our dreams? What if we found ourselves in great difficulty and confusion? What would sustain us then? Where would we turn?

The answer, Beloved, is always the same. We must go to the Word of God. We must search the pages of Scripture for His commands, insights, and precepts. Know it or not, believe it or not, this is precisely where you and I can discover the answer to every life situation. With every ounce of passion and confidence within me, I declare to you that the Bible is *the* book of life. It is the only book in the world that is absolute, pure, unadulterated truth. Within its pages are the very laws of life by which we gain understanding and the ability to discern right from wrong, good from evil. Its counsel can shine the light of truth on any situation in which we find ourselves, no matter how tangled or torn.

Everything to Gain

Do you realize, my friend, that the reason we are so messed up, so bruised and wounded and bleeding as a society, is because we refuse to turn to this Book of books? Even many who say they know the Bible often ignore its counsel or simply refuse to believe it. We deceive ourselves into imagining that we are an "exception" to God's precepts and that we can live as we please without facing the consequences.

The words of the Bible, however, aren't to be compared with advice we might receive from a secular counselor or pick up on a talk-radio program. As Paul told his young disciple, Timothy, the Bible is "inspired by God" (2 Timothy 3:16). Deuteronomy 8:3 tells us that we are to live by every word that comes from God's mouth. Jesus pulled this very verse out of His arsenal when He came under savage attack by the evil one (see Matthew 4:4).

Perhaps at this point in your journey of faith you don't have the same bold confidence in the Bible that I just expressed. May I ask you to continue reading, Beloved? After all, what do you have to lose? Give it a try, and see if it works. Announcers on television and the radio are always talking about a "ten-day free trial" to persuade people to buy their products. And now here you are with a book in your hands that holds forth the possibility of building a marriage without regrets.

Could it be true? Let's move on together and see what we can learn from the Bible on the subject of marriage and family and see if it makes sense. Not only do you have nothing to lose, but you have everything to gain!

Connecting with the Word

You may have read dozens of other books on these subjects or spoken with numerous counselors and "experts." But maybe you've never taken the time simply to focus on what *the Bible* says about marriage. In the long run, it doesn't matter how many books you've read, how many counselors you've consulted, or how many weekend conferences you've attended. What matters is this: Have you *connected* with the counsel in God's Word? Are you truly hearing God? Are you obeying His precepts? Are you being guided by His Holy Spirit? Eloquent prose and celebrity opinions fade away, become inconsequential. What you and I desperately need to do is connect with God's eternal counsel and wisdom. If this simple book can be the tool God uses to do that, nothing would thrill me more.

I certainly don't have all the answers, nor do I claim this book is an end-all cure-all. But with God's help, we will soon find ourselves uncovering truths from the book that *does* have all the answers. I cannot tell you how many people—men and women, singles and divorced, older folks and teenagers—have been transformed, turned-around, rescued, and set free by the biblical principles you will encounter on these pages. And it all came about because they discovered what God said and ordered their lives accordingly.

"But the Bible is a big book," you say. Where do we begin? As it turns out, many of the answers we seek are on the first few pages!

The Book of Beginnings

In Genesis, we have God's account of the creation of man and woman. Do you like weddings? There was never a wedding like this one before. God Himself conducted the ceremony, planned the honeymoon, stood beside the groom, and gave the bride away! It all begins with the dramatic words recorded in Genesis 1:26-28:

> Then God said, "Let Us make man in Our image, according to Our likeness; and let them rule over the fish of the sea and over the birds of the sky and over the cattle and over all the earth, and over every creeping thing that creeps on the earth." God created man in His own image, in the image of God He created him; male and female He created them.

> God blessed them; and God said to them, "Be fruitful and multiply, and fill the earth, and subdue it; and rule over the fish of the sea and over the birds of the sky and over every living thing that moves on the earth."

After God made the heavens and the earth and everything on the earth, He scooped up some dust from the ground and formed it into the highest form of all His creation—man and woman. God made them in His image and breathed the breath of life into them. He then told them to "fill the earth and subdue it."

Adam and Eve were to be God's vice-regents, co-rulers over all the earth. If you observe the text carefully, you'll see God gave this rulership not just to the man, but to the woman also. *They* were to reign side by side as partners. Woman was not less than man in God's eyes and that's important to remember whether you are a man or a woman. God has very specific roles for men and women, as we will see later, but one sex is by no means superior to the other in the eyes of God. As a matter of fact, Christianity has elevated the role of woman through the centuries above the place many societies would seek to assign her. In Galatians 3:26-28, we read: "For you are all sons of God through faith in Christ Jesus. For all of you who were baptized into Christ have clothed yourselves with Christ. There is neither Jew nor Greek, there is neither slave nor free man, there is neither male nor female; for you are all one in Christ Jesus."

Genesis 1 gives us the big picture, the overview of creation, a panoramic snapshot that tells at a glance what happened from day zero to day six. In Genesis 2, God fills in with some wonderful details (never as much as we might want, perhaps, but certainly all that we need). Some people look at the different accounts in chapters 1 and 2 and imagine them to be contradictory, but they're not. The two chapters simply look at the same events from different perspectives.

Genesis 2 focuses on the how and why of woman's creation. The chapter begins by telling us that man was created first. In verse 7 we read, "The LORD God formed man of dust from the ground, and breathed into his nostrils the breath of life; and man became a living being." Verse 8 goes on to say that God placed Adam in the Garden of Eden. One of Adam's first tasks was to name all the living creatures God had made—quite a job when you think about the vast scope of the animal creation! But then Scripture adds this poignant footnote: "But for Adam there was not found a helper suitable for him" (verse 20).

God's work was not finished. Man was not yet complete. God said, "It is not good for the man to be alone; I will make him a helper suitable for him" (Genesis 2:18).

This is where the role of woman first appears in Scripture. For now, you simply need to note that even though both man and woman were created in God's image, one was carefully designed for the other. That's why people want to get married. (Dr. Howard Hendricks called it "the urge to merge.") The majority of us are designed for marriage. God tells us that it was not good for man to be alone, so He fashioned woman to be "a helper suitable" for Adam. Woman has a very essential place in God's creation—a high and noble calling—and when she discovers this, it is *so* liberating!

Now how did God bring about the creation of woman? Genesis 2:21-23 describes what happened next:

> So the LORD God caused a deep sleep to fall upon the man, and he slept; then He took one of his ribs and closed up the flesh at that place. The LORD God fashioned into a woman the rib which He had taken from the man, and brought her to the man. The man said, "This is now bone of my bones, and flesh of my flesh; she shall be called Woman, because she was taken out of Man."

The Hebrew word for woman is *Ishshah*. Man is *Ish*...woman is *Ishshah*.

So what can we conclude, my friend, from simply observing the text? We see that woman was created *after* the man, she was created *for* the man, and she was created because it was *not good* for man to be alone. She was created as someone specially suitable—a helper—for man. As others have said, woman was not taken from man's feet to be trampled upon, nor from his head to rule over him, but from his side as an equal, to stand beside him.

Later to be called Eve, the mother of all living people, woman was a unique, delightful creation who, with Adam, was to rule over all creation. Man needed woman, and our gracious Creator (who knows so well our every need) created her to meet those needs. This was to be Adam's bride, the mother of all mankind, with whom he would truly "live happily ever after."

There was no reason why they shouldn't. This was no fairy tale or Hebrew myth; it was a beautiful, perfect reality as real as today's headlines. This was not a world of man's imagination, but one of God's instigation. God had placed them in a perfect environment, supplied all their needs, and walked and talked with them day by day. There was no sin in their world, nothing to cast a shadow, stir a worry, provoke a resentment, or spark an argument. Adam and Eve never knew what it meant to lie down at night with a tinge of regret in their hearts. And when the sun peeked over the horizon in the morning releasing a mighty chorus of bird songs in the Garden, there was no waking thought of guilt or bitterness or anxiety. How wonderful it must have been! Adam and Eve enjoyed complete lightness of heart.

We're not told how long they lived in this paradise. If they had so chosen, they certainly could have lived in this wonderful situation forever; "happily ever after" would have been literally true. That was God's intention and desire.

But it didn't happen that way.

Which explains, my friend, why you and I are where we are. That is why we are reading a book like this, searching for answers, wrestling with difficulties, wanting to better our lot in our marriages and help others do the same.

So Where Do We Begin?

What's the key, the answer, the solution? It begins right where God begins…right in this "book of beginnings," the book of Genesis. God introduces precepts in Genesis that He develops throughout the rest of His holy book, the Bible. Primary among these are the relationships between God and mankind, between man and woman, and between parent and child.

When we gain a proper understanding of these relationships and give them correct priority in our lives, we take hold of the building blocks for enjoying great marriages and deeply fulfilling lives. But if these relationships are allowed to drift, then our marriages—and our lives and families—can easily fall apart.

That old longing to "live happily ever after" may not be a fairy tale after all. The principles in God's timeless Word can enable us and empower us to reorder our lives and lift the shadow of regrets from our hearts.

It all begins with three primary relationships. We'll look at these in the following chapter.

CHAPTER 3

WHAT'S THE GLUE THAT HOLDS A MARRIAGE TOGETHER?

IT WASN'T AS THOUGH BILL AND RUTH SAW eye to eye on everything. They didn't.

In fact, each came from families with very different understandings of the role and purpose of a woman in the home.

They married anyway, and soon they were traveling a road full of bumps and turns. Ruth, raised on the mission field by Presbyterian parents, felt highly valued as a woman. Before she met Bill, she was aiming toward a missionary career in Tibet. In the sovereignty of God, however, she met Bill...and life changed. Bill felt called to preach—and Tibet just didn't figure into those plans.

The young man's convictions about the role of a woman became clear when he told her, "If you believe that God has brought us together, and if you believe that the husband is the head of the wife, then if the Lord is leading me, it's up to you to follow."

In later years, Ruth would reflect that it was her relationship with God that sustained her in a wonderful, if sometimes difficult, marriage. And we can all be happy that her marriage made it through the hard times. Had that union fallen through, it might have ended the ministry of Billy Graham.

In a recent article, Ruth Bell Graham recalled her early desire to serve in Tibet. "I think that the Lord must have given me that intense longing for a purpose," she wrote, "so that I could have the understanding and sense of fulfillment that I now receive from Bill's work. I knew from the very beginning that I would not be first place in his life. Christ would be first. Knowing that, accepting that, solves an awful lot of problems right there. So I can watch him go with no regrets, and wait for him joyfully."

No Perfect People...No Perfect Marriages

As you read that account of Billy and Ruth Graham, you may have found yourself wistfully thinking, *If only I had a mate who loved God like that—someone willing to follow Christ and do His will.* If you are a woman, you might be thinking, *If I had a mate who walked with God like Billy Graham, I would gladly step into second place.*

Yet assuming a "second place" role isn't easy for anyone, as Ruth Graham's biography bears out. In fact, their marriage could have ended in disaster had they not discovered and lived out the truths we will consider in this chapter.

When you look at another couple's marriage from afar—or even "up close and personal"—it may seem far easier than it really is. Don't be deceived; marriage in our fallen world is not easy. It isn't easy even for those who belong to Jesus Christ and serve Him in some prominent way. Each of us faces a unique set of circumstances in life, with challenges, heartaches, and struggles no one may ever know about but the Lord Himself. No one has a perfect situation because there are no perfect places or perfect people on this planet.

Some marriages, of course, are much better and happier than others, but each of us has his or her own difficult situations and circumstances to deal with. Why? Because we don't have the Garden of Eden as our address. Paradise was lost and will not be regained until we step through the gates of heaven. No matter what anyone tells you, marriage is the union of two people born into sin and living in bodies of flesh inclined toward profound selfishness.

Whoever you are then, whomever you may be married to, you're going to face stresses and sorrows and pressures that will seek to pull your marriage apart. What is the glue that can bond a man and a woman together for life? What is the secret that can hold your marriage together?

The answer lies in the first of those three primary relationships I mentioned in the previous chapter: God and man (male and female).

The Most Important Relationship of All

Broadcaster Paul Harvey at one time promoted a certain brand of glue on his daily radio program. In his own inimitable style, Mr. Harvey praised the virtues of a bonding agent that will cement anything from glass and porcelain to metal and plastic. Testimonials abound from those who have repaired everything from earrings to vases, from snowmobiles to a cracked engine block.

But where in all of this wide world can you find a glue that will rebond a fractured marriage? How do you cement a husband and wife who are being pulled apart from a hundred directions? Only our Lord God has such glue. The One who created marriage in the Garden of Eden, the One who blessed marriage at the wedding feast in Cana, and the One who gave His own body and blood to redeem us from our sins can provide a bonding agent the very forces of hell cannot break.

An intimate, daily walk with God is the most crucial element for holding a husband and wife and a family together. It is the most vital relationship in all of life—even more important than your relationship with your spouse or children, though they may be as dear to you as life itself.

This is the relationship that kept Ruth Graham on track and made her a great woman of God. It is this relationship that becomes the foundation for everything else.

It *must* begin here. It cannot begin anywhere else.

You can talk about the specifics of a marriage—communication, money, sex, child-rearing, in-laws—but unless you give priority to *this* primary relationship, to your relationship with your Creator and God, your marriage will always be in peril. When the cold winds blow, when the pressures and cares of life pull and tug at you, you will not be able to find the agent to hold it all together if you ignore your relationship with God.

God designed Adam and Eve for a unique relationship with Him. No other created creature enjoys this kind of union. The first couple was made in God's own image, given dominion over the rest of creation, and gloried in daily fellowship with the Creator along the winding, sunlit paths of Eden.

Adam and Eve were not mere puppets—marionettes on strings—lurching and dancing as God moved His fingers. No, they were rational, volitional beings who could choose of their own free will whether to trust and obey God. At the same time, however, they were created to live in total dependence upon Him. In fact, the Lord placed a tree in the Garden that would give them the opportunity to express their trust and dependence…the tree of the knowledge of good and evil. Although the tree grew in Eden, a garden planted by God, God soberly warned Adam that if he ate the fruit of that tree, he would surely die. No ifs, ands, or buts about it. Death was the consequence of disobedience. Not only would he begin the downward spiral toward physical death (Wrinkles! Gray hair! Osteoporosis!), but he would immediately experience spiritual death—a separation from God.

Tragically, Adam and Eve made the wrong choice. They ate the forbidden fruit, and in that dreadful instant, the stain of sin came upon their hearts. What was their first response? Suddenly aware of good and evil, they sought to cover their nakedness and hide from God. They knew the sound of God "walking in the garden in the cool of the day" (Genesis 3:8). Until that moment, it had always been a welcome, joyous sound, but now it filled them with guilt, shame, and dread. Instead of rushing to meet their Creator and Friend, they crouched behind trees hoping He wouldn't see them. The intimacy they once knew with God had evaporated like water under a desert sun.

Yet in God's unfathomable grace and love, their relationship with Him did not perish in the Garden. As the Bible later reveals, God in His omniscience already knew what had to be done to restore that relationship. He knew that He had to provide a way. And He knew it would cost the life of His own dear Son.

The Way, the Truth, and the Life, the One through whom He created all things, the *Logos* of God, would become flesh, born of God's seed placed in a virgin's womb. Jesus Christ, the only begotten Son of the Father, would be born a man, yet born without inherent sin. He would become flesh and blood so that He might taste death for every man and woman and bear the consequence of sin, which is death.

Through His death, Jesus Christ would deliver those who would believe in Him and receive Him as their God and Savior. They would be set free from Satan's dominion, from the one who held the power of death because of sin. It is only through Christ's sacrifice on the cross and His resurrection from the dead that they could be reconciled to God and experience the renewing of the Holy Spirit.

We still live in a fallen world destined for judgment; we still face the prospect of physical death. Yet we have the unspeakable privilege to walk and talk with the living God. Praise His name! Through Jesus, God's rightful position is restored in our lives. He becomes our God and we become His people as He takes up residence in us by the power of His indwelling Spirit.

> *Christ in us*—the hope of glory.
> *Christ in us*—the Lord of our lives.
> *Christ in us*—a very present help in time of trouble.
> *Christ in us*—who will never leave us or forsake us.
> *Christ in us*—so that we can boldly say, "The Lord is my helper,
>   I will not fear what man shall do unto me."

Christ's death and resurrection made it possible to restore the most important relationship ever created—that between God and mankind.

Isn't That Enough?

Is that enough, then, to keep a marriage together? Having Christ in you? Does that guarantee a life, a marriage, a family with no difficulties? Is Christianity a magic carpet ride to wedded bliss and tranquility? I wish I could say that were true, but simply being a Christian is no iron-clad guarantee of a happy marriage. Marriage takes work, massive infusions of God's grace, and a solid understanding of the precepts and commands in His Word.

Years ago, I had neither a relationship with Christ nor a knowledge of His Word. To my deep regret, my first marriage failed. In those days I faced all the hurdles and adjustments of a marriage relationship, but I had no "inward help," no sustainer, because I didn't know Jesus Christ. When life began to come unglued, there was no one I could run to with the broken pieces.

Even in my second marriage, with Christ in my heart and married to a man who knows and loves God and is so dear to me, there still have been adjustments. There have been dark times and times when I wondered if I had really been in God's will when I married Jack. Our personalities are so very, very different. In reality, the only thing we have in common is God—and the work of God in our lives. Besides that, I had two sons who had to get used to a new father while I was getting used to a new husband (not to mention him getting used to me!). It wasn't an easy time. And when difficulties sweep into life like a storm, we can find ourselves gripped by the "seasickness" of doubt.

Sometimes I will be talking to someone who has observed our marriage, and she will ask something like this: "What has given you a good marriage and a fruitful ministry all these years? What has kept you and Jack together and faithful to one another when other Christian leaders have divorced their mates or live separated from one another? What kind of superglue did you use?"

It is the glue of maintaining an intimate, surrendered relationship with our Father, of determining that God and His Word will have priority over self. Nothing more, nothing less.

Isn't this the life to which Jesus called every child of God? Jesus said to the multitudes, "If anyone wishes to come after Me, he must deny himself, and take up his cross and follow Me" (Matthew 16:24). He also said, "If anyone comes to Me, and does not hate [in comparison with our love for Him] his own father and mother and wife and children and brothers and sisters, yes, and even his own life, he cannot be My disciple" (Luke 14:26). Jesus did say those things. And He meant them. They are not idle words. It is truth coming from the lips of the One who is Truth. He is God; He expects to be believed and obeyed, and He has given us the power to do so by giving us His Spirit. That life, that reliance, that obedience, is the glue that makes a marriage last in a day when marriages fall apart everywhere. It is a process of walking daily with God, knowing His Word, respecting Him, fearing Him, and obeying Him.

God says, "If you love Me, you will keep My commandments." In other words, "Your love for Me needs to be something more than positive words and a nod of the head." Real love for God isn't some vague, stained-glass glow or the warm, fuzzy feelings you may get when you sing a praise chorus.

Words can be cheap, can't they? Perhaps at one time or another you "bought stock" in someone's words and assurances—only to have that stock crash, bringing about a depression. Perhaps people have told you they loved you, but when the hard times came, where was the evidence of that love?

Love is not a feeling; it is an action. In fact, Beloved of God, all through this book we are going to talk about our relationship with God and how it is played out in the various challenges and hard places of marriage. This relationship is the master key to a marriage without regrets.

I know very well that some who read this book are living in horrendous situations that are cruel, twisted, and brutal. We will talk about such situations in the pages to come, for God's Word has a remedy for every circumstance of life. He has promised His children that He will never give them more than they can bear. Scripture says He offers us a way of escape—but it is His way, and not the one we might imagine or desire. So be patient, do not despair, and please…keep reading!

The Second Most Important Relationship

Let's take a moment to talk about the second relationship we encounter in Genesis: the union between man and woman.

After God created Eve, He presented her to Adam. Now, how do you suppose Adam might have responded? We might guess he would say something like, "Wow!" Or maybe, "Where have you been all my life?" Actually, we don't have to guess. Scripture gives us his precise words: "This is now bone of my bones, and flesh of my flesh; she shall be called Woman, because she was taken out of Man" (Genesis 2:23). The account goes on to say, "For this reason a man shall leave his father and his mother, and be joined to his wife; and they shall become one flesh. And the man and his wife were both naked and were not ashamed" (verses 24,25).

What is the significance of Adam's words? It seems obvious, doesn't it. When God presents Eve to Adam, that very act makes it an issue of stewardship for Adam. After all, the woman was created by God for man and presented to him. Surely such a gift from God brings with it some serious accountability.

It is inherent in a man to care for a woman. The feminist movement, for all its noise and propaganda, cannot quench that inborn desire in a man to care for a woman…or a woman's inborn desire to receive such care. Through the annals of history we can read countless stories of men laying down their lives for the protection of their women, defending them to the death.

Once God presents Eve to Adam, the first thing you hear from Adam's lips is the unshakable recognition that Eve is part of him—not just an appendage tacked on, extraneous baggage, but a deep and profound sense of identification. How important this is to marriage—identifying with one another, owning one another, treasuring one another! The woman was in no sense a "lesser creation." She, like her counterpart, was created in God's own image. This special creation was called *Ishshah* because she was taken out of man.

Paul tells us in 1 Corinthians 11:7,8 that "woman is the glory of man. For man does not originate from woman, but woman from man." The word "glory" (*doxa* in the Greek), means "to seem," thus to give a correct opinion or estimate of. As we shall see later, the identification is so intrinsic and so real that when a man loves his wife, he is actually loving himself.

In marriage as God intended it to be, the man and woman become an expression of the other, even as between the heavenly Father and His Son. Jesus was the glory of the Father. He told Philip, "He who has seen Me has seen the Father."

Not only did God establish the marriage relationship with the principles of stewardship and identification built in, He also made it clear that this was a relationship that would have priority over all other relationships, with the exception of the relationship of a man or woman to God Himself. Scripture says: "For this reason a man shall leave his father and his mother, and be joined to his wife; and they shall become one flesh" (Genesis 2:24).

Marriage supersedes the relationship of a child to his parent, especially a son to his mother and father, because in marriage husband and wife are joined. With these words, Scripture acknowledges for all time the priority of the husband-wife relationship. The man is to leave his father and mother and cleave (like glue!) to his wife.

Leave and Cleave

The two words chosen by the Spirit of God, "leave" and "cleave," succinctly demonstrate just how crucial and unique the marriage relationship is. It is so singularly important that the man is to move from the home of the parents who nurtured and raised him to another home, where he will take on the role of lover and provider for the woman who is to be his wife. Together they will establish a family...and a home of their own.

It is this very act of leaving that demonstrates the new priority in the man's life. By making known his commitment and allegiance to the woman he is taking for his wife, he is saying to the watching world, "I am uniting myself to this woman for life." Can you imagine, Beloved, what might happen if this were more clearly understood before marriage—and if greater preparations were made to educate and facilitate such a transition?

First, the leaving…and then the cleaving. To cleave is to glue together. The Hebrew word for "join" or "cleave," *dabaq,* occurs just over 60 times in the Old Testament. It means "to cling, cleave, keep close." In modern Hebrew, the same word means "to stick to, adhere to." *Dabaq* yields the noun form for "glue," and also the more abstract ideas of loyalty and devotion.

This is the application of the glue that brings oneness to two persons. It is a oneness portrayed and consummated on the night when he takes her into his arms to bring her to himself in the beauty of sexual intercourse. That act, in the design of God, symbolizes as nothing else the unique oneness of their marriage. In their physical union they literally become "one flesh."

And what does this one-flesh relationship show us about marriage? *Permanence.* Marriage is to be a permanent relationship.

A Last Try

When Tom and I were having all our marital problems, I begged him to go to counseling with me. "I don't need to go," he told me. "I've taken counseling in seminary. You can go if you want to."

That was that. A slammed door I didn't know how to open. Tom thought he knew it all, but I hadn't been to seminary. I didn't know what he knew, what he had been taught. And the little I thought I knew hadn't worked. In desperation, I got on a plane and flew from Ohio, where we were living, to Virginia, to talk with the man who had been our priest when Tom was in seminary. Ned and his wife lived next door to the church. His office was on the ground floor of their house, with a separate entrance. When I arrived, I moved into their guest bedroom.

I'll never forget the day Ned and I talked. We sat across the room from each other, each smoking a pipe! I had forgotten my cigarettes, and he didn't have any. So he simply lit up one of his pipes for me. (I know what you're thinking: "What an interesting scene!" You're right. It was.)

I smoked Ned's pipe and poured out my heart to him while he smiled, puffed, and listened. He was a big man—and tall. His clerical collar and his quiet sympathy made him seem more appealing than he really was. His questions, probing regarding our physical intimacy, charged the air. And in situations like I was in, almost anyone who seems to care and understand seems better than who you left at home.

When I finished my sad story of bitter disappointment, Ned rose from his chair, put down his pipe, came across the room and put his arms around me. I was crying. He leaned down, kissed me on the neck, and whispered in my ear, "You sure are a good-looking gal, Kay."

I thought for a moment or two that I might find solace in this man's arms. But it only deepened my despair.

The man in the clerical collar, the man who called himself a minister, never even made an attempt to open up the Bible. He was a false shepherd who cared only for himself. So I flew back to Ohio without ever learning God's plan and provision for marriage. I never realized that when you glue two objects together, they become one. And when you divide that united one, you don't get two again. You get halves. Pieces.

Imagine a little girl with a sheet of construction paper and a pair of scissors. Biting her lower lip with concentration, she cuts out the shapes she has penciled onto the paper: a house, a tree, and a girl. Carefully daubing each cut-out with glue, she affixes them to another sheet of paper.

Some time later, she comes back to look at the picture with a critical eye. Somehow, it seems wrong. The house is a little crooked. The tree is too close to the house. The paper girl should have been under the tree. So the little artist comes running to her mother to ask her to fix it.

"Move her, Mommy. I don't want her there. I want her here." She jabs at the picture with her finger to indicate the change she wants to make.

Can't you just see the mother patiently stooping down to her daughter's level and explaining to her what would happen if she tried to change the picture now?

"Honey, if Mommy does that, then it will ruin your picture. It's been glued together, and if we take it apart now, some of the picture will stick to the little girl, and some of the little girl will stick to the picture. I may not even be able to get the little girl off without tearing her in half."

"I don't care!" the little one shouts, stomping her foot. "I want it moved! I don't like it there!"

As I have used this illustration through the years and sought to apply it to myself, I honestly can't tell you how I would have responded to God's gentle wisdom if I had understood His counsel as a young woman. I don't know if I would have stomped my foot when I heard God explain the permanence of marriage, the oneness it brings, and the damage that results when you seek to pull that marriage apart.

I only know that I was never told.

It was never explained to me.

All I knew was the Bible was "against divorce." I didn't know that although God hates divorce, there are times when He will permit it for very legitimate reasons. I only knew God didn't like it, but I never knew why. Nor did I know what He taught about marriage.

I Want You to Know

My ignorance, of course, in no way excused me. I possessed a Bible, and I might have discovered these things on my own. But I didn't. I turned to the arm of the flesh, to my own way, and reaped a marriage I deeply regret having destroyed, children whom I wounded in the process, a husband who hung himself, three years of immoral relationships, and a stronghold of immorality in my life.

Yes, I am who I am today. Redeemed, regenerated, restored. Set free from Satan's strongholds. But I might have had an opportunity, a shot at staying married though I would experience sorrow, if I had known what God said in His Word.

But I didn't know.

That's why I so deeply want you to know these things. And that, Beloved, is why I sit here in my office at home on this Saturday evening at 10:15, writing this book instead of resting after a full day's work. I have a passion to teach others what God's book has to say about marriage, for His words are life itself. Through His mighty precepts, you will gain understanding of truth…pure, unadulterated truth.

Let's take time now to kneel before the Lord of Truth, precious one, and seek His help and healing as we ponder these important insights from His Word.

> *O Father, You are the sovereign ruler of all the universe, the One who created us male and female, the One who created us for Your pleasure. We want to please You. If we are fighting an inner battle between pleasing You and pleasing ourselves, help us to see the folly of placing our will above Yours.*

> *Father, only You know all the questions, concerns, doubts, and fears that race through the mind of the one who prays with me right now. Dear Lord, please help this woman, this man, to see that the one thing most to be feared is not knowing what You have said in Your Word and acting in the flesh or according to the counsel of people.*

> *As we continue through the pages of this book, help this one whom you value so highly to listen and examine the precepts of Your Word. Show him, show her, Father, how to find the peace and joy that all of us desire so much.*

> *Thank You for being a God who is near, a God whose mighty counsel is within reach. Thank You for caring, for speaking, for promising that as Your children You will not permit anything to come into our lives that will be more than we can bear. May we rest in You. We ask these things in the name of the One who sits at Your right hand, who lives to make intercession for us, in the name of Your Son, our Lord Jesus Christ. Amen.*

CHAPTER 4

I Didn't Know Marriage Was Going to Be Like This!

c∞9

The Sin Factor

She sat on the chair beside the bed fully dressed, putting on her panty hose. As she stretched her beautifully curved silky leg into the air, she pointed her toes toward the hotel bed and the man whose passion had been spent on her.

"Welcome to the world of AIDS, my friend." Her voice was filled with rancor—she would not go to the grave alone.

His hand flew to his head. Covering his eyes, he rolled away from her as his body knotted into a ball and he cried out in disbelief.

It was a decision he had made with his eyes wide open, his mind fully intact. When the firm who had trained the men told them their reward for a week of grueling work would be a classy companion and a night on the town, he knew he shouldn't take it. He knew what God said. He knew that marriage meant one woman—and only one. But as he listened to their description of "the reward," the offer grew more tempting. It was something he had never done before and something he told himself he would never do again. Besides, he didn't want to face the jeering of his buddies who all thought it only a fitting end to their hard labors.

It was only one night, only one time. But, oh, the ramifications of his "one-night stand." He died of AIDS. His wife died of AIDS. Their children were left parentless.

His experience was not dissimilar to what happened in the Garden of Eden almost 6000 years ago, if you follow biblical chronologies. It was only one bite—one time, yet Eve's and then Adam's single act of disobedience impacted the whole course of mankind as it brought sin and death onto the stage of life.

What was the X-factor in these true accounts that destroyed lives, blasted hopes, dashed expectations, and brought death when God intended life?

It was sin.

Sin is always *the* factor. The human race can trace all of its problems back to that single source. You and I can do the same when we recall the struggles and dark days of our lives. And if you and I are going to understand the role of man and woman in marriage and live accordingly, we must understand the sin factor.

What is sin? When you look up what the Bible has to say about sin, you discover sin is refusing to believe God and take Him at His Word.

It is knowing to do good and not doing it.

It is a lack of faith—for what is not of faith is sin.

It is crossing the boundary lines drawn by God.

It is going your own way, rather than His way.

Sin is breaking God's commandments.

Sin lurks somewhere behind every blowup, every regret, every sigh, every moment of frustration and grief in marriage. And since sin is here to stay—until King Jesus opens the curtains on a new heaven and new earth—we had better know what we can about it. We had better learn how to deal with this deadly enemy so that it doesn't sabotage our dearest relationships.

Genesis 2 lays out a summary statement of marriage as God intended it. Every bit of it is good and reasonable and would work forever—if only the Bible ended with chapter 2.

But it doesn't.

Following the beauty and glory of Genesis 2, we plunge into the horror and tragedy (with a glint of hope for future redemption) of Genesis 3. It is in this third chapter of this book of beginnings where the relationship between man and woman underwent drastic and far-reaching change. It began with a broken relationship with God, extended to the relationship between the sexes, then kept rippling outward to touch their children, their extended families, their neighbors, their communities, and eventually the nations of the world.

And it all began with an action that took no more than a moment.

A friend of mine told me about an accident he suffered while camping with his family this past summer. Wanting to hang a tarp and lacking a stepstool, he decided to trust his weight to a round of firewood. As soon as he stood on it, it flew out from under him. He fell, seriously damaging his arm muscle. Following surgery and physical therapy, he has use of his arm once again, but it will never be the same. The wide scar on his skin will never go away. The stiffness of movement will be with him always. What amazed him is how one foolish decision (using an unsteady piece of wood for a ladder) will impact the rest of his life. The accident took only a second, yet will have a lifelong impact the rest of his life. He will never escape from the consequences of his action.

Isn't that the way it is? One brief act can lead to a lifetime of consequences. In Adam and Eve's case, it wasn't stepping onto a treacherous perch; it began with listening to the wrong voice.

Where Sin Began

All the serpent in the garden had to do was convince one of the marriage partners, Eve, that she couldn't trust God—His words, His commands, or His intentions—and he would have her! It was that simple.

> Now the serpent was more crafty than any beast of the field which the LORD God had made. And he said to the woman, "Indeed, has God said, 'You shall not eat from any tree of the garden'?" The woman said to the serpent, "From the fruit of the trees of the garden we may eat; but from the fruit of the tree which is in the middle of the garden, God has said, 'You shall not eat from it or touch it, or you will die'" (Genesis 3:1-3).

Listen to the tempter's first recorded words: *"Indeed, has God said?"* As a matter of fact, God *had* said something. He had issued a single command and made it very clear. It was a commandment first uttered to the man before God put Adam to sleep and woke him up with a wonderful woman by his side. The Creator told the man, "From any tree of the garden you may eat freely; but from the tree of the knowledge of good and evil you shall not eat, for in the day that you eat from it you will surely die" (Genesis 2:16,17).

It couldn't have been clearer. It was like a red, octagon-shaped sign bearing the bold letters S-T-O-P. What was there to misunderstand? What part of S-T-O-P needed explaining? The command was given; the consequence of disobedience was clearly spelled out.

When the tempter threw a curve of doubt at Eve, she swung blindly and struck out. From the text it is obvious that God's command was given to Adam and apparently relayed in some form to Eve. Listen to her reply to the serpent of old, the one whom the Bible refers to as the devil, Satan, the liar, and the deceiver.

> Eve: "From the fruit of the trees of the garden we may eat...."

> *So far so good. That was exactly what God had said in Genesis 2:16.*

> Eve: "But from the fruit of the tree which is in the middle of the garden, God has said, 'You shall not eat from it....'"

> *To this point, she was still accurate. From this moment on, however, God's Word gets watered down.*

> Eve: "You shall not eat from it or touch it...."

Touch it? God said nothing about touching the fruit.

Eve: "Or you will die."

God didn't say "or you will die." He said, "You will surely die."

There was a twist in what Eve said—a slight distortion of God's word that hardened the prohibition and maybe even softened the consequences. There's a hint in her words that possibly the outcome wouldn't be as grave as advertised.

Isn't that usually the way it works? We see ourselves as the exception to God's commands. *(Moi? Surely not moi!)* Yet Scripture tells us again and again that God is no respecter of persons. God says what He means, and means what He says, whether or not the words seem pleasant or convenient to us. God watches over His words to perform them!

But the conversation between Eve and the serpent wasn't over. The smooth, hissing creature moves in closer and whispers, "You surely will not die!"

This was a direct and blatant contradiction to what God had said. Finished with subtlety, the enemy declares, "No way! Couldn't be! Such a terrible thing could never happen to *you*, dear woman."

As I type these words, I cannot shake a true-life illustration from my mind. I close my eyes and see a young face, a face full of promise and hope and the thrill of living. Yet it is the face of a young man just moments from tragedy.

The Day Dano Died

Two of our grandsons, born five days apart, had just turned 16. That's quite an occasion: a day usually celebrated by taking a driver's test and picking up a license. It's a coming of age—driving age!

If you happen to have boys that age, you know that birthday cards are just not a big deal (unless there's a gift tucked inside!). I've come to believe that birthday cards for 16-year-olds are written for the parents' or grandparents' sake, rather than for the teenager. What do teenage guys care about rhyming verse and mushy sentiments? So I came up with what I believe to be a creative alternative. I bought a magazine that covers one of their interest areas and created an extended birthday card, by writing or tucking clever notes (or money) throughout its pages.

Scanning the shelves at Barnes and Noble, I found a strong prospect for John. For a young man interested in history and military battles, the magazine seemed perfect! (What I tucked in wasn't so bad, either!) Joseph, on the other hand, is into rock climbing. I looked for a magazine in his interest area, too—and bingo! I succeeded once again.

The only thing I wasn't wild about was the cover article. The cover featured an awe-inspiring photo of a young man flung into space, his white-gloved hands gripping red ropes stretched to the max. Pink and yellow straps trailed from his purple pants.

Everything about Dano Osman looked taut. The purple straps over his broad shoulders clamped to a black harness, seeming to vie in strength with his bare, bronzed chest. The glistening sun delineated every well-developed gleaming muscle, etching it in gold. His long hair flew away from a face chiseled like that of an Indian warrior.

To the left of that startling picture brief copy let you know that Dano never expected to fall to his death on that day so sunny, so bright with anticipation. The text reads:

> On November 23, Dano stood atop Yosemite's Leaning Tower and prepared for his biggest rope jump ever—over 1,000 feet of free fall. He called friends in Tahoe on his cell phone, and kept it on so they could hear him jump. He let out a wild laugh, counted aloud, "Three, two, one," then yelled, "See ya!" Dano's friends on the phone heard the wind roar as he approached terminal velocity, and then nothing.

Dano was only 35 years old. Too experienced to miscalculate. Too young to die. He didn't expect anything to go wrong. He expected to enjoy the rush of his life, then laugh with his friends back in Tahoe. If he had thought something would go wrong, if he had really believed his equipment would fail, he never would have jumped. But the equipment *did* fail, there was nothing to catch him, and there was no going back. On a day he meant to live, he died.

It was the same for Adam and Eve. God had told them what the consequences for disobedience would be. But they didn't believe it. If they had believed it, if they could have looked down through the long years and seen what was to be, they never would have eaten the fruit. But in the critical moment they entrusted their lives and their destiny to a faulty piece of advice. Someone told them they could take their fruit and eat it too!

They listened to the lie.

And ate.

And died.

On that day, death entered into the world, and our first parents experienced spiritual death. Physical death would come later, but it would surely come. With one bite, sin entered the picture and their relationship with God shattered, *as did their relationship with one another.* Beyond that, the shadow of their act would bring death to their children and their children's children through all the ages of mankind including now, reaching you and me. As the apostle Paul wrote, "Just as through one man sin entered into the world, and death through sin, and so death spread to all men, because all sinned" (Romans 5:12).

What a fall! The plunge forever changed the face of marriage and the relationship between man and woman. It changed everything because the people themselves were changed. They were separated from the life of God. Immediately Adam and Eve tried to hide from God in the Garden of Eden. *Hide from God? Hide from the all-powerful, all-seeing One who created them and loved them and treasured them?*

Ridiculous, isn't it? Crouching behind a palm tree trying to hide from the Almighty? Yet that is exactly what they did. Now they were afraid of Him. With their newly found knowledge of good and evil, they became painfully aware of their nakedness. And in the next moment, in their newly found selfishness, they began to point the finger and blame others for their sins. Adam pointed the finger at Eve. Eve blamed the serpent. Neither wanted to accept responsibility for rebelling against God.

Could that be where you are, Beloved? Hiding from God? Internally aware of your shame and yet blaming others? If you are going to build a marriage without regrets, you will have to deal with these things. We don't have to hide behind bushes (or excuses); God already knows we have sin in our lives. It's no news to Him! And yet if we humble ourselves and come to Him for cleansing and help, He will become our strength when we have none of our own.

Biblical Geometry

The root of all sin is self—choosing our way rather than believing God and living according to His commands and precepts. This is why the key to a marriage without regrets is first and foremost a living, moment-by-moment relationship with God through the Lord Jesus Christ.

When I teach this material in person, I illustrate an ideal relationship by drawing a triangle on the board. At the apex of the triangle is God in heaven. The line at the base is earth, where you and I live out our threescore-and-ten. The lines on each side of the triangle are man and woman, respectively. As you move them up on that line toward the pinnacle—God—the husband and wife not only draw closer to God, they also draw closer to one another. When they do not grow toward God, they also cease growing toward each other!

And how does a person draw close to God? It happens through communication. First, through spending time in the Bible where God reveals His character, His ways, His thoughts, and the course of those who follow Him and those who don't. Second, there is communication through prayer—talking things out with God, committing and sorting out every situation, making every decision with Him and in the light of His Word. This two-way communication is further reinforced through worship—honoring God for who He is, valuing Him, respecting Him, trusting Him, and yielding to Him in obedience and service.

As we explore what God says about marriage, my only purpose in writing is to introduce you to what God says in the Bible. I will not give you pat, man-made solutions or a series of interesting stories; rather, I want to bring you face-to-face with the timeless precepts of God's Word. My desire is that you might know what God says, and in knowing it, that you might learn how to overcome the sin factor that plagues every one of our lives, that causes us at times to wonder why on earth we ever married whom we married.

As you learn these things and put them into practice, you will not find yourself in the position of Dano Osman on that bright November day in Yosemite Park. Your rope will hold when the crisis comes. You will be able to tell your children and grandchildren how the strong arms of God saved you, directed you, and upheld you through your marriage.

Let's pray together once again.

O precious Father, I—we—have sinned against Your great love. Time after time, we have believed a lie. We have heard what we wanted to hear and disregarded the rest. We thought we could escape sin's consequences for somehow, in our blind pride, we thought ourselves to be smarter and wiser than You. Consequently, we walked in sin, choosing what pleased us at the moment, following after our own confused desires. But now, Lord, we want to deal with those issues. We want to face up to the sin factor in our lives. Speak to our hearts in this moment. Show us truth and we will embrace it. Say to us through Your Word, "This is the way," and we will take it. We will trust You, follow You, and obey You.

We acknowledge, Father, that we can speak only for ourselves, not for the mates You have given us. Nor can we blame them for things we need to face in our own secret hearts. We will listen, and by Your grace and power we choose to say yes to Your Spirit.

Yet in the same breath, Lord, we plead for You to also be working in the hearts of our mates. You are God, and You have asked in Your Word, "Is anything too difficult for Me?" O Lord, we know that the answer to that question will always be no. So we place all our situations and burdens and anxieties into Your capable, loving hands.

All of this we ask in the name of the One who redeems us from the curse of sin, the One who sits at Your right hand interceding for us at this very moment. In the name of Jesus, amen.

CHAPTER 5

WHAT DOES GOD EXPECT OF THE HUSBAND?

GEORGE PICKED UP HIS RAZOR AND GAVE the can of shaving cream a vigorous shaking. Pausing before he filled his palm with the rich, white lather, he evaluated the image that stared back at him from the mirror.

Hmmm.

He definitely looked a little older, but he wasn't sure he looked any wiser. Time had begun to do its work on his face. When he squinted, he noticed how deeply wrinkled he had become around the eyes. And there seemed to be more gray sprouting around his temples.

All that gray hair and those wrinkles were the price extracted from all the stress and worry in his life, the result of trying to meet a thousand expectations that seemed to come from all directions.

Expectations of being a good employee—one who did his work well and gave that extra effort to make sure that he met every deadline.

Expectations of being a good friend, of being available to his buddies, especially those who were facing really tough times in their own lives.

Expectations of being a good father, giving his kids the love and attention they needed. Of finding the time to attend his son's basketball games and his daughter's piano recital.

But most of all…expectations of being a good husband.

Man, oh man. How could he do it all? How could he measure up on what seemed like a dozen fronts at the same time? The responsibilities. The competing expectations. The pressures. Those feelings of guilt and failure that washed over him.

When it came to doing his job, he pretty much understood what he needed to do to be counted as a success. But when it came to his marriage—well, that was another matter altogether!

Here was the question that haunted him, the age-old question that most men despair of ever being able to answer:

> What does it take to make a woman happy?

Unlocking the Mystery

Let's face it. Both sexes are kind of a mystery to each other. No matter how hard men try, it's pretty difficult to figure out what makes women tick.

George had listened to some marriage experts on television and the radio, had shared his personal marital triumphs and failures with his friends, and had even snuck a peek or two at the articles in some of the women's magazines his wife left lying around. But none of these provided the answers he needed.

Where on earth could he go for advice?

That's when it hit him. Maybe he'd been chasing "earthly" advice so hard that he'd forgotten to check in with heaven. He had failed to search the very best source for answers to such questions—the Word of God. If he could count on the Bible to teach him how to be a better Christian, perhaps it would be the best place to go to learn how to be a better husband.

Manufacturer's Specifications

If we are to walk in the truth, we must set aside all our own personal views about "what works and doesn't work" and look to the Word of God for guidance on the husband's role in marriage. When you buy a new car, it comes with an owner's manual inside the glove box. Within that little book is all the information you need to maintain that car and keep it running smoothly. Why wouldn't God, the Creator and Designer of man and woman, put into His eternal book the insights and instructions we need to live together in harmony and joy?

In fact, He has done just that! So let's get into God's book together and see what He says about a husband's responsibility to his wife.

When we study what the Bible says, we see that God's expectation for the husband is every bit as challenging as His expectation for the wife—and maybe more so. The high calling of the husband is to love uncon-ditionally—to love his wife as Christ loves the church.

The classic Scripture passage on marriage is Ephesians 5:25-33. Take a moment to read it through, and then let me ask you a few questions that will help you see for yourself what God says to husbands. So you get the real impact you might want to underline "love," and circle every "as" or "just as."

> Husbands, love your wives, just as Christ also loved the church and gave Himself up for her, so that He might sanctify her, having cleansed her by the washing of water with the word, that He might present to Himself the church in all her glory, having no spot or wrinkle or any such thing; but that she would be holy and blame-less. So husbands ought to love their own wives as their own bodies. He who loves his own wife loves himself; for no one ever hated his own flesh, but nourishes and cherishes it, just as Christ also does the church, because we are members of His body. For this reason a man shall leave his father and mother and shall be joined to his wife, and the two shall become one flesh. This mys-tery is great; but I am speaking with reference to Christ and the church. Nevertheless, each individual among you also is to love

his own wife even as himself, and the wife must see to it that she respects her husband.

These verses in Ephesians 5 are so crucial to a healthy and strong marriage that we mustn't miss a thing that God is trying to teach us. Let's look closely at this passage.

First, what is the husband commanded to do in respect to his wife? This can be wrapped up in one word: love. He is to love her.

How much is he to love her? To what degree or extent is the husband to love his wife? Look carefully at the phrase "just as." Yes, that's right. Husbands, Paul is writing directly to you and telling you that you are supposed to love your wife *just as* Christ loved the church. And Christ loved the church so much that His goal was to make her "holy and blameless."

There is a second way that husbands are told to love their wives: "as their own bodies." Men, you are told to cherish and nourish your wives just as you would your own body. You wouldn't starve yourself, so is it right to starve your wife of affection? No, you must give yourself as Christ gave Himself: unconditionally, fully, sacrificially.

This is a high calling. An awesome responsibility.

Remember, Genesis 2 insists that when a man takes a wife, he is to be guided by the principle of stewardship. God holds a man accountable for the welfare of his wife, and while it may seem that many who violate this stewardship get away with it, never forget that we haven't yet read the final chapter.

Jesus Christ *is* coming.

His reward *is* with Him.

He *will* give to everyone—lost and saved—according to their deeds.[1]

If Jesus Christ were to return to earth today, would you be ready, my friend? If He were to ask your wife for a report detailing your marital stewardship, what would He hear? Would you smile with gratitude (and relief) as your wife opened her mouth in praise…or would you shrink

1. Revelation 22:12.

back in shame because you didn't treat your wife as your Lord would have you treat her?

O my friend, there is no reason why you can't start making needed changes today—even at this moment. There is no need for anyone to feel ashamed when Christ returns. (No regrets, remember?) God has made it clear in His Word that He wants us to "have confidence and not shrink away from Him in shame at His coming."[2]

God cares about how husbands treat their wives. Although many nations around the world treat women as if they were livestock, God insists (in both the creation account and in His instructions in Ephesians 5) that a woman is not chattel, a slave, a person of less worth than a man. When God created mankind male and female, *both* were to subdue the earth and rule over it. Certainly the role of a woman is different from that of a man, but that is why God created us male and female. If men were intended to do it all, there would have been no reason to create women. *(And wouldn't that have made for a boring world?)*

But women are every bit as indispensable and vital to mankind as are men. They are to be honored and treated as precious vessels made in the very image of God, just as men are. When it comes to value and worth in the sight of God, women and men stand together on perfectly level ground.

In fact, to demonstrate how seriously He takes all of this, God has laid down clear parameters in His Word, telling us how to relate to one another. God calls these parameters "commands." And He expects them to be obeyed.

A Love Like God's

God commands the husband, for example, to love his wife. You saw this in Ephesians 5:25. In the original Greek, the verb translated "love" is *agapao*. The Greek language uses several words that in our English

---

2. 1 John 2:28.

Bibles are equally translated "love," but this particular love, an *agape* kind of love, is the highest and most lofty. To describe the love of God— the love that God gives freely, unconditionally, regardless of response— the ancients took a little-used term and invested it with deep, rich meaning.

The full meaning of *agape* burst into full blossom in the New Testament as holy men of God were moved by His Spirit to write down the Word of God. In the Gospels, *agape* was carefully chosen to picture God's immeasurable love toward mankind. In the Gospel accounts, we have a precious record of God's coming for us, of leaving the glories of heaven to take on our human nature so that He might taste suffering and death on our behalf. He died for us when we were yet enemies, when we were helpless, hopeless sinners.[3]

Of all the words used for love, *agape* is the noblest. It's the word God uses to describe His love for you. It's the kind of love you have always longed for in your mom, your dad, your wife, your child. It is the word used in the most precious of verses, John 3:16: "God so loved [*agapesen*] the world, that He gave His only begotten Son, that whoever believes in Him shall not perish, but have eternal life."

Now stop and think about this. God loves all the people of the world, but all the people of the world certainly don't love Him. Rather, the great majority ignore, deny, or even blaspheme Him. Yet God still loves them and invites them to turn from their rebellion and accept His offer of eternal life by believing in His Son.

Isn't that an awesome thought? It ought to stop us right in our tracks no matter how many times we've heard it. It doesn't matter what an individual has done; God loves him and will take him just as he is. What's more, He will help that individual step out of the ashes of his past and really begin to make something of his life. What a love! What a God! You know very well how amazing this all is if you've ever experienced it. I hope with all my heart that you will never get over that sense of wonder and awe in what God has accomplished on your behalf.

---

3. Romans 5:6-11.

And this—*this*—is the same love God asks husbands to lavish on their wives? Could it be? Could the Word of God really mean that a husband is to love his wife with the same sort of self-giving, unconditional, sacrificial love that Jesus demonstrated when He laid down His life for sinful mankind?

Yes. That is exactly what the Word of God means.

Do you see now how necessary it is to walk in the power of the indwelling Spirit of Christ day by day?

Let me take a moment now and share a few interesting insights hidden in the tense, mood, and voice of this all-important Greek word. When God tells husbands in Ephesians 5 that they are to love [*agape*] their wives, He puts the verb:

—in the *imperative mood,* which means it is a command

—in the *present tense,* which indicates continual or habitual action

—in the *active voice,* which tells us the subject carries out the action of the verb.

Are you still with me? What does all of that mean?

First, it means that God takes this matter of husbands loving their wives so seriously that He mandates it. Hear me carefully, Beloved. God will *never* accept the excuse that "I just don't love her anymore" because of the kind of love He commands. (We'll study the subject of love in a later chapter. I think you'll find it very helpful.) God does not ask husbands to "feel" a certain way or to work up an acceptable emotion. He simply commands them: "Husbands, love your wives."

Second, it means that husbands are to love their wives in a consistent, ongoing way—moment-by-moment, day-by-day, year-by-year. Special occasions like anniversaries, birthdays, and holidays present wonderful, creative opportunities to show such love, but they are no substitute for the *agape* love that is like a mountain stream that continually bubbles up bracing and fresh from the ancient rocks to bring life and vitality to the lush meadows below.

Third, it means that God expects a husband's love for his wife to be proactive. A husband cannot wait around for some outside source to prompt him. He can't sit in front of the ballgame on TV and wait for the Spirit to "move" him to some act of sacrificial love. No, this is the sort of love that takes the initiative. A husband is to plot the ways he can love her, cherish her, and make her feel as if she is the most blessed woman on earth. Oh, men, believe me—if you will love a woman as God would have (and enable) you, you will know that you are a success, a winner, a man above most men! You will find looking in the shaving mirror a more encouraging activity each morning.

Love Is a Choice

Isn't that an awesome thought? A husband is commanded to continuously love his wife *in and of herself, regardless of who she is or what she does.*

And if that were not awesome enough, think about this: Love is not merely an emotion, otherwise it could not be commanded.

Love requires action.

Love demands deeds.

Love calls on a man to step up to the plate each day and give even when he doesn't feel like giving at all.

Love wills.

Love acts.

Love moves on behalf of its object.

How different this is from the concept held by most of our society! How many times have you heard someone say he was getting a divorce because "I just don't love her anymore," meaning, "the feeling's gone"? How many sad, pitiful songs have you heard on the radio, bemoaning the fact that "he or she just doesn't love me anymore…the feelin's gone, and my, oh my, we just can't get it back again."

How absurd! How shallow! As if love were some sort of vague, hazy cloud floating through the air that dissipates at the first puff of wind. In God's estimation, that sort of reasoning just won't hold water. It's full of holes. It leaks like a sieve because it misses entirely the true nature of love.

Love is *not* merely a feeling that comes and goes, a shiver in your liver caused by elevated blood hormones. (No, I'm not saying love is nothing more than a dead and passionless obedience, a bloodless decision to do one's duty without a hint of affection or tenderness or emotion. At its best, it is infinitely more than that!) At its core, however, love *acts* whether the emotion is there or not. Love decides to do something, and then it picks itself up and does it.

It is a courageous, thoroughly manly thing to do.

It is committed to positive action for the benefit of the beloved. Love acts and the emotions follow—and even if they don't, love acts anyway. This is how God commands a husband to love his wife.

"But what does this love look like?" you ask. "If I can't see it, how am I to mimic it? Especially when it seems so hard?"

Ah, there's the captivating part! Our God doesn't leave the husband scratching his head, wondering what *agape* love looks like. In the same breath that He gives the commandment to love, God also gives us two perfect pictures of this love.

Two Portraits of Love

The first picture of love God gives us is by far the most instructive. The husband is to love his wife, God says, "just as Christ loved the church."

Wow! Are you choking? Remember—God said it, not me! What an overwhelming responsibility falls on those broad masculine shoulders. "Just as Christ loved the church." And how did Christ love the church?

> He humbled Himself, girded on a towel and washed filthy feet, that she might be "cleansed by the washing of water with the word."

> He offered His flesh to be torn by evil men, that she might be without "spot or wrinkle or any such thing."

> He died on a cruel cross, that she might be made "holy and blameless."

O, Beloved, our Lord loves us warts and all! Unconditionally, sacrificially, patiently, enduringly, endearingly.

God forgives and does not forsake. Read the Gospels and see Him in action; read the epistles and see Him explained. *Then* you will know how a husband is to love his wife.

Of course, it is quite true that a husband has been given the role of headship over his wife, just as Christ is the head of the church. But if you observe Ephesians 5 carefully, you will see this headship acting in a servant's role, a role that stoops down and washes feet, just as Jesus did in John 13:1-17.

Have you read that startling story lately? Think of Jesus in the Upper Room, facing His greatest hour of trial and testing and knowing the agonies that await Him. And yet at that Passover meal He rose from dinner, took a pitcher and a towel and washed the filthy feet of His disciples. Although His hour had come, "having loved His own who were in the world, He loved them [literally] to the end."

How can we observe our Teacher and Lord girding on a towel and washing the grimy feet of His disciples and not see that Jesus Himself modeled headship in a servant's role? He never ceased to be the head; but it was precisely because He *was* the head that He bent down and cleaned the soil from between dusty toes. "I gave you an example that you also should do as I did to you," He told His men that night.

Please take note that this was no dictator angrily barking out that no one had washed *His* feet and that one of His disciples had better be quick to rectify the error. You don't hear the Master shouting, "Hey, you! Get a basin, get water, get a towel—and get with it!" Rather, we see a divine, committed love that bows its head, stoops down, and picks up a towel.

Men, may I ask you a personal question? When your wife drops something around the home, are you quick to stoop down and pick it up for her? Or do you eyeball the floor, look at her, then look down at the floor again to signal, "Hey, you! Didn't you *drop* something?"

Agape love stoops down and gets to work.

Agape chooses to soil its hands.

Agape expends itself.

Agape inconveniences itself.

Agape offers itself.

Agape doesn't have to be asked.

Agape looks for ways to help and encourage.

It is no accident that the Bible tells us Jesus came not to be ministered unto, but to minister and to give His life as a ransom for many.

How about you, Beloved? How can you practically encourage your wife today? How can you show her this *agape* love? How can you minister to her needs?

Does she need a break from grocery shopping? Maybe tonight you could pick up a cartload of food.

Does she need a good neck massage? Maybe your fingers could do the walking.

Does a drab winter make her long for spring? Maybe you could visit the florist.

Can you imagine what would happen throughout the homes of America if husbands would begin to love their wives in this *agape* way? Can you picture what would happen to the divorce rate? It would plummet like the stock market did in the Great Depression—only instead of depression the greatest boom this nation has ever known would arise. Homes would be restored and children would find the security, peace, and joy that their little hearts crave.

That's what can happen when a husband chooses to love his wife "as Christ loved the church." Christ stayed at it all the way until His last breath—and then battled (and conquered!) death itself to ensure that we, His bride, would *never* be parted from Him.

And yet there is more to this picture.

A husband is not only to love his wife as Christ loves the church; he is to love her *as he loves his own body.* Now, healthy men don't inflict wounds and bruises on their own bodies (unless they play football). What the body needs, the body usually gets. Why? Because the man *lives* inside that body.

Men don't hate their own flesh; therefore, they should never hate their wives. Why? Because when a man and a woman are joined in marriage, they become "one flesh." Remember, Genesis 2 taught us that when a man marries a woman, he leaves his family and cleaves to his wife, and the two become one flesh. Therefore a man who hates his wife is really hating his own flesh—and that is not only foolish, but ultimately destructive.

This word from God came at just the right time, for until Jesus Christ appeared on the scene, women were held in low esteem, even in Judaism. Jewish men often gave thanks to God that He had not made them a Gentile dog...or a woman. The scene was no more pleasant in the society of the Ephesians. In the Roman Empire, men expected to have a wife at home and a prostitute in the brothel or temple. Women existed merely as bearers of children, as satisfiers of desire, as servants to do the bidding of men—until Jesus came and set us on a whole new path.

When I think about this kind of visible, attractive love, my friend Robertson McQuilken comes to mind. I told a little of his story in my book *As Silver Refined: Learning to Embrace Life's Disappointments.* There could be no greater disappointment, I would think, than to watch your loved one waste away under the merciless talons of the disease we call Alzheimer's. What a heartache to see your beloved, sound in body but not in intellect or emotion. That was Robertson's great tragedy.

But my friend did not merely *see.* He *acted.*

His story is told in a beautiful book that I believe every married couple ought to own, *A Promise Kept, the Story of an Unforgettable Love.*

Robertson tells of the incident that led up to his resignation from the presidency of Columbia Bible College and Seminary. Speaking of Muriel's love and devotion to him, he wrote, "And Muriel loved me, too. By then she couldn't speak in sentences, only words—and often words that didn't make sense. *No* when she meant *yes,* for example. But she could still say one sentence. And she said it often: 'I love you.'"

"She not only said it, she acted it. During the latter years of my presidency at Columbia, it became increasingly difficult to keep her at home. As soon as I left for the office, she would take out after me. With me, she was content; without me, she was distressed, sometimes terror-stricken.

"The walk to school is a mile round-trip. She would make that trip as many as ten times a day—*ten miles,* speed walking. Sometimes at night when I helped her undress, I found bloody feet. When I told our family doctor, he choked up. 'Such love,' he said simply. Then after a moment, 'I have a theory that the characteristics developed across the years come out at times like these.'"

His wife's bleeding feet precipitated Robertson's letter to the Columbia constituency:

"Twenty-two years is a long time. But then again, it can be shorter than one anticipates. And how do you say good-bye to friends you do not wish to leave?

"The decision to come to Columbia was the most difficult I have had to make; the decision to leave 22 years later, though painful, was one of the easiest. It was almost as if God engineered the circumstances so that I had no alternative. Let me explain.

"My dear wife, Muriel, has been in failing mental health for about 12 years. So far I have been able to care for both her ever-growing needs and my leadership responsibility at Columbia. But recently it has become apparent that Muriel is contented most of the time she is with me and almost none of the time I am away from her. It is not just 'discontent.' She is filled with fear—even terror—that she has lost me and always goes in search of me when I leave home. So it is clear to me that she needs me now, full-time.

"Perhaps it would help you understand if I share with you what I shared in chapel at the time of the announcement of my resignation. The decision was made, in a way, 42 years ago when I promised to care for Muriel 'in sickness and in health...till death do us part.' So, as I told the students and faculty, as a man of my word, integrity has something to do with it. But so does fairness. She has cared for me fully and sacrificially all these years; if I cared for her for the next 40 years I would not be out of her debt. Duty, however, can be grim and stoic. But there is more: I love Muriel. She is a delight to me—her childlike dependence and confidence in me, her warm love, occasional flashes of that wit I used to relish so, her happy spirit and tough resilience in the face of her continual distressing frustration. I don't *have* to care for her. I *get* to! It is a high honor to care for so wonderful a person."

All who caught wind of the sweet fragrance of love's sacrifice took notice as Robertson poured himself out on the altar of sacrifice (as Paul speaks of in Philippians chapter 2).

The response to Robertson's letter was a mystery to Robertson until an oncologist who lived constantly with the dying told him, "Almost all women stand by their men; very few men stand by their women." What a sad observation when the man is to portray to his wife, their children and society the love of Christ who would never leave nor forsake His bride.

It might embarrass my humble friend if he should read this, but I saw in him the nobility of man. In Robertson's tender nourishing and cherishing of his ailing wife despite the pain and heartache, I saw a living picture of Ephesians 5:29. In that verse, Paul uses the word *ektrepho* ("nourishes") to describe the care men use to pamper their bodies.

Ordinarily *ektrepho* is used of children. It means to nurture them, to rear them, to care for them as one cares for one's own flesh. It is the word the apostle Paul uses later in Ephesians 6:4 when he tells fathers to "bring up" their children in the discipline and instruction of the Lord. The second word, *thalpo* ("cherishes"), means "to heat, to soften by heat," and by extension "to keep warm, as of birds covering their young with their feathers." Metaphorically, it means "to cherish with tender love, to foster with tender care."

It wasn't always easy for Robertson to nourish and cherish his Muriel in her deteriorating condition; in fact, often it was more a struggle than a joy. My friend makes that confession in his small book *Until Death Do Us Part*. But when Robertson failed, he felt a godly sorrow and corrected himself.

Robertson loved Muriel as he loved his own body. And when her body began to fail, he loved her all the more. Because that's what real love does.

The Heart of God

The love Robertson showed is the love that is God's heart, that is His design.

Yes, I know. There is the sin factor. No man can completely live up to such a high calling of love. And if we are honest with ourselves, most of the time we just don't *want* to love like that. It takes too much work, too much sacrifice.

But as Christians we are without excuse, for we possess the Spirit of God who loves to strengthen us "with all power."[4] He dwells within us, and if we walk by the Spirit, we will not fulfill the lusts of the flesh. Then will burst from our lives the fruit of the Spirit, which first and foremost is love—*agape* love.

"But," someone says, "I don't *feel...*" Hold it right there. None of that. Feelings are not the issue! It is a matter of the *will.* The question is, by God's strength, what do you *resolve* to do? That is the issue.

According to God's Word, the husband is to give himself up for his wife. She is to take priority, even in the face of contrary personal desires. Christ modeled for us a sacrificial love—but not a sacrifice without purpose. Why did Christ sacrifice Himself? "That He might sanctify her, having cleansed her by the washing of water with the word, that He might present to Himself the church in all her glory, having no spot or wrinkle or any such thing; but that she should be holy and blameless."

Where did Christ focus? He focused on His bride. She was to be loved even though she was yet unlovely and covered with many spots, wrinkles, and blemishes. Christ loved her to the utmost so that she might blossom into her full beauty, holy and blameless.

That's also the prescription for Christian marriages. A husband is to focus on his wife, even though he notices spots and wrinkles and blemishes that he wishes were not there. His role—his sacred calling, his holy task—is to love her until she blossoms into her full beauty as a woman, radiant and stunning as she reflects the very holiness of Christ.

What a treasure, this *agape* love!

Listen, my friend, don't we all blossom under love? Is it not the dew of morning, the soft gentle rain, the fertile soil, the warming sun, the sheltering shade? Love makes the world go 'round, to be sure, but it is also what created the sun and the earth itself in the very beginning and what keeps them both sparkling like diamonds in the black void of space.

---

4. Colossians 1:11.

The Bottom Line

So what's the bottom line of this chapter? It's simple, really. *The husband is to love his wife just as Christ loved the church, even as a man loves his own body.*

If husbands would follow this single rule, it's doubtful any Christian wife would find submission at all distasteful. Why? Because such a wife would be fully assured of her worth and value. She would enjoy a security beyond words. And submission would simply never become an issue. (But since many husbands do not follow the example of Christ, submission *is* an issue. And that, Beloved, is what we will consider in the next chapter.)

But for now, what do we do? If you are a woman reading this, you long for exactly this kind of love. And there's nothing wrong with that. You were made for it. God knew that, because He made you and He wants you to have it.

If you are a man reading this book for yourself, I urge you to act not only on your own behalf, but also for others. Pray that God will give you an opportunity to make plain to other men God's principles on marriage. Pray that you may model these things in the way you speak of and care for your wife. I know this: If you do pray like this, you will be praying according to the Word of God and you will gain the petitions that you ask of Him.[5] This is what God promises—and He watches over His Word to perform it. Isn't that reassuring!

So let's pray. Let's pray for the men, for the husbands, for the sons being raised to become husbands and fathers. And let's pray with conviction.

> *O Father, what do we say? We have read Your Word; we have studied Your precepts. We have seen them for ourselves. We have come face-to-face with truth. We know Your heart; we have seen Your commands. In many situations, in many marriages, they will be difficult to obey. But may the many who read it bow*

---

5. John 15:7.

their knees in humble submission, knowing that "faithful is He who calls us and who will also do it." This, Father, is holiness— living set apart from the world to do Your will, to believe You, to honor You as God, no matter the personal cost.

O Father, somehow move in our society, in our homes, in our communities, and in our nation. Give men the boldness to speak out, to call others to this sacrifice, to give themselves for their wives just as Christ gave Himself up for the church. May men love their wives as they love their own bodies. May they begin to nourish them and cherish them. And may their wives blossom under their gentle, tender warming.

May their children take notice and remember what they have seen lived out at home. And may these little ones be nurtured in the security of seeing a mother and father who are so committed to each other, so in love with each other, so united in purpose, that the children can rest and put away all fears of separation. May the yelling, the threats, the slandering, the slaughtering words be cast into the sea. May the swords be bent into plow- shares and be used for planting seeds of affection that will blossom into a harvest of love.

Father, as judgment begins at the house of the Lord, so too may this begin in the house of God and in the church of Jesus Christ. Oh, how we appreciate Your patience with us, Your longsuf- fering, as You have waited for the men of the church to come to this holy sacrifice of themselves.

May each wife treasure every move her husband makes, and may she be quick to pray and slow to retaliate when he falls short of Your call.

Father, in the privacy of our own lives and days, may we know that Your ears are open and attentive to the prayers of Your people. Help us to remember that we have not because we ask not. Help us to see when we ask amiss, for we would not gratify our own desires. O beloved Father, we ask this for the sake of the church, for the sake of Your kingdom, for the sake of all those created in Your image. We ask all this in the name of the One who models His great love for us every moment, every hour, every day—even when we ought to be further along than we are. Amen.

CHAPTER 6

I'M A WOMAN!
WHAT IS MY VALUE?

MY, HOW YOU HAVE CHANGED, LITTLE GIRL," Belinda murmured to herself, shaking her head in a bemused way. In the midst of her spring cleaning and digging through old boxes, she had come across a May 1976 issue of *Highlights,* her old high school newspaper.

There in an opinion piece on the editorial page, Belinda read the militant words of a 16-year-old girl—her own words. She had to laugh in disbelief. Could she really have considered herself the "Queen of Women's Lib"?

> A woman can successfully compete in almost all walks of business life with a man....Being a career woman is a full-time job because of the male competition. You've got to give it everything you've got to hold down and keep a man's job....Whatever you do, don't settle for the traditional role in life of marriage and family life, because TODAY, LIFE HAS FAR MORE TO OFFER WOMEN!

Belinda had been a junior in high school when she penned these words. How could she forget? It was the year her parents separated. Over the next 12 years, this young "Queen of Women's Lib," the "unshackled woman" who was out to grab her share of fun and make her mark on the world, found her life deteriorating rapidly. Now, in retrospect, she saw the limits of her "liberated" dreams.

"Little did I realize," she wrote to me, "that I was rapidly becoming the person I would end up being for a very long time. The choices being made set up habits and a way of life that took me on a roller coaster ride I had not bargained for....It was as if I were on some kind of downward sloping ride at an amusement part and I could not get off. I was confronted with more sin in my life than I thought I was capable of...."

These were years of immorality, adultery, alcohol, drugs, and even an abortion.

Then Belinda met Jesus.

Eventually she was invited to a Precepts class (part of Precept Ministries). She noted, "I began studying the Bible in a way that I never had before. It wasn't dry and impossible to understand anymore. Before long the things I learned reshaped my goals for life....How different my life has turned out from the claims I made of independence and success 20 years ago."[1]

What was it that made the feminist message so appealing to Belinda's attention at the age of 16? How did she come to the conclusion that life has far more to offer women than what they might find in a traditional marriage and family? And what was it she learned from studying the Bible that reshaped her goals for life and helped her as a mother and wife to fulfill those traditional roles she once disparaged?

Deceived Again?

In 1963, Betty Friedan concluded that the women of her generation felt unhappy and stifled. She became one of the prominent voices in a

---

1. "My, How You've Changed! Confessions of a Former BCHS Women's Libber." At the end of her paper that she gave me to share, Belinda wrote, "My prayer for those of you who read this story is that you would seriously consider the invitation to allow Christ to take control of your life, too."

growing "feminist movement." The word "feminist" first appeared in a book review in the April 27, 1895, edition of *Athenaeum*. It described a woman who "has in her the capacity of fighting her way back to independence."[2]

It sounds like a concept with some merit, doesn't it? The word "independence" sounds sweet to the ear. But in this context it amounted to a rerun of an old tune first heard in a beautiful garden, long, long ago.

The Garden of Eden.

As in that Garden at the dawn of time, women have believed a fine-sounding lie. Only this time, the promise isn't that they will be wise...it is that they will be *free*. As a result of this lie, many women shunned marriage and motherhood for a career. Believing that "sex is power," women have bought into the idea that it's okay to sleep with men—just don't marry them. These changes have been trumpeted as a new day, the day of liberation. Liberation from the shackles of caring about others over yourself.

In 1972, the United States Congress passed a so-called "Equal Rights Amendment."[3] In 1973, *Roe v. Wade* legalized abortion on demand. In three rapid decades since these pivotal years, the number of divorced people would quadruple, and 62 percent of mothers with children under three would join the workforce.[4] And for the first time in 60 years, the majority of firstborn children would be conceived by unmarried women.[5] The percentage of families headed by a single parent would triple. One-fourth of all adolescents graduating from high school would have a sexually transmitted disease.

Such is the fruit of the lie.

The "freedom" promised by the serpent has come at a very dear price.

---

2. Susan Faludi, *Backlash* (New York: Anchor Books, 1991), p. xxiii.

3. The Equal Rights Amendment was not ratified by the states within the time limit set by Congress, so it was not added to the Constitution.

4. Census Bureau, *American Demographics,* May 1999.

5. Ibid.

Declaration of Dependence

Something else happened in 1963 that had little to do with Betty Friedan's year of realization. It was the year that I discovered Truth.

It was truth that would take me from independence to dependence upon a God who has never failed me.

It was truth about His only begotten Son, the Lord Jesus Christ.

It was truth that would take a bitterly unhappy woman, stifled by her own sinful, selfish ways, and set her free.

It was truth that would help me understand my vital, critical role as a woman.

It was truth that over the next 30 years would heal the damage done to my two sons by the lie I had embraced.

It was truth I would eventually teach on radio, television, and in print, touching the lives of millions across the world.

It is *this* truth, dear reader, that I want to share with you right now, a truth that can not only change the course of your life, but impact and influence the lives of your loved ones. And what is that truth? It is what God has to say about the role of woman.

Distinctively Female

First, wives, you need to know you were created by God—made distinctively female. Your role and your physical and emotional construction are decidedly different from that of a man.

"Well, how obvious," you might say. "Tell me something new." And yet it is at this very point—the distinction between the sexes—where Satan has attempted to blur the lines and create unhappiness and vast confusion in our culture. It's when we refuse to embrace the truth of our gender differences (and all they imply) that our society begins to tear apart at the seams.

In God's eyes women are equal with men, but we certainly aren't like them. The differences that begin to manifest themselves six weeks after conception delineate very clearly that, just as Genesis 1:26,27 attests, God created us male and female. Woman, created as a helpmeet for man, differs physically, emotionally, and biochemically from the man from whose rib she was fashioned.

I could fill a book with examples, but I will only cite a few. Men excel in brute strength over women by about 50 percent. The verbal part of our brains (the left hemisphere) develops earlier with girls, while the visual part of the brain (the right hemisphere) develops earlier with boys. Generally this difference is seen in the old-fashioned and much-needed 3 R's: reading, (w)riting and (a)rithmetic. Girls are quicker to read and write; boys usually begin to grasp math at an earlier age.

It's our biochemical differences, our hormones, our larger thyroid, that gives us that sometimes complex emotional makeup that makes it difficult for a man to understand us. Remember Professor Henry Higgins, in *My Fair Lady*? He vented his frustration with the song, "Why can't a woman be more like a man?"

Well, there's a simple answer, Professor Higgins.

Women aren't like men because God created us different!

And the sooner men and women realize this, take it into account, and order their lives accordingly, the quicker our society will be able to recover from the disaster wrought by the lie so many of us have bought into.

Now, just as I said to the men in the previous chapter, let's consult that Manufacturer's handbook and see what God's Word has to say about women, their roles, and their relationships to men and to society. Understanding this and living accordingly is an all-important key to a marriage without regrets.

How Does God View Women?

Never doubt it, Beloved, God places a high value on women. For all her physical differences, she is not less than man when it comes to value. Nor is she less because her role is different. As you have already seen in Genesis 1 and 2, woman is an equal creation of God, made in His image, and given not only equal dominion with man over God's creation but the mutual responsibility to multiply and fill the earth. When describing the headship of man in 1 Corinthians 11, God quickly highlights the fact that no man exists apart from woman: "However, in the

Lord, neither is woman independent of man, nor is man independent of woman. For as the woman originates from the man, so also the man has his birth through the woman; and all things originate from God."[6]

So how did we get to the place of devaluing women in our world? As with so many things in our world today, it all began back in the Garden.

Woman had been created from man for man. Her role was highly valued. The Lord God said, "It is not good for the man to be alone; I will make a helper suitable for him."[7] The word helper is *ezer* and comes from the root word *azar,* which means "to help, to succor." The word translated "suitable" is *neged,* which means "in front of, in sight of, opposite to."

Woman, the helper suitable, was made to be man's counterpart, his completer (note I did not say *competitor).* I often illustrate the relationship of a man to a woman by using the fingers on one of my hands. Pointing to the tips of my spread-out fingers, and then the gap in between my fingers, I say, "Usually where a man is strong, the woman is weak. And where the woman is strong the man is usually weak." Then I slide my hands with their spread-out fingers together, inserting the fingers on my right hand between the fingers on my left. It's a simple little demonstration meant to show how we become counterparts, completers, complementary to each other. Together, with our differences, we become more than we could ever be without each other.

Once sin entered into the world, however, this harmonious integration was jeopardized. Both partners now had a knowledge of good and evil. Instead of interlocking, they would now find themselves deadlocking. Eating from the fruit of the tree of the knowledge of good and evil brought heart disease to the man and the woman—and to us. As Jeremiah and Ezekiel tell us, our hearts became like stone, deceitful and desperately wicked.[8]

---

6. 1 Corinthians 11:11,12.

7. Genesis 2:18.

8. Jeremiah 17:9; Ezekiel 36:26.

Life changed in one terrible heartbeat. The former oneness of man and woman was severely damaged. Now they were two individuals, feeling their independence, each functioning according to a whole new way of reasoning. God's pronouncement of judgment brought huge, crushing consequences to bear on that first couple—and to every man and woman since. Man would now earn his bread by the sweat of his brow, wresting crops out of stubborn, weed-choked soil. Woman would now bear her children in great pain and travail. Furthermore, God told her, "Your desire will be for your husband, and he will rule over you" (Genesis 3:16). The chaos wrought by sin had to be brought into some kind of order for mankind to survive on earth. Someone had to rule.

Who's Going to Rule?

The responsibility for ruling fell on the shoulders of men. Although headship was established by the sequence of their creation and demonstrated in Adam's naming of the woman, an *order of authority* had to be instigated.

And so we come to the submission of women.

And we don't like it at all.

It is something that sparks rebellion within us. Something that incenses us deep down. Yet submission (*hupotasso* in the Greek) in Ephesians 5:22 and Colossians 3:18 is a word chosen by God and issued as a command. We will look at it in a minute or two, but first, Beloved, we need to backtrack for a minute and look at those God-uttered words, "Yet your desire will be for your husband." What in the world does that mean?

The word translated desire is the Hebrew word *t'shuqa*. It comes from a little-used term, *shuwq*, which means to overflow or overtake. It is used only three times in the Old Testament, and in each incident it is translated "desire." Yet there are differences in how this word is to be understood. Hang in there with me for a minute, and we'll zero in on these.

T'shuqa appears for the first time in Genesis, in a context of sin and judgment. After Eve sins, God informs her that she will now suffer multiplied pain in childbirth—*yet* (notice the word!) her desire will be for her husband.

It sounds as if God is saying, "Although having children will be painful, it is not going to stop you from desiring your husband physically. It is not going to curb your longing." There are others, however, who give the word a different spin. These commentators believe that, in this context, *t'shuqa* does not mean to "desire" but "to run after, to overflow." In other words, because of sin Eve now desires to overtake Adam, to rule over him.

Regardless of which interpretation is correct, the next consequence of Eve's sin is perfectly clear: "And he will rule over you." For the first time in the narrative, the issue of who is in charge is brought up. And the responsibility falls to the man. In *God's* economy, the husband is to rule over his wife. Please note that the text does *not* teach that man is to rule over woman; rather, it is the *husband* who is to rule over his *wife.*

The second use of *t'shuqa* is found in the very next chapter of Genesis, once again in the context of sin and judgment. In Genesis 4:7, God tells Cain, "Sin is crouching at the door; and its desire (*t'shuqa*) is for you, but you must master it." Sin "desired" Cain; it longed to overtake him like a lion crouching at his door. Cain was warned to master it, to bring it into subjection.

T'shuqa makes its third and final appearance in the Old Testament in a book noted for erotic passion expressed in love between a husband and wife. In Song of Solomon 7:10, the Shulammite woman says, "I am my beloved's, and his desire (*t'shuqa*) is for me." The translation of the verse in this context clearly speaks of desire.

However one interprets *t'shuqa* in Genesis 3:16, it is clear that God ordained the man to rule over the woman. Therefore, for a wife to declare her "independence" from her husband's headship is to fight against the wisdom, will, and choice of Elohim, our Creator.

And that, my dear friend, brings untold chaos.

To fight what God has ordained isn't wise. In fact, it is patently foolish. We will *always* lose. Even when we seem to win, we will lose! It is the way God has ordered His universe in these days after the fall. And *losing* is the very word that describes what is happening in our society today. We are suffering great losses because we are going against God.

God has established His order in marriage. If you want to have the best marriage possible—one without regrets—then you will follow His order. If you fight it, you will be fighting God—and be assured that there are consequences to such rebellion. You can see those consequences as you look around you, can't you, Beloved? Look at the fragmented families. Look into their eyes. Listen to their pain. See it etched on their faces.

What Does Scripture Say?

Does understanding God's order in marriage help you grasp what He means in Ephesians 5:22 when He commands wives to submit to their husbands? The best way to avoid any confusion on the subject is to allow the Scripture to speak for itself. So let's begin by looking at this famous passage on submission, which says simply, "Wives, *be subject* to your own husbands, as to the Lord."

Here, as everywhere, context is everything. To make sure we don't take these words out of context, let's consider the whole passage, Ephesians 5:18-33. You've looked at Ephesians 5:25-33 in the previous chapter; this time, however, I want us to focus on its *setting*—and what God says about the woman's role.

18 And do not get drunk with wine, for that is dissipation, but be filled with the Spirit,

19 speaking to one another in psalms and hymns and spiritual songs, singing and making melody with your heart to the Lord;

20 always giving thanks for all things in the name of our Lord Jesus Christ to God, even the Father;

21 and be subject to one another in the fear of Christ.

22 Wives, *be subject* to your own husbands, as to the Lord.

23 For the husband is the head of the wife, as Christ also is the head of the church, He Himself being the Savior of the body.

24 But as the church is subject to Christ, so also the wives ought to be to their husbands in everything.

25 Husbands, love your wives, just as Christ also loved the church and gave Himself up for her,

26 so that He might sanctify her, having cleansed her by the washing of water with the word,

27 that He might present to Himself the church in all her glory, having no spot or wrinkle or any such thing; but that she would be holy and blameless.

28 So husbands ought also to love their own wives as their own bodies. He who loves his own wife loves himself;

29 for no one ever hated his own flesh, but nourishes and cherishes it, just as Christ also does the church,

30 because we are members of His body.

31 FOR THIS REASON A MAN SHALL LEAVE HIS FATHER AND MOTHER AND SHALL BE JOINED TO HIS WIFE, AND THE TWO SHALL BECOME ONE FLESH.

32 This mystery is great; but I am speaking with reference to Christ and the church.

33 Nevertheless, each individual among you also is to love his own wife even as himself, and the wife must see to it that she respects her husband.

The word "subject" in verse 21 (where God tells us to be subject to one another) is the Greek word *hupotasso,* which means "to place under" or "to arrange under." The context makes it clear that submission is one of the results of being filled with the Holy Spirit.

In the original Greek, the verb "be filled" in Ephesians 5:18 is in the present tense, which means the action is performed continually, habitually. The mood of the verb is imperative—a command. "In the middle voice, the present imperative is used to give a command for something which concerns particularly the recipient of the command."[9]

(Please stay with me, Beloved. I promise that it will be worth your while to wrestle with this crucial teaching.)

The various activities we are commanded to perform in the Ephesians passage—speaking, singing, making melody, giving thanks, and being subject—all appear as present participles. The present participle expresses continuous or repeated action and relates to the main verb; in this case it is the command: "Be filled with the Holy Spirit." In other words, these are specific actions that accompany the filling of the Spirit.

Why did I go into all this? Because, beloved learner, it is crucial for us to see that only *after* God gives us these instructions does He delineate the specific roles of wives, husbands, children, fathers, slaves, and masters!

Mutual Submission: Evidence of Spirit-Filling

God intends that all who are filled with the Spirit will gladly submit to one another and place themselves under whatever authority God has ordained. If you are a wife, that means that you will voluntarily place yourself under the authority of your husband.

Look again at verse 22. Did you notice that "be subject" appears in italics? That means it was added by translators for the sake of clarity. Literally the passage reads, "and be subject to one another in the fear of Christ. Wives, to your own husbands as to the Lord." In other words, your submission to your husband is out of obedience to your Lord. You do it as a sacrifice of obedience to the very Word of God.

All right, you say, but should a husband *force* his wife to submit? Please note that the Scripture tells a woman to subject *herself.* The passage says nothing about husbands compelling their wives to submit. The apostle's only command is that a husband love his wife as Christ loved the church. Don't miss this because there are many who teach

---

9. Spiros Zodhiates, *The Complete Word Study New Testament, King James Version* (Chattanooga, TN: AMG Publishers, 1991), p. 857.

that it is the husband's "duty" to somehow bring his wife into submission. If that were true, God would command it, or Jesus would model it. But God *doesn't* command it—and Jesus certainly doesn't model it!

Christ certainly commands the obedience of His bride, but He doesn't *force* it. It is the bride's choice (yours and mine as believers). If we're wise, we'll obey and reap the blessings. If not, we will feel the consequences—and they are devastating!

In God's order, the wife is to subject herself to her husband. That is His clear command. But what is His reason? God doesn't leave us in the dark, for He is quick to explain: "for the husband is the head of the wife, as Christ also is the head of the church, He Himself being the Savior of the body." The wife is to submit because the husband is the head.

Period.

End of reason.

But not the end of reasoning!

Should a Woman Bury Her Gifting?

Living under her husband's headship and submitting to him does not mean that a wife can never open her mouth, never give an opinion, never disagree with a decision, or never warn her husband that he's about to make the wrong decision. We must not carry the text on submission and headship beyond its true limits.

Women were created for more than procreation, although that is a high honor. We are right up there with men—created in God's image, capable of ruling over His creation, designed to be man's counterpart, his completer.

Man needs a woman for more than his existence. We are intelligent, gifted, and talented in so many, many ways. And it is our very differences from the male gender that allow us to see, feel, understand, and evaluate people and situations from a fresh perspective. Men and women need to recognize and honor each other's gifts, talents, and strengths.

This is important because many times the man or woman's role in a marriage is defined arbitrarily according to old tradition or practice. For instance, some believe if the man is the head, it is his task to handle the money—to pay the bills and handle the checkbook—even though he may be all thumbs in this area. What if the wife is better at handling money? Should she suppress that ability simply because she's a woman and not the head? How silly! There is nothing biblical in that kind of thinking.

When looking at the role of a man or a woman, we should be careful not to make unbiblical judgments and conclusions that ignore a person's area of giftedness or ability. This is one of the things that provoked the feminist movement. Women felt stifled—and too many men refused to honor and respect women as partners and equals.

Biblical or Cultural?

Remember, when two people get married they come into marriage with a set of expectations based on what was taught to them or modeled by example as they were growing up. For instance, my father never ironed clothes. Nor did he work in the kitchen or vacuum the house until much later in life—after I left home. These were considered a woman's job, not the man's. And no man loved a woman more than my dad loved my mom.

I was raised understanding that my job as a woman was to iron my husband's clothes (and these were the days before permanent press!). I would have felt like a failure if Tom, my first husband, had to iron anything. Yet as my understanding grew, I saw to it that our sons could wash, iron, and function in a kitchen, too. I trained them to do it, and it didn't strip them of one inch of their manhood. How grateful their wives are that they can iron their shirts and are willing to help in the kitchen and with the kids!

Now Jack, my husband, is another story.

After our sons married and left home, my dear husband would sit in his recliner with his remote, watching television, while I cooked and cleaned. (This was after a full day of working at Precept Ministries.)

What absolutely amazed me was that this dear, godly man thought nothing about it. It stunned me—and upset me, too. I thought to myself, *Can't you see what's happening here, Jack? There's something very wrong with this picture! One is resting, enjoying himself, while the other is dog-tired and cleaning this kitchen.*

For a long time I didn't say anything about it. I was raised in the same culture as he was. The man got to sit and relax in the evenings; his work was done. But a woman's work, as they say, was never done!

As I scrubbed and cleaned, I did it with great vigor as I let him have it in my mind: *You keep telling me to rest more—that I shouldn't stay up all night working. Well, if you mean that then why don't you get up out of that chair and help me? Then I can rest! Don't tell me you love me when you sit there doing nothing!*

I guarantee you that on those nights when I went to bed, I hung over the edge on *my* side. I didn't want him to come close to touching me. I was not in the mood for love.

Now, in my husband's defense, let me explain that Jack was raised on a farm. He plowed, harvested, milked the cows, killed and plucked the chickens and sold them door to door in Greencastle, Indiana. He and Pop, the grandfather who raised his grandson, worked outside the house in the barn and in the fields. Consequently, it just didn't occur to Jack that he should help me in the kitchen.

Finally, over the course of several long walks, long talks, and not a few tears, I reminded Jack as sweetly as I could that I needed his help. Now we have our routine and it includes both of us. (Well, most of the time!)

Who Makes the Decisions?

If the man is the head, is he to make all the decisions? Some people insist that this is so. Any successful CEO of a large organization, however, would tell you that is not wise leadership. He or she would tell you that you need to tap the human resources in your company. You need to listen to those under you. And then, after you've received all the counsel and insights you can gather, you make a decision.

Do you hear, what I'm saying, Beloved? It may be traditional for a man to make all the decisions in your family, but it is not biblical. And it doesn't even make good common sense. Remember, husbands, your wives are your counterparts, your completers. You need them. A wise and prudent man won't move independently of his wife.

But what happens when you don't agree? When it comes to a bottom-line decision, the man rules and the wife is to submit. But that leadership carries with it great responsibility. A wise man will consult the helpmeet God has given him, then move prayerfully and carefully forward.

Submission and Abuse

Just how extensive should a wife's submission be?

Ephesians 5:24 tells us it is "in everything," even as the church is to be subject to Christ in everything.

Does the "in everything" include abuse? Is the wife to be a physical punching bag? A doormat for his feet? Is she to steal, lie, cheat, or commit adultery if he commands her to?

No, Beloved. True submission means *none* of the above—or anything approaching such an abusive relationship. The context of this passage does not permit anyone to take submission that far. This passage was written to the church, to those who called themselves believers. In earlier verses, Paul had already warned them not to be deceived by people who talked the talk but didn't walk it. Unfruitful deeds of darkness were not to be tolerated or covered up. Rather they were to be exposed, made visible by the light. The very wrath of God would come upon such people.

Therefore, to say that a wife is to submit to an abusive husband is to deny the context of this command. Paul, in verses 18-33, is delineating how submission to the control of the Spirit is lived out in relationships. The wife is to submit as unto the Lord. The Lord would not call her to obey her husband in such a way that would violate the clear teachings of Scripture.

The wife, remember, is the one who *chooses* to submit. To submit to abuse or to fulfill her husband's desire by committing sin, would bring harm and degradation to the *holy* temple of God (see Ephesians 2:19-22). God neither wants, asks, nor expects such a thing—and nowhere does Scripture support it.

A woman devoted to God should not allow herself to be physically abused under the guise of submitting to a husband out of obedience to God. You may have heard such teaching from some well-intentioned Christians, but it is not biblical.

Hear me, precious one. If this is what is happening to you, if you are allowing yourself to be abused and abased, please, please see that your thinking is twisted. In no way do you deserve this. Nor should you endure it. God created you for *His* pleasure. For anyone to do something like this to you makes God angry, and He will judge the one who harms you.

You have worth, you have value, you have purpose. Abuse is not of God, nor is it pleasing to Him. So cry out to God and ask Him to show you His means of deliverance, for it is there for the asking. His ears are open to your cries.

What If My Husband's Not a Believer?

Let's consider another familiar scenario.

What if my husband is walking in disobedience to the Lord—or if he's not even a believer? How can I submit myself to him "in everything"? Does God say anything about that?

Yes, and we can find the instruction in the little book of 1 Peter. "In the same way," the apostle writes, "you wives, be submissive to your own husbands so that even if any of them are disobedient to the word, they may be won without a word by the behavior of their wives" (1 Peter 3:1).

There it is. An explicit instruction regarding a husband who is not bowing his knee to God. Now, before panic sets in or a hundred "but what ifs?" bombard your mind, let's check out the context of this verse. The subject of submission first comes up in verse 13 of 1 Peter 2. This is preceded by the command to keep one's behavior excellent among the

Gentiles in verse 12. Believers are to do this so that when they are slandered as evildoers, the Gentiles might see their good deeds and glorify God. As Christians respect the established authorities, their submissive behavior silences the ignorant comments of foolish people.

So how was a wife who had been set free in the Lord to behave toward a husband who didn't know Christ or obey the Word? How was she to keep her behavior excellent and silence her critics?

Sweet Silence

To put it bluntly, she was to shut her mouth. She was to refrain from verbally pressuring her husband. She was to let her godly actions and attitude woo and wow him. She was to get beyond merely looking great on the outside, and look fabulous on the inside, too. She was to adorn herself with commendable behavior, with the winsomeness of submission, and a "gentle and quiet spirit" (see 1 Peter 3:4).

The word translated gentle is the word "meekness," a word of power, not of weakness as many think. If meekness governs the circumstances, rather than the circumstances governing it, it has to be powerful! Meekness is defined as an inwrought grace of the soul primarily toward God. It is an attitude that accepts God's dealings with us as good without disputing or resisting. It's the opposite of self-assertiveness and self-interest. It's an equanimity of spirit that is neither elated nor cast down because it is not occupied with self at all. This is how Jesus walked and responded, even to those who mistreated and falsely accused Him. Go back to 1 Peter 2:18-25 with me for a minute, so we can see the example Peter directs wives to when he writes, "in the same way, you wives be submissive to your own husbands."

> 18 Servants, be submissive to your masters with all respect, not only to those who are good and gentle, but also to those who are unreasonable.

> 19 For this finds favor, if for the sake of conscience toward God a person bears up under sorrows when suffering unjustly.

20 For what credit is there if, when you sin and are harshly treated, you endure it with patience? But if when you do what is right and suffer for it you patiently endure it, this finds favor with God.

21 For you have been called for this purpose, since Christ also suffered for you, leaving you an example for you to follow in His steps,

22 who committed no sin, nor was any deceit found in His mouth;

23 and while being reviled, He did not revile in return; while suffering, He uttered no threats, but kept entrusting Himself to Him who judges righteously;

24 and He Himself bore our sins in His body on the cross, that we might die to sin and live to righteousness; for by His wounds you were healed.

25 For you were continually straying like sheep, but now you have returned to the Shepherd and Guardian of your souls.

Did you notice the "meekness" of Jesus? He didn't operate with deceit. He didn't return derogatory remarks. He didn't threaten, even though He was God Almighty. Instead, He kept His mouth shut and prayed. He continually entrusted Himself to God, knowing that God knew and would judge righteously. His was not to judge; His was to win over the sinner. And if the sinner would not be won to God, then God would sit as his judge.

This, Beloved, is our example, our role model, and—most importantly—our enabler. Remember 1 Thessalonians 5:24? "Faithful is He who calls you, and He also will bring it to pass." He will keep you blameless if you will let Him (see 5:23). Do all you can, dear wife, to win your husband with your meekness and with a quiet spirit, with that tranquility that arises from within and remains unshaken by circumstances.

It's not an easy command, is it? Especially in a day when women are taught independence and self-assertion. Yet this is what God says—and it is God who knows and understands the hearts of all mankind. That is why God tells us not to lean on our own understanding, but to acknowledge Him in all our ways.[10] He assures us that His thoughts and ways are so much higher than ours. How I pray God will use the teaching within this chapter to create a fresh determination in your heart—a determination to take His high road that you might live life on His highest plane.

"I Was Married, but I Felt So Alone"

Let me tell you about a woman who took this high road and what happened in her life as a result.

Susan attended a "Marriage Without Regrets" seminar some time ago after nine years of a frustrating marriage. "My main complaint during those years was that I was all alone," she wrote. "I would feel so sorry for myself, always being alone at church, ball games, and school functions. I kept telling myself someday I would have a companion… even if it wasn't Jerry. I would have *someone* in my life who cared about my feelings."

In that despairing state of mind, Susan took the course and discovered what God had to say about unbelieving husbands. "God took that opportunity to let me know that I didn't need to 'work' on Jerry, that He was doing that for me," Susan explained. "He took the hurt out of my life and helped me to keep a warm, loving heart and godly manner, with no nagging."

And what happened? No miracle occurred overnight, but a miracle is exactly what Susan says she got:

> I learned as a wife of a husband who was disobedient to the Word to continue to love and follow the Lord. To be a perfect example to my husband and that he would be "won without a word." At that time in my life, I probably did not believe that a miracle was taking place. But it was! With just prayer and faith on my part, the Lord turned Jerry into the most wonderful husband and father I could ever ask for. I worry now about him keeping his health because I don't ever want to lose him! He takes me to church. He

10. Proverbs 3:5,6.

tells our children to revere their mother because I kept everything together and they had the life they had because I was obedient.

On our twenty-fifth wedding anniversary, he bought me a beautiful diamond ring and slipped it on my hand during silent prayer. This is a man who let me sit in church for years alone with my heart breaking.

I often tell women it's not their job to make their husbands holy. That's *God's* job! Ours is to do what we can within reasonable bounds to make our husbands happy. Remember, as a wife, you're his counterpart, his completer, so he won't be alone.

I love how Susan wrapped up her letter to me: "Jerry encourages me daily, and makes me a content woman."

Wow! Is that what you long to be? "A content woman"? Is your husband's disobedience to the Word frustrating that contentment? Then determine right now to follow God's instructions. Submit to your husband. Win him over without a word by your gentle and quiet spirit. And not to knock your socks off, but Peter says that Sarah even called her husband "lord."

Understanding Your Husband

Sometimes as wives we get so caught up in our own personal struggles that we don't take into account the struggles our husbands face. This is what happened with me. Women are so much more prone to talk about the pain and insecurity they feel than men are. We'll talk about it with friends, but men tend to stuff it all inside. However, just because your husband doesn't say much about his personal struggles doesn't mean he isn't struggling.

Many times, unless a husband is totally secure in his wife's love and acceptance and knows he's not going to get an immediate solution, he won't tell his wife about all the things he is dealing with. Men tend to have a difficult time talking about such things. It may be hard to coax his feelings out of him. Issues related to the male ego and expectations of being "tough and together" get in the way of being honest and vulnerable. But we need to realize that men in this generation are facing fears and insecurities that are very real to them and can feel very overwhelming. The wise woman will take these issues into account in the way she interacts with her husband.

What are the issues men face today? Well, whole books have been written about the subject, but I'd like to suggest three things that every wife should be aware of.

First, men deal with self-image issues, just like you do. As they compare themselves with movie stars or athletes on television, they find that they can't measure up. They may not feel that they look good enough or are sexually attractive enough to compare with others. Beloved, your words can bring much needed encouragement to your husband or do further damage to his ego. Ask yourself, how do I speak to my husband? Do I compliment him often? Do I let him know he is still attractive to me? These are things men need to hear—more than once! In fact, they thrive on it!

Second, many men have grown up without the benefit of a good relationship with their father. They may feel that there was never anyone there to show them what a man should be like or to mentor them in a biblical perspective of masculinity. Their father may not have provided them with a very positive example of how to treat a woman. So don't assume that he knows what he should know! Be willing to be patient and clear on what you need and want from him.

Finally, many men today feel overwhelmed. There are just too many expectations placed on them by others…and often by themselves. Pressures. Expectations from work, from their family, from their church. The stress just builds and builds. It's everything from keeping up with the odd jobs around the house to meeting the needs of his wife and kids. Men fear that they can't live up to all that is expected of them, yet they are afraid to admit their own feelings of inadequacy. Often they get to the point where they just want to give up, to run away from the responsibilities and stress.

Which brings me to something that every woman needs to know about the man in her life: men struggle with fear, just like women do. But their fears are uniquely masculine in nature.

Men's Two Basic Fears

These are two basic fears woven into the warp and woof of every man's being. I would call these fears innate. In other words, they're in the male genes. Here they are:

Fear #1: The dread of being ruled over by a woman.

It goes against the male grain to be bossed around by a woman. God knows this; He built that trait into all males. It's the common denominator among men. And why does it go against the male grain? I believe it's because of what we have so clearly seen: Man was made first. He was given headship, and he's to rule. That's why God commanded the wife to submit! (Remember, whenever you have problems with that, it was *God's* idea. So talk it out with Him!)

Fear #2: The anxiety of being found inadequate.

I believe that if we could get under the skin of most men in our nation, we would find them suffering from the wounds of feeling inadequate. Deep down, they feel they just don't measure up. They may compensate by strutting, barking, swaggering, and boasting—but inside they are like boys wanting to be seen on the playing field…turning around constantly to see if you are watching. They desperately want women's applause from the grandstands, our encouragement even when they miss the goal, the basket, the ball. They want us to cup our hands and shout, "Don't worry! You'll get it next time. You're the greatest." Without ever saying the words to a woman, the man is thinking, *Just look. Just notice. Just admire. Just encourage me!* This is what they want, what they need—and what will help them live like a man!

A teacher in a women's Bible class gave her students the assignment of complimenting their husbands on one thing they admired about their men. The assignment, she would find out later, brought great consternation to one woman.

This was a lady who simply did not know what to do. There was nothing, absolutely *nothing,* she appreciated about her husband. She didn't admire him. She didn't even like him. She just lived with him because it was the thing to do. Even so, she determined to complete her assignment. She didn't want to be the only woman in the class who had nothing to report.

She sat at the dinner table that evening, looking at her husband and searching her mind—rummaging through the past—for any single noteworthy thing she could identify. Suddenly relief washed over her.

"I…" she began, then hesitated. Words of praise never came easily. "I want you to know that I, uh, I've been thinking. I-I admire what you did five years ago when you saved that money on our income tax." The words came out sounding stilted and lacking in emotion.

Yet her husband's fork froze in mid-air, until his hand dropped like a stone to the table. He sat there, shaking, unable to speak. Tears flooded his eyes. In all their years of marriage, it was the first time his wife had ever mentioned even one praiseworthy thing about him.

That story always brings tears to my eyes. I wonder how many husbands are starving for some little affirmation of their worth, their ability, their value. I wonder how many long for a kind word, a simple praise, a warm declaration of acknowledgment, of appreciation, of admiration. Men so need to be affirmed.

If you have sons, surely you have seen this as they conquered new territory, moving from a three-wheeler to a two-wheel bicycle, as they hit their first ball, caught their first fly, ran fast, jumped high—performing with all their hearts, watching for your nod of approval. It's innate in a man, this need to succeed, to be admired, respected, trusted.

So I wonder, Beloved, how quick are you to let your man know he's appreciated and valued? When was the last time you thanked him for bringing home a paycheck (regular or not)? When was the last time you complimented him on a job completed around the house (done to your satisfaction or not)? When was the last time you told him you were glad to be his wife? When was the last time you praised him in front of your children?

We wives cannot afford to forget Ephesians 5:33: "The wife must see to it that she respects her husband." It is a command because God made men and He knows they need it! The word translated "respect" is literally the word for "fear," as in we are to "fear God." Just as we are to have an awesome respect for and reverential trust in God, so are we to respect our husbands.

The Male Ego

Does all this sound as if men have egos that need to be stroked?

Well, as a matter of fact, they do.

I used to think it was a sin for a man to have a strong ego. For that reason, I quickly volunteered for duty to help God shatter the one I saw in my husband. I didn't think it was "spiritual," so I assumed it had to go.

Bless Jack's sweet heart and patient spirit!

Honestly, my conclusion was supremely dumb, uneducated, and hasty. So eventually I began to think it through. I reasoned like this:

Men have egos. *All* men have egos (although some are so trampled, so traumatized, and so flattened that they have been relinquished for the sake of peace, quiet, and safety). But if God made man, and all men have egos, then wouldn't it follow that their egos must come from God?

Could it be? Did *God* really create the male ego?

Yes, indeed, Beloved.

When at last I saw this, I finally came to my senses. Not only did God create man with an ego, but He sought to preserve and protect that ego by commanding the man's helper—his counterpart, his complementer, his completer—to reverence and respect and trust him (Ephesians 5:33).

If you are a wife, it does not demean you to respect your husband, to reverence him, or to submit to him. Nor does it lower your status. It does not reduce you to the level of a doormat. Rather, it places you on God's pedestal, where all can see your inward beauty and recognize it as a living image of the bride chosen by God for His Son. In your reverent submission to your husband, you are a picture of the church in all her glory, living in subjection to her heavenly bridegroom, honoring Him and trusting Him.

And not only are you a picture of Christ's bride, you also have something in common with Christ Himself. In 1 Corinthians 11:3, God tells us that "Christ is the head of every man, and the man is the head of a woman, and God is the head of Christ." So even Christ lives in submission to the Father, though He is equal with the Father and one with Him. Think of it: Christ, too, has a head!

Beloved, isn't it encouraging in this analogy to see that the woman holds the position of Christ? That's not so bad, is it?

The Landscape of God's Order

This, then, is the landscape of God's order in marriage. God has a purpose, a plan. We can deny it, we can fight it, we can ignore it, we can scorn it—but God will not alter it. He is God and is perfect in all His ways. And this is His way concerning marriage: Wives are to submit to their husbands and reverence them; husbands are to love their wives as Jesus loves us, giving themselves up for their wives.

It's awesome, isn't it? Oh, if only we would trust and obey. If only we would choose to live this way. Think of how it would change our society; think of what it would do for the emotional health of our nation. And closer to home, think what it would do for your own marriage and family.

What struggles would cease?

What arguments would end?

What anger would cool?

What peace would reign?

My friend Jane knows the answer to those questions. After her third divorce, she began looking for the causes behind her failed marriages. Some of the problems were obvious enough: Her last husband was an alcoholic. He always seemed to have a "girlfriend" in the wings. And Jane thought he did not support her in the way she felt she deserved. As she began learning God's principles of marriage, however, she discovered she shared the blame.

"I did not allow him to be head of the household, make the major decisions, discipline the children, or have responsibility for the money," Jane told me in a letter. "I did not respect him as I should have, nor did I allow him to do any of the things the husband is supposed to do. The only thing important was whatever Jane wanted. I also put my children before him and told him if the time ever came to make a choice between him and the children, he would lose. If I wasn't getting my way, I would boot him out and file for divorce."

The couple remained in contact even after the divorce, and soon they began discovering God's Word together. They enrolled in a "Marriage Without Regrets" course and remarried, this time determined to do it right.

They succeeded.

"Before this time, our sexual relationship was not as it should be," Jane admitted. "I used it as a tool to get what I wanted, mostly. Afterward, it was the greatest thing I had ever experienced. Before, we both did everything wrong. Once we learned our individual roles, we couldn't seem to do anything wrong."

A happy ending? Yes, but not completely. Only 11 months after Jane and Don reunited, he died from injuries sustained in a terrible accident. Jane wrote to me 4 years after Don's death, on the day before her late husband's birthday.

"Kay, I am still so very grateful to God for those 11 months we had as truly one in God as husband and wife. I do regret we did not listen for the 18 years before. What bliss we could have had…."

Beloved, there is no time like the present to begin to live as God ordained. There is no time like now to commit ourselves to learning His precepts and obeying His Word. There is great bliss to be won and terrible regret to avoid.

Precious Father, thank You for being a God of order, for having a plan, a way for us to live. Thank You for not leaving us to fend for ourselves, to figure out life as best we can. O Father, we ask that we might so love You, so trust You, that we will live according to Your precepts rather than our presumptions. We want to be doers of the Word.

There is so much to learn, and we want to learn it all. We want to be the wife, the husband, You desire us to be. Help us! When we feel unable to measure up, may we remember that if we are

Your children, we have the Holy Spirit living within us, able to guide us, to give us grace sufficient for any situation, and to provide us with wisdom from above. Thank You for making Jesus Christ our wisdom, our righteousness, our sanctification, and our redemption. Thank You for supplying all our needs through Him, according to His riches in glory. May we appropriate Your all-sufficient grace in whatever situation or circumstance we find ourselves. May our marriages reflect the relationship of Christ to His church.

And, O Father, we realize there are so many who are in abusive situations. We recognize that for them, reading about what a husband or wife is to be may be excruciating because they live so far from Your ideal. May our disappointments in our mates, in ourselves, never rob us of our hope. May we remember that You are the God of the impossible, and nothing is too difficult for You. Whatever our circumstance, may we cling to You as the waistband clings to the waist of a man—and there may we find Your grace sufficient.

We ask this in the name of the One we call Lord. Amen.

CHAPTER

YOUR HOME:
A LITTLE BIT OF HEAVEN?

LET ME WARN YOU RIGHT AT THE START. This chapter may challenge you. We need to look at what the Bible says about the importance of the home and how the roles of men and women relate to it. You may find that it is very different from what you've always believed. But I want to challenge you to hear what the Word of God has to say on this important issue. Ultimately, Beloved, it doesn't matter what you think or what I think. What matters is what God thinks!

Are you worn out, stressed out, running on empty, and afraid you're going to get stuck on some deserted road, never arriving at the destination of your dreams? Could the reason for this desperate feeling be that your home life is not all that it could be?

If you have read this far without skipping around (which I don't recommend because one truth builds upon another), you're aware that we've just finished laying out the basics on marriage and on the roles of the man and the woman. Now we need to integrate what we've seen in a very practical way. We need to add the color, see how these truths should be lived out in our daily lives, and customize them for where *we* are now.

A Pattern and a Plan

In Ephesians 3:14,15, the apostle writes: "I bow my knees before the Father, from whom every family in heaven and on earth derives its name."

The pattern for relationships within a marriage, and within a family, has already been set in heaven. And so we should bow our knees and say, "Father, my heart's desire as a woman (man), a wife (husband), a mother (father), is to pattern my relationships and my home according to Your design—*and no one else's!*"

Our goal in marriage and in establishing our homes ought to be to bring to earth a little heaven—a picture of our spiritual family in the heavenly home that awaits us. This picture is not only for our own benefit, but also for those who don't know the Lord. The way we live in our homes can be a powerful witness. There are so many dear people who know something is missing in their lives, but they have no idea what it is. They don't know the Word of God. They don't understand the principles of Scripture. And what's more, these principles have never even been modeled for them. They've never been taught the basics of marriage, family, and establishing a home. Consequently, multitudes are groping in the darkness looking for just a glimmer of light, trying to find a better path—a path that leads to joy, peace, satisfaction, and fulfillment.

In the Lord's prayer we read, "Your kingdom come. Your will be done, on earth *as* it is in heaven."[1] If our heavenly home is to be a pattern for our earthly home, then let's take a few brief moments to look at some of the ways heaven is described and some of the parallels.

---

1. Matthew 6:10.

1. In heaven there are three that are one in purpose; the Father, Son, and Spirit "give birth" to children who become part of the family.[2]

On earth, there's a father and mother who give birth to children to form a family.

2. In heaven it's the Father who first loves the children, and teaches the children to love.[3]

On earth, we are the ones who first love the children...and so teach our children to love. (How many of our problems come because we haven't understood or experienced the unconditional love of God or our parents?)

3. In heaven, the Father is the Builder, the Maker[4]...the One who shows the path of life.[5]

On earth, shouldn't the father be the builder, the maker of the home, and the one who shows us the path of life? (Many men feel cheated by their fathers, suffering because they were never mentored by them, never taught, tutored, and trained for life.)

4. In heaven, the Father is the giver of good gifts,[6] the One who disciplines His children for our good that we may share His holiness[7] and is worthy of our reverence.[8]

Men, in your families are you known as fathers who give *good* gifts? Are you recognized as the ones who faithfully discipline the children for their good, thereby earning their respect and reverence?

---

2. John 1:12; 3:3; 1 John 5:1.

3. 1 John 4:10-12; 3:14-18.

4. Hebrews 11:10.

5. Psalm 16:11.

6. Matthew 7:11.

7. Hebrews 12:5-12.

8. Hebrews 12:9.

Is Your Home Like Heaven on Earth?

Shouldn't our homes be like heaven on earth?

What does the Bible tell us heaven is like?

- Heaven is a prepared home…a place of peace,[9] righteousness,[10] joy, pleasure.[11]

- Heaven is a place where you are fed and nourished.[12]

- Heaven is a place of singing…extolling righteousness, sacrifice… things that are worthy.[13]

- Heaven is a place where one receives an abundant entrance.[14]

- Heaven is a place where tears are wiped away.[15]

- Heaven is paradise.[16]

When you read Revelation 21 and 22, Beloved, and look at the glorious New Jerusalem, it is a place of order, peace, safety. It's a place of nurturing, brimming over with light and joy. What is your home like? Is it a place of order or chaos? Is it a dark, depressing place, lacking the light of life that lifts our souls? What is the atmosphere when you or someone else in your family walks in through the front door? Is it a place of criticism and sarcasm? A place of cutting words, angry looks, or demeaning comments? Or does the weight of the world slip from your shoulders when you walk through that door because now you are shut out from the clamor, the pressure, the crudity, the meanness of people who live and move under the domination of the prince of this world?[17]

---

9. Revelation 21:3,4.

10. 2 Peter 3:13.

11. Psalm 16:11.

12. Revelation 7:15-17.

13. Revelation 5:9,10.

14. 2 Peter 1:11.

15. Revelation 7:17; 21:4.

16. Revelation 2:7; 2 Corinthians 12:4.

17. 1 John 5:19; Ephesians 2:2,3.

When a family member walks through your front door, does he know that someone is glad to see him? Are there arms that reach out? A face that lights up? Ears ready to listen to the events of the day? A shoulder to cry on? A voice to speak a kind word of encouragement?

Reason with me for a minute. Imagine dying, being absent from the body and present with the Lord. Imagine entering into heaven and finding no one "home" to greet you. Imagine walking through the portals of Paradise crying out, *"Hello! Hello! Anybody home? I'm here! I'm here!"* Not likely, is it?

Can you imagine entering the doorway to eternity and hearing a rather gruff or wearied voice shout back words like these: "Is that you? So, you finally came home! Where in the world have you been? Hang up that coat—then get in here and help me for a change."

Can you imagine stepping into heaven and hearing a voice that says: "I just got in. I've had a terrible day. Nothing went right. Don't talk; I don't want to hear it. I just can't handle any more. And by the way, don't go sniffin' around the kitchen. There's no food in the house; we'll have to go out."

No, you can't imagine such a thing…because heaven isn't like that! And coming home shouldn't be like that, either. Coming home ought to cause you to quicken your step instead of drag your feet.

You won't find the Father, Son, or the Holy Spirit at odds with one another—arguing, raising their voices, clenching their teeth, demeaning one another. In God's family there's total regard for one another, open communication, and harmony because they are "one." Heaven is where we'll behold our Lord's glory and sense the incredible love[18] shared by the Father, Son, and Spirit.

Heaven, as we have seen, dear one, is a place of safety and security. A place of love, joy, peace, and total acceptance. Is that what it's like in your home? If not, are you working on it—or haven't you even thought about it?

---

18. John 17:20-24.

Don't you think it's a worthy goal to have a little bit of heaven on earth? We all long for it, and we so desperately need it. And it would certainly ease the stress of life. Isn't such a place worthy of all we can give it? Of course it is, so let's talk about it.

How Do We Create a Home?

In order to understand how we can bring heaven into our homes, we need to take a closer look at the role of the man and the role of the woman. The way these roles are played out is the key to bringing heaven to earth in your home. Be prepared for the fact that what I am going to say about this doesn't fit with the world's biases. But don't argue with *me*—let's see what the Word of God teaches!

In God's order, the man is to be the provider of his household. Paul tells Timothy, "But if anyone does not provide for his own, and especially for those of his household, he has denied the faith, and is worse than an unbeliever" (1 Timothy 5:8). This responsibility dates all the way back to Eden, when God told Adam that he would earn his bread by the sweat of his brow.

Normally the act of earning a living puts a man outside his home and into the world. That's where he works, but that is not where he is supposed to *live*. He's supposed to live at home. Home is to be both his haven from the world and his launching pad into the world. But running the home was not in his original job description; that was given to the woman.

Now, hang on. I told you this chapter would cut right across our contemporary culture's biases. But I believe with all my heart that it is what multitudes of women are feeling. Women are longing to get out from under all the pressures and return to their homes. I am constantly talking to women who long to be better wives and mothers, but they find it impossible because there simply aren't enough hours in the day.

What's the Problem?

Recently, I spent a small fortune for an armful of women's magazines. It wasn't because I lacked reading material. No, I made that purchase so

I might better discern the "hot issues" among today's women—or at least what the editors felt would sell magazines. Besides feeling almost soiled by what I read, my heart ached, and my spirit groaned.

So much bad advice.

So much unnecessary unhappiness.

As I read I could almost hear the call of the trumpet of the Lord rallying His children to war against such a depraved culture. From that point on, I was even more determined to press on for the cause of Christ, no matter the cost. I knew I must speak God's truth about the home.

Listen to what one dear young woman wrote to a magazine advice columnist:

> My Problem: Two months ago, I had my first baby. Before she was born, I was convinced I'd never be a stay-at-home mom. In fact, my friends and I have always looked down on women who stayed home with their kids. But since I've returned to work full time, I'm totally miserable. All I want is to be with my daughter. My husband would like me to quit my job, too, and though it would be a bit of a stretch for us, we've saved enough that we could swing it financially, at least for a few years. But I feel so much pressure to be true to my original idea of myself—I'm just not sure I'd respect myself if I gave up my career. I'm completely confused. Please help.[19]

Doesn't that just break your heart? Why is she confused? It's because she is torn between motherhood and a career. God made her a woman, and part of a woman's heavenly job description says that children go with marriage. It isn't a cultural issue at all; it is the Lord God's design and doing. God is the one who forms us in our mother's womb, who numbers our days before a single one comes to be. Motherhood is part of God's design (unless God has kept you single). If we lose touch with this part of ourselves in pursuing worldly success, we become disconnected from God's plan for our homes.

---

19 Harriet Lerner, Ph.D., "Good Advice," *New Woman* magazine, June 1999, p. 48.

God's Habitat for Mothers

So what is God's plan for women? How will they find the truest fulfillment? The Word of God holds the answer. Let's let God speak for Himself:

> Older women likewise are to be reverent in their behavior, not malicious gossips nor enslaved to much wine, teaching what is good, so that they may encourage the young women to love their husbands, to love their children, to be sensible, pure, workers at home, kind, being subject to their own husbands, so that the word of God will not be dishonored.[20]

According to God's design, the proper habitat of mothers is the home. The word "workers at home" is *oikouros* in the Greek, which means the "keeper of the home." Yet an even stronger word than that, *oikodespoteo,* is used in 1 Timothy 5:14,15, where Paul gives instructions, under the inspiration of the Holy Spirit, as to what widows are to do. He writes:

> Therefore, I want younger widows to get married, bear children, keep house, and give the enemy no occasion for reproach; for some have already turned aside to follow Satan.

When He says "keep house" and uses the word *oikodespoteo,* did you notice that this word contains the root for the word "despot"? Have you ever known a despot that was not in charge? According to this verse, women are to be the masters of their houses, governing them and managing them along with the domestic affairs of the family.

Talk about career! What greater career could a woman have? None. Through their mothering and fulfilling their calling as a keeper of the home, mothers mold the next generation. We are raising presidents, kings, government officials, doctors, lawyers, scientists, business people, philosophers, poets, pastors, inventors, and good, solid, salt-of-the-earth

---

20. Titus 2:3-5.

workers who know how to give full measure of themselves for an honest day's wages.

What happens if women fail to follow this calling? Just look around at the moral devastation in our culture. Take a good look at the younger generation, and tell me who we are raising. What are our sons and daughters like? What are their moral values? Where is their integrity? Their commitment? Are you pleased with what you see? Where do you think we are headed as a society?

Or look at yourself. How were you raised? What's the end product? Do you want to produce the same? Have you found the answers? Do you have a model you want to follow?

Read the stories of people who have made major contributions to our society for good and for evil. Watch television's "Biography" on A&E, and observe the role of the mothers in the lives of important people…and also take note of the role the fathers play in their children's futures. By their presence and influence, parents have the power to build a new generation. By their absence and neglect they have the power to destroy. Some of the wealthiest, most famous people have raised the most self-destructive children. The destinies of nations have been changed because the homes the rulers were raised in were hell on earth, rather than heaven on earth!

A number of years ago, Dr. Guer Litton Fox, director of Wayne State University's Family Research Center, wrote, "There's a lack of family cohesion now, a product of the celebration of the individual. As a result, we are almost like strangers living in the same household. If society continues to encourage parents and kids to live out their own lives, we're going to start seeing some dire results."

His words were prophetic. Just look at the statistics:

- At the turn of the millennium, S.A.T. scores had dropped 73 points in the last 30 years.

- There have been almost 45 million abortions in the last 28 years.

- The divorce rate has more than doubled. And marriages with two full-time workers are more divorce prone.

• Suicide is the third leading cause of death among young people.

• At least one out of every four women are victims of incest.

• The incarceration rate in America is higher than any other indus-
trialized nation in the world.

Need I go on? These are dire enough to show the depth of the
problem.

This is what happens when we don't order our marriages and our
homes according to God's pattern. His pattern is that the man is the
provider and the woman is the keeper of the home. He is the One who
has called us to seek His kingdom and His righteousness. He assures us
that if we do so, He will see that we have shelter, food, and clothing.
What we *need*…not what we *greed*.

What About Self-Esteem?

God knows the importance of the family and the home. He knows what
gives a man or a woman a sense of accomplishment and well-being. It
has been proven over and over again: A man's esteem generally comes
from the workplace, while a woman's is found in her husband and her
children. You can be the most successful career woman in the world, but
if your relationships with your husband and your children are not right,
your job cannot deaden the pain in the innermost part of your being
because you will feel as though you have failed at the very thing you
were born for.

According to 1 Timothy 2:15, women find their salvation—their
health, their wholeness—when their children continue "in faith and
love and sanctity with self-restraint." In other words, all of a wife and
mother's hard work, sacrifice, and selfless love pays off if her children
turn out well.

Am I saying that the woman should not work outside the home? No,
I am not saying that. In Proverbs 31 you can read the biography of an
amazing woman. She not only keeps her home in order and cares for her
household, she also manages a staff and conducts business on the side,
considering and buying fields. With her earnings, she plants vineyards.

She makes linen garments, sells them, and deals with tradesmen. She cares for the poor, stretches out her hand to the needy, and does it all in such a way that her children rise up and bless her, along with her husband who praises her highly.

What I am saying is that our priorities have become introverted. It all started with the philosophy that all of our society's foundations need to be questioned and abandoned. Liberal theologians taught that the Bible was not the Word of God; it was merely a sublime collection of human documents reflecting evolutionary thinking. Instead of looking into God's Word, we were told to look inside ourselves.

Once again, the serpent of old whispered in Adam's ear, "Yea, has God said?" As a culture we bought the lie. Turning from the Word of God and its restraint of truth, our minds were taken "captive through philosophy and empty deception, according to the tradition of men."[21] The effects of the industrial revolution, the World Wars, and other factors brought about the separation of wives from their families, and men ceased to love and cherish their mates as they ought to. Women believed the feminist lie and went out to make their own way in the marketplace. Self became our focus. Marriage and children would have to wait while woman made a place for herself in this man's world.

And where are we today? Our homes, our children, and our relationships are in shambles. Women are worn out, stressed out, wrestling with doubt, and battling guilt. Our relationships are broken; our lives are filled with pain.

But listen, beloved man, beloved woman, *it doesn't have to be that way.* You can chose to restructure your home in accordance with God's Word.

The Challenge to Change

Don't plan on everybody congratulating you when you decide to order your home by God's principles. Some will be threatened or feel personally challenged when you determine to live as the Word of God

---

21. Colossians 2:8.

teaches. The biblical pattern for the home is at odds with what many psychologists and sociologists tell us is the optimum way to live.

If you determine to conform your life and your home to the biblical pattern, be prepared for sarcasm, ridicule, and put-downs among those you have named as your friends. Everyone is *not* going to clap their hands in delight or throw you a thumbs-up and say, "You've got it, man, you're right on target. You're going to be a winner, lady!"

Instead, you may very well hear words more akin to these: "It's impossible. You'll never make it. You're crazy! How are you going to survive? If I—if we—did that, I'd be giving up everything I've worked for!"

This is part of the warfare—among other tactics and devices of the enemy that you will encounter. Just remember that according to 1 John 5:3-5, God's commandments are not burdensome, and you are an overcomer because you belong to God's family. The victory that overcomes the world is faith—taking God at His Word and living by it without flinching.

Where Do I Start?

Take a day. Get alone. If you're married, ask your mate to join you. If you're a single parent, ask someone you trust to stay with the children, then go somewhere quiet where you won't be distracted. When you get there, get on your knees and tell God that you need to hear from Him. Tell Him to help you honestly evaluate where you are and to examine where you are headed.

God understands. And He will meet you right where you are, wherever it is, as long as you cry to Him. Meeting with you will be His delight, for more than anything else He wants to see His children walk in truth. He is a God who wants to help you accomplish His will "on earth as it is in heaven."

Tell God that you want to consider your ways…your marriage…your career…your family…your walk with Him. As you ponder these things, ask yourself if you are satisfied with where you are and where you are headed. Write down the things you really want and what you would like to change.

Then, Beloved, cost it out.

What will it take in order to accomplish what you want to do? Do you think you could ask God to underwrite it? Would it be something He could back? If so, are you willing to trust Him? Remember, without faith it is impossible to please God. If you're going to come to Him, you need to believe that He is God, and that He rewards those who seek Him in a disciplined way.[22]

Ask yourself individually, and then ask each other as a couple, if you are willing to stop blaming others, to stop looking back, to stop dwelling on the past wrong turns and failures, and move on. Are you ready to take full responsibility for your future under the sight and care of God? You might as well do it now, Beloved, because when you stand before God someday (in the not too distant future), there won't be any finger-pointing or excusing. We will be totally accountable before the One whose "eyes are a flame of fire."

Ask yourself if you are willing to believe God—to take Him at His Word and order your life day in and day out according to His principles, precepts, and commands. (Or do you really imagine that when God wrote the Bible He couldn't foresee our times and cause His words to apply to our precise circumstances? Oh, Beloved, we serve a greater God than that!)

Discuss with yourself and with God the role that the Bible is going to play in your life. Will it have the lead role or simply play a bit part?

Finally, my friend, write out some action steps that you need to take in order to achieve your goals, change your direction, and establish what you want in your marriage and family. Then, next to these, put down a reasonable time frame. When you finish, get back on your knees and lay it all out before God.

He will hear and answer, just as He always has.

He is faithful to His promises...and to His dearly loved children.

> *O Father, thank You that Your ears are open to our cry. Thank You for Your promise that when we seek You with all our hearts, we will be found by You.*

---

22. Hebrews 11:6.

Find us…and lead us from here as we build according to Your blueprint.

We ask this for our sakes—and for the sake of Your kingdom.

In the name of our King, the Lord Jesus Christ. Amen.

CHAPTER 8

WHAT HAPPENED TO LOVE?

IT WAS LATE. SHE WAS IN BED, READING, waiting for him to come home. When he walked into the room she looked up and smiled. She opened her mouth to say something, but he walked past her without a word.

They had been married for years. She knew how these trips exhausted him, and she had learned when to be quiet. In just a moment he returned from their closet—clean shirt, suit, pajamas, underwear shirt, and shorts draped over his arm. Pausing beside the bed, his only words were, "I'm leaving. It's over. I just don't love you anymore."

With that he tossed the keys to the house on the bed and walked out of their bedroom, their home, and their life together.

What happened to love?

Where did it go?

Why did it fail?

Isn't this the claim in almost every case of divorce or infidelity? And if love is really gone, well, why stay married? Why stay monogamous? It's that simple, isn't it?

No, it's not. Not with God. According to God, the One who designed and instituted marriage, love is a *choice*. It's a matter of *obedience*, not emotion.

And please hear me, Beloved. If you can grasp this single truth, then you will understand why it is completely possible to have a marriage without regrets. If you can untangle the confusion created by this word "love," if you can catch a glimpse of *God's perspective* and begin to live in the light of His changeless truth, then you will find that little bit of heaven within reach of your marriage and your home.

Love is a choice!

Out of all that I cover in this book, precious one, this single precept from God's Word could be the most important to your well-being. While it may not cure your pain, radically change your spouse, or remake your marriage, it can bring a whole new depth of understanding, purpose, and healing into your life.

Four Ways to Say "I Love You"

New Testament Greek uses four different words for "love." Once we grasp their meanings, I think we will be better able to understand why people talk about "falling out of love." We'll gain some insight as to how a man or woman can abandon a mate, walk away from his or her own flesh and blood, and rationalize a lack of love as reasonable grounds for divorce. At the same time, we will also see a shining solution to this very old, sadly common human dilemma.

Storge—The love of natural affection

The Greek word *storge* is a term of natural affection or obligation. Its basis is in one's own nature. It is a quiet, abiding feeling within a man or woman that rests on something close to him or her. It's that natural affection of soul that wells up within for your mate, your child, your close friend, or even your dog.

Because it finds its source in fickle human nature, it is a love that can come and go. It is a also a natural affection that can be virtually destroyed in early childhood. A child who endures years of isolation or brutality may simply no longer be capable of this basic emotion.

Interestingly, this term is used primarily in a negative way in the New Testament. In Romans 1:31 and 2 Timothy 3:3, for instance, it is used with a negative prefix, rendering it "unloving," or "without natural affection."

That describes what happened in the illustration that opened this chapter, doesn't it? The man had no natural affection for his wife. Somewhere in the space of time, events, and circumstances it disappeared—and with it went the relationship and the vows.

Eros—The love of passion

The second word for love so typifies our culture. It is *eros,* the word for erotic love. Eros is a love of passion—a passion that seizes and over-masters the mind. Its source and object are one and the same—*self!* This is the sort of love that has dominated the pop music charts for years. It's a word with chemistry in it; it's a "feel good" love. Some characteristic in a person of the opposite sex pushes a button in you and you get a "shiver in your liver." You're "turned on," as the saying goes. You've "fallen in love."

But what happens if that characteristic that so charms and dazzles you is no longer apparent or even ceases to exist? What happens when the shiver goes away? What happens if you get up one morning and no longer feel anything at all? Is love gone, too? Is it time to end the relationship because the pleasure isn't there?

As you can see, eros is a self-centered love; it looks for what it can receive, what can bring pleasure, happiness, and satisfaction. "Being loved," then, depends on being attractive—and staying attractive—to another person. It is strictly conditional.

How I remember my "before Christ" days, when as a divorcée I would ask a man if he would still love me if I had to have my breasts removed. It may sound crass to write this in a Christian book, but the concern was very real. I asked the question more than once, more than twice. To me, my breasts are a symbol of my womanhood, my femininity, my beauty—a very crucial part of my physical appeal. But what if cancer suddenly stripped me of this pleasurable symbol of womanliness? Would my lover still love me...or would he be turned away?

Without even knowing it at the time, I was asking for a different kind of love—one that would supersede all other loves. I was asking for a love I had no ability to give—and I didn't even know it! How blind I was. And how thankful I am that I discovered it.

By the way, you'll never find the word "eros" in the Bible. Isn't that interesting? Even in the Greek translation of Song of Solomon, that passionate love poem between a bride and a groom, that word does not appear.

Phileo—The "I really care for you" love

To me, this is the most enjoyable of all loves. It's the love that makes marriage so pleasurable, a delight and joy for couples of all ages. It is the love of fond companionship, the love we so long for in our relationships through the years. If we're not experiencing this love in our own marriages, it's so difficult not to be envious when we see others enjoying it.

Kenneth Wuest defines it as a "love that is called out of one's heart as a response to the pleasure one takes in a person or object."[1] Knowing the definition of "phileo" helps you understand why you can say almost in the same breath that you love chocolate, a sunset, a painting, and someone who is very special to you.

It's a love—a feeling—you must carefully watch. It's an affection that can be sparked by another outside your marriage in all innocence. Yet as soon as it is recognized for what it is, it must be quickly dismissed or it could lead you into trouble. You can't believe how quickly phileo can

1. Kenneth Wuest, *Wuest's Word Studies in the Greek New Testament* (Grand Rapids, MI: Wm. B. Eerdmans Publishing Co., 1975), vol. III, Bypaths, pp. 111-13.

slip into eros! I think this is how people sometimes slip into affairs when it was never in their hearts to even consider another!

Phileo is an "I like you" kind of love that responds to kindness, appreciation, or acts of tenderness. Different than eros, it's a love that wants to give as well as receive—and yet it doesn't give merely in order to get. It's not a "my happiness only" kind of love; it's more noble than that. It's an "I want your happiness" kind of love.

Even so, for all its warm, wonderful, and delightful qualities, phileo doesn't have the "stickability" of *agape,* the next kind of love we will consider. Why? Because phileo is called out of one's heart and affections by the *qualities* in another. So, as with the other loves we have considered already, it is still possible for an individual to say "I don't love you anymore" when those appreciated qualities begin to fade for one reason or another. A marriage partner may abandon even the most companionable of phileo love if he or she comes to the conclusion that the price tag for further investment has gone too high. "Yes," he or she may reason, "we shared some wonderful love together, but I have lost the desire to go the distance."

Agape—The love without limit

Agape is a love called out of one's heart by the preciousness of the object loved. It's not that something about the person makes him or her precious. Rather, it is because every human being created by God has worth, value, and purpose. Agape is a love of esteem, of evaluation. It carries the idea of prizing and is the most noble word for love in the Greek language.[2]

Yet for all its value and nobility, it is a word rarely used outside the pages of Scripture. Within the pages of the New Testament, however, it shines off the page at least 320 times. What makes this word so unique? Just this: *Agape* is not kindled by the merit or worth of its object; it has its origins in the nature of God Himself!

God is love—*this* kind of love.

---

2. Ibid., pp. 111-13.

God's love gives and gives and gives—even when the loved one is unresponsive, unkind, unlovable, and unworthy. It is a love that never falters or fails. It is the love that caused God to love us when we were helpless.[3] It is a love that does not grow weary. Shakespeare captured the spirit of this love in one of his sonnets, when he wrote: "Love is not love which alters when it alteration finds, or bends with the remover to remove....It is an ever-fixed mark."[4]

This, Beloved, is the love we need.

This is the love our heart craves.

It is the distinguishing mark of true believers through the centuries and in every culture throughout the world. Christians are known by their love...*this* kind of love. By *this* love, we are recognized as Jesus' disciples.

Jesus modeled agape love for us. He is a divine plumb line dropped from heaven by which we might measure our love for others. Agape is a love that proves its existence in demonstrable activity. It's a love that can be commanded—and obeyed. It is the love of a marriage without regrets. It is priceless. And it is a love that is available to every one of us!

Our Lord calls us to love our mates in this agape way...even if our marriages are no longer what they used to be...even if we never receive love in return.

God *is* love. He loved us when there was nothing to love and everything to despise. And now He has thrown open the door of His infinite storehouses of love so that you and I might experience it to the full and parcel it out to others.

If we begin to understand the extent and nature of His limitless love, we may also begin to grasp how we can become better conduits of this love to those who so desperately need it. And the place to begin, of course, is with your own husband or wife.

An Unconditional Love

God's agape love is unconditional. The apostle John writes: "In this is love, not that we loved God, but that He loved us and sent His Son to

3. Romans 5:5-8.
4. William Shakespeare, Sonnet CXVI: "Let Me Not to the Marriage of True Minds," 1609.

be the propitiation for our sins" (1 John 4:10). We didn't do anything to deserve God's love. He reached out to us even though we were living in total darkness and rebellion. That's what unconditional love does. It takes the initiative to show love no matter what response it might receive.

Many years ago, a friend of mine was invited to have lunch with the roommates of a young woman he had just begun dating. These roommates wanted to let him know that although they were happy he had begun to spend time with their friend, he faced some major challenges. For one thing, they said, this young woman refused to open up to anyone. She tended to make a joke out of everything. Her sense of humor made her the life of the party—but he should forget about having any deep conversations with her. She just wouldn't allow it.

When my friend asked what had been done to crack through this good-times veneer, one roommate replied, "Well, we even tried unconditional love. But it didn't work!"—meaning that the attempt had been abandoned.

My friend, that is not "unconditional love." Love that abandons the beloved when it receives the wrong kind of response is highly conditional. Love that stops giving when it "doesn't work" is far from unconditional.

Unconditional love never gives up. It digs in and continues to love despite hardship or disappointment and right in the face of apathy, anger, frustration, and failure. As we have said, agape *chooses* to love, no matter what.

That's the kind of love God displays toward us, and that's the kind of love He calls us to display toward our spouses.

An Everlasting Love

Agape love has no limit and no end. In Jeremiah 31:3, we hear God say to His wayward adulterous wife, Israel: "I have loved you with an everlasting love; therefore I have drawn you with lovingkindness." God's love for us is eternal. Forever. It springs from His own being and nature and is not affected by our actions. It does not change depending on how we respond to it.

Once God sets His love upon an individual, that person will be loved through all eternity. God will never withdraw His love from His beloved. Of course, someone may choose to spurn God's love. If such a person spurns it long enough, the day will surely come when justice, not love, will become the issue. Never think that God dismisses His justice in favor of His love! He *never* does that. But in His love He provides us with an escape from the consequences of His justice—the awful consequences already paid by Jesus. If we reject His love, we reject the only provision He has made for escaping the horrors of His judgment. And those who make such a foolish choice despise heaven and choose hell.

Think of it like this: God's unconditional love never stops flowing from the depths of His infinitely gracious heart. Forever it pours out in gushing torrents of living water. But a man or woman may choose to build a dike against this blessed flow. He may divert its rushing waters and prevent them from ever touching him. She may choose to die of thirst with living water swirling all around.

God's love never ceases. Day by day, moment by moment, year after year it is being poured out upon all mankind. While man breathes, God loves the just and the unjust. "God so loved the world, that He gave His only begotten Son" (John 3:16). That love continues to be showered upon us today—and will continue to flow at flood stage through all eternity.

A Sacrificial Love

Agape love is a sacrificial love, a love that's willing to lay down its life for another. John 15:13 says, "Greater love has no one than this, that one lay down his life for his friends." In the original Greek, the word translated "love" is agape, so you could read the passage this way: "Greater *agape* has no one than this, that one lay down his life for his friends."

It was Jesus who made that statement, and it was Jesus who lived it out most fully. He loved us so much that He laid down His life of His own free will, gladly, on our behalf. No conditions had to be fulfilled for Him to do what He chose to do. But because He was (and is) the embodiment of agape love, He chose the cross and died as our substitute.

Agape love takes the first step (and the second and the third and the fourth…) and willingly sacrifices itself for the sake of its beloved—even with no promise of anything in return.

A Ministry-Oriented Love

Remember the Gospel story in which James and John ask Jesus if they can have the honor of sitting on either side of His throne in heaven? Immediately after their request, we find Jesus having a little heart-to-heart chat with all His disciples. The brothers' request had stirred up a hornet's nest of resentment, and Jesus used the tense moment to explain something none of them had grasped.

"Whoever wishes to become great among you shall be your servant," the Master told them. "And whoever wishes to be first among you shall be slave of all. For even the Son of Man did not come to be served, but to serve, and to give His life a ransom for many" (Mark 10:43-45). The King James version translates the passage, "The Son of man came not to be ministered unto, but to minister, and to give his life a ransom for many."

Agape strives to minister to others. It doesn't look for ways to be served; instead, it searches out new avenues for service. It doesn't insist on being treated in a certain way, but rather looks for fresh ways to show love toward another. It is outward focused not inward focused; other-conscious not self-conscious.

In His agape love, God is always seeking to minister to us and our needs. And because He wants us to become increasingly like Him, He calls us to minister to those around us—especially to our spouses.

The Love Chapter

The apostle Paul's famous words about love in 1 Corinthians 13 reflect each of these four characteristics of love. Paul insists that God's love truly is unconditional, everlasting, sacrificial, and ministry-oriented. Read this passage slowly and put yourself into these words.

> Love is patient, love is kind and is not jealous; love does not brag
> and is not arrogant, does not act unbecomingly; it does not seek its

own, is not provoked, does not take into account a wrong suffered, does not rejoice in unrighteousness, but rejoices with the truth; bears all things, believes all things, hopes all things, endures all things (verses 4-7).

That, my friend, is agape love. Does it describe your relationship with your mate? I have to admit that it doesn't always describe the way I treat Jack. I know I'm not always patient with him or quick to forgive him. And every now and then, I give in to my flesh and cry out for what I'd like and what I wish could be. At times I have allowed circumstances to get in the way of my love for him.

But God knows I'm trying!

My heart's desire is to please God, to obey Him, to show His love toward others, including my mate. I want the Lord to refine me, teach me, mold me, and make me into the Christlike woman that He wants me to be. As I say in my book *As Silver Refined,* God is the true Refiner and He can shape us if only we will let Him. He can take what is impure and make it pure. And as He does so, that which was dull becomes shining, bright, and beautiful.

Allow Him to remake life's disappointments into His appointments. Let Him use even dark events to draw you closer to Him, make you more like Him, and transform you into a great marriage partner.

Love in Action

It is impossible for God's kind of love to be passive. It *must* act. God couldn't merely say that He loved us and then allow us to die in our sin. He acted by sending His Son to pay the penalty our wicked deeds deserved. In the same way, we cannot merely *say* that we love our spouses and then do nothing. How hollow such words would be! We, too, must act. We must demonstrate our love.

In his excellent book *The Friendship Factor,* Alan Loy McGinnis includes a chapter titled "Love Is Something You Do,"[5] in which he says we need to learn the gestures of love. Little kindnesses help to bind you

---

5. Alan Loy McGinnis, *The Friendship Factor* (Minneapolis, MN: Augsburg Publishing House, 1979).

and your spouse together—and can serve as a warning signal when something has gone amiss, as one man learned too late.

I talked to a man whose marriage had gone bad after 18 years. "How did you know it was over?" I asked. "When she stopped putting toothpaste on my brush in the mornings," he replied. "When we were first married, whoever got up first would roll toothpaste on the other's brush and leave it lying on the sink. Somewhere along the line we stopped doing that for each other, and the marriage went downhill from there."[6]

Meaningful rituals and gestures of love can go a long way in your marriage. The hello and good-bye kisses, the hugs, the squeeze of a hand under the dinner table, the tender secrets and "inside jokes," the celebration of birthdays and anniversaries, the sharing of "our song" can all serve to make your relationship more special.

What rituals and gestures of love do you practice in your marriage?

One way to help keep the flame afire is to demonstrate your love in visible ways. How can you show agape love to your spouse today? How can you set yourself aside for the benefit of your mate with no thought of getting anything in return? Now would be a good time to write down your ideas and save them as reminders for the future. Consider some possibilities:

- wash the dishes together
- play his or her favorite game
- read aloud to one another at bedtime
- write a mushy love note and put it where it will surprise him or her
- bring home some flowers for no special reason
- make your mate's favorite dessert
- buy a tiny "I love you" present
- compliment even the little things she or he does well
- wash the car together (and expect to get wet!)

6. Ibid., p. 53.

• go out for breakfast early on Saturday before doing house or yard chores

• dream up special pet names for one another that no one else knows

What's so marvelous about these little expressions of love is that they pave the way for bigger ones. The saying "It's the little things that count" is especially true in marriage. Start small and you'll find your affection and appreciation for one another growing—naturally—ever deeper.

Love When There Is No Love

"Oh, if only it were that easy," you may be thinking. "My marriage is on the rocks, and little gestures of love just won't cut it. What should I do when I no longer feel any love for my partner?"

Not long ago, I received a letter from a woman who said almost exactly that. Her husband constantly criticized others. He never had anything nice to say. He was forever making choices that hurt himself, his wife, and their marriage. From the day they walked down the aisle, she would beg him to stop and to change. She pointed out the ways he was injuring people, including her. As the months and years passed, her begging turned to pleading, then shouting, then rage.

"I have decided to divorce him," she declared in her letter. "I feel nothing but anger whenever I see him." Then she softened a bit. "I know divorce is not God's way," she admitted. "But I can't stand my husband anymore. Is there no way out? If I divorce my husband, I sin. If I stay married and remain bitter, I sin. Why isn't there a way out for me? Where is God?"

What a wrenching dilemma! Sadly, I can promise you that she's not alone. I have met hundreds, maybe thousands, of husbands and wives who feel as if they're trapped in a no-win situation. They fear nothing will change and they're destined for a lifetime of misery. Their marriage lies in shambles and the love that once drew the partners together has grown icy cold.

Maybe you can identify. Maybe you're concerned that your own marriage has taken a turn for the worse. Or perhaps you feel as if you're already at the end of your rope. What should you do? Just what is the key to loving someone when you don't *feel* love for him or her? Is it possible to bring back the love?

God says it is.

Through Christ, it *is possible* to love even in the most difficult of circumstances. And God proved it, Beloved! He loved us with an agape love even when we turned our backs on Him, even when we were "sons of disobedience . . . by nature children of wrath" (Ephesians 2:2,3). The expression of agape love is always a choice.

With God it was a choice.

With you it is a choice.

It's always a choice.

In no uncertain terms 1 John 4:11 tells us, "Beloved, if God so loved us, we also ought to love one another." The unconditional love God showed us is the very same love we're to show our spouses. And when I say "unconditional," that is exactly what I mean. We are to love our mates regardless of the results.

Thank God that love is already available within us! Romans 5:5 says, "The love of God has been poured out within our hearts through the Holy Spirit who was given to us." If you're a Christian, the Holy Spirit lives within you. And if He lives within you, the agape love of God can flow into your heart and refresh the hearts of others—including your spouse!

You might be saying, "But, Kay, you have no idea what I put up with. My partner is absolutely *impossible* to love!"

You're right that I don't know what it's like to be in your shoes. But I do know that if it's possible for God to show agape love to the worst of sinners, and you have that same agape love within you, then you can love your mate. Of course it may be difficult, but it's not impossible. God never calls His children to do that which they cannot do.

If your love for your mate is not all that it could be, Beloved, take the matter to God. Pray to Him and yield your heart to Him. One woman who took this advice years ago wrote me to say, "Kay, you were right. I didn't think I could possibly love my husband anymore. But after the conference, I went home and immediately put my marriage into the

Lord's hands. I can't explain it, but for the first time in years, I can say I really do love my husband. He hasn't changed, but *I* have! It's definitely made our marriage better!"

Commit yourself, dear one, to making agape love a priority in your marriage. Believe me, it *will* make a difference. If not in your spouse, then definitely in your own life.

Yes, this may be very, very difficult. But it is certainly possible. It's possible because love is a choice. A hard choice? Perhaps. But an impossible choice? Never. At least not as long as God's Holy Spirit dwells in our hearts through faith.

What About Marriage to an Unbeliever?

Many Christians who married unbelievers wonder if their situations should be considered differently. That, in fact, was the very question asked by some first-century believers in Corinth. And the apostle Paul had an answer for them.

As the apostles traveled from city to city proclaiming the gospel, large numbers of people came to faith. In many cases, one spouse would receive Christ while the other would not. Suddenly many new believers found themselves in a situation they hadn't anticipated. Were they to leave their unbelieving spouses? Were they free to marry someone else, only this time believers? Or were they to stay married to their unbelieving partners?

In 1 Corinthians 7:13, Paul gave his answer: "A woman who has an unbelieving husband, and he consents to live with her, she must not send her husband away." That works the other way as well. If an unbelieving wife is willing to live with her Christian husband, then he should not send her away.

So leaving is not an option. God wants husbands and wives to stay married. Why? Paul tells us in the next few verses: "For the unbelieving husband is sanctified through his wife, and the unbelieving wife is sanctified through her believing husband..." (verse 14).

Now, there's no doubt a believing spouse married to an unbeliever will face difficulties. In some marriages this creates constant tension. In many cases the Christian is ridiculed or even persecuted. But consider this: When one partner in a marriage belongs to God, the union brings blessing to the entire home. The family is better off because the Christian brings grace and blessing that otherwise would go wanting. This is the sanctification Paul just spoke about. So rather than view an "unequally yoked" situation in a negative way, we need to see it as a blessing for the unbeliever.

"But what about my children?" you might ask. "Aren't they going to be affected by my unbelieving partner's opinions and behavior?"

Paul addressed that problem as well: "For the unbelieving husband is sanctified through the wife, and the unbelieving wife is sanctified through her believing husband; *for otherwise your children are unclean, but now they are holy* (1 Corinthians 7:14, emphasis added). If both parents were unbelievers, Paul says, the children would be unclean. But if just one parent is a Christian, there's a special sense in which the children are holy.

Even if you are married to an unbeliever, God calls you to minister agape love to your spouse. You can let life's problems defeat you or strengthen you, Beloved. It all depends on how you choose to respond.

But whatever you do, dear friend, remember this: If you are a Christian, God has already made His agape love available to you. His love is the wellspring of agape love, and He boasts an infinite supply. According to Romans 5:5, His love was poured out within your heart through the Holy Spirit who was given to you. Therefore, when you need help in showing this kind of love to your spouse (and who doesn't, now and then?), then walk instead by the Spirit and He will give it to you freely for it is one of the ninefold elements of the fruit of the Spirit. It is yours for the taking. Only let your heart serve as the channel through which God's love can pour into the life of your spouse.

Remember, love is a choice.

A Portrait of *Agape* Love

Recently a man named David came to one of our training seminars and told a heartbreaking story that beautifully portrays agape love in action. It also shows just how profoundly God can work through life's disappointments to refine us into vessels that can be used in ways greater than ever before.

At this point I'm going to turn my pen over to my husband, Jack, for he is the one who first heard David's story.

During our training seminars at Precept Ministries, Kay and I often separate at mealtimes so we can meet more people. That's when I met David.

David found us "accidentally" on the radio, between a couple of programs he enjoyed. "I noticed her program was different from the others," David said. "The words were so gentle, out of the Word of God, and they just seemed to go deep into my heart. I couldn't shake them, and they began to change my thinking."

David's wife neither loved the Lord nor wanted anything to do with Him. In 1982, she was diagnosed with colon cancer, and when David told her that he had become a Christian, she began to cry.

"Oh, no!" she wailed. "I want my old husband back. I don't want a Christian husband."

That very day their son had been born, and David's wife handed the baby back to him and said, "Just go back and undo it if you can. I really don't want a religious fanatic as a husband."

So began 18 years of struggle. Her bitterness toward God and David deepened until she finally took their two boys and moved back to her parents' home. In the meantime, David continued to listen to Kay's program and grow spiritually. He also began to serve as an assistant pastor at a local church.

Some time later, David received a phone call. His wife was dying, and she wanted him to spend time with her. Yet the unbelief of both David's wife and in-laws made the atmosphere in the home tense. Hatred for God permeated the air.

One day David's wife asked him to get a prescription filled. After David made the purchase and began to leave the drugstore, he noticed a book rack. One title caught his eye. In bright gold letters it asked, *God, Are You There? Do You Care? Do You Know About Me?*

"It hit me so strongly that tears came to my eyes," David said. "I myself was asking those questions. I knew the Lord had called me; I knew the sound of His voice; I knew the Word said He would never fail me. But everything *looked* like it was failing. I was about to lose the one I loved, and she didn't know the Lord. The book asked the very question that cried out in my mind: God, are You there? I then noticed the author was Kay Arthur, the woman on the radio programs I'd been listening to. I knew that she had always spoken from the Word of God and that I could trust what she said. I began to hope that maybe my wife would be willing to read the book if I gave it to her."

David took the book home and put it on the nightstand next to his bedridden wife. He asked her to read it only if she wanted to; she didn't have to. He also said that he heard Kay on the radio and knew she didn't have an agenda of any sort. "So if you would like to know about God," David said, "I know you'll find it in this book."

David's wife neither answered him nor acknowledged the book. But each day thereafter, David noticed his wife was writing in the book's margins. She continued to do so until she grew too weak to write. A couple of days later, she amazed David by asking, "Could you read the Bible to me?"

The question startled David. *Is this for real?* He wondered. *Is she really saying this? Is she just desperate?* But she wasn't desperate— this was for real! She had read that God was telling her, in essence, "I love you and I really mean it." So each day David began to read from the Gospel of John—and he noticed a definite change in his wife.

One evening one of David's sons started giving his dad a hard time. When David erupted in anger, a weak voice piped up from across the room. It was his wife. "Don't do that," she said. "Don't let Satan ruin the very first day of my new life."

What am I hearing? thought a surprised David. *What is she saying?*

"Don't let Satan ruin our night," his wife repeated. "He's the one who wants to ruin it. This is the first day of my new life. This is the first time that I have known the love of God that you've been telling me about all these years."

Shock, elation, surprise, glee, and bewilderment—they all hit David together. He didn't know what to do except to cry. His wife now knew the Lord!

For the first time in 18 years the couple became like brother and sister. They poured out their hearts to one another, exulting that now they both adored the same Lord.

David's wife died two days later, but she didn't die in fear. Even the nurses saw a glow about her. They said they noticed something "different" about her. She had become as peaceful and pleasant as could be.

"Of all the things that ever could have happened to the one I loved," David declared, "this was the best—that she had come to know the Lord."

I do not tell David's story to claim that every problem marriage has a happy ending. None of us can predict what the future holds. But even if David's wife had never accepted Jesus as her Savior and Lord, David still would have been able to stand before God and say, "I was everything you called me to be—and therefore I can say I had a marriage without regrets." David willingly made the choice to love his wife despite the difficulties. He showered her with love even when she showed no signs of returning his love or receiving Christ into her heart.

You can do the same.

Beloved, even if your marriage has avoided major problems, is there room for improvement in the love you give your spouse? I admit there is always room for growth in my love for Jack. That's why we must constantly place our marriages in God's hands. He knows what is best for us, just as He knew what was best for David.

One thing is certain: As the Refiner, God is in the business of shaping us into something better, something more beautiful. Maybe we won't see how that's so on this side of heaven, but it's a promise we can trust completely because we know that God loves us unconditionally...sacrificially...forever. And He's called us to give to others what He gives us.

It's a choice He leaves up to us.

CHAPTER 9

COMMUNICATION: THE GREAT PRIORITY

FROM EVERY OUTWARD APPEARANCE, THIS WAS a couple who had it all together.

She was attractive, warm, and loving. A good mother.

He was attentive, affectionate, and successful. A terrific dad.

But when the Christmas card arrived signed only with her name and the names of the children, I felt a sinking sensation in the pit of my stomach. The enclosed note confirmed my apprehension.

Oh, Kay it's been so hard. Frank has remarried and moved away. These words were followed with these simple but pleading words of advice: *Don't ever lose the ability to communicate!*

Communication tops nearly everyone's list of marriage problems. And too many times it is the final straw that brings the roof down on a marriage and a home. Perhaps you have heard words like these—or even said them yourself:

- "We just don't talk."

- "We never get below the surface."

- "We don't have anything in common anymore."

- "Every time we share our real feelings we end up in a fight."

- "We'll never understand each other. It's just not worth it. Life is too short!"

It's no secret that many volumes have been written on this subject. Techniques, principles of "how to" and "how not to" flood the bookstores. Yet for all of those resources on the shelves, all of those books with the clever titles—homes and relationships continue to disintegrate at a rate that has escalated through the years.

Husbands and wives *still* aren't communicating. And marriages are still falling apart all around us.

The Power of Our Words

Communication is the art of listening, watching, and sharing. Communication God's way is certainly not "unloading"—backing up your dump truck of gripes, disappointments, and frustrations and releasing the load on the head of your mate. It is the *free exchange of thoughts, ideas, and opinions shared between two or more people who are willing to be open, honest, and, yes, vulnerable.*

But it's more than words. Communication specialists estimate that only 8 percent of our communication is verbal. Beyond that, 35 percent is emotional, 55 percent is body language, and 2 percent is intuitive. These observations may be true, but never discount the sheer power of verbal communication. Who can begin to imagine how critical are those words we allow to spill out of our mouths?

- They are like seeds that can grow into trees that bear fruit for generations.

- They are like arrows that pierce and kill and cannot be recalled.

- They are like sparks that can ignite a conflagration.

- They are like ropes that can pull a drowning person out of the deep.

Carefully chosen, wisely offered words can change a countenance, soften stony resistance, splash cool water on a hot temper, release tension, and rein in raging emotions. Thoughtful, well-timed words can soothe savage passions, lift up the downcast, give hope to the depressed, and grant new life to those who just want to die. Like a signpost on a lonely road, they can change the very direction of a person's life.

This is why we need to learn what we can about communication if we truly want to have a marriage without regrets.

Two Basic Needs

When my father-in-law called me with the news that Tom, my first husband, had committed suicide, my mind raced back to two conversations. In both instances, Tom told me he was considering taking his own life. Back in the mid-fifties, the common wisdom was that "those who talk about suicide never do it." (How dreadfully wrong we were.) All you had to do, according to my limited understanding, was to make them mad and bluff them out of it.

So how did I respond in that first conversation? I actually said these words: "Well, do a good job, Tom, so I can get your money."

The second time he mentioned it, I suggested a good method. He could fly his plane into the side of a mountain so there would be no questions asked and I could collect his insurance.

Once spoken, I could not call those words back. And all the while I was completely ignorant of my husband's desperate reaching for significance. How I wish I had known then what I am about to share with you now!

The truth is, Beloved, that our Creator built each and every one of us with two basic needs:

• the need for love (or security)

• the need for a sense of worth (or significance)

I so well remember the day when I stood in the living room of my rented apartment and shook my fist at a God I didn't even know. I was separated from Tom, filled with bitterness and disillusion, and as lonely as I could be. "To hell with You, God!" I raged. "I'm going to find someone to love me!" Oh, the grace of God that finally let me discover the love we are all looking for, someone who will love us no matter what. Someone who will care for us and stand beside us whether we are ugly or pretty, sick or well, in a good mood or bad mood. Each of us longs for someone who will look at us and say, "I know all about you—and love you still."

We need a love that goes beyond our bad moments and everyday mistakes. We want someone who will bear with us in our weaknesses and imperfections, someone who won't give up on us or walk out on us or write us off when we stumble and fail. We want someone who will love, nurture, and care for us, no holds barred. If someone would love us like that—unconditionally—then we would feel secure.

Rivaling this desire for love is our deep need to sense our own worth. We all need to know that our lives have significance, meaning, value. I believe that is the reason Tom threatened suicide. He battled manic depression and was haunted by the memory of his first failure, the first time this very capable man had attempted something and did not succeed. He had dropped out of flight training when he was a naval officer, and he never recovered from that decision. It gripped his mind and emotions, literally, from then on. That was why he flew as a private pilot. He was driven to prove himself, to somehow compensate for the loss of those Navy wings he never attained.

Tom's real problem was mental illness—a body chemistry that was out of balance and warping his thoughts and emotions. I wish we would have sought help for him, but we could never manage to talk about it. The problems were never out on the table; they were always pushed back, back beneath the surface. He never shared his struggles with me, and I had no idea how to help him with his private nightmares.

Love and worth, security and significance. Don't kid yourself, Beloved, all of us need both in megadoses. And nowhere do we need them as profoundly as we do in our marriages. Yet so often that is the very place where they seem hardest to find! And when we ache for those things and never receive them, we lash out in bitterness, in the frustration of disappointment, or in anger, saying things we should never say.

A Most Effective Weapon

When I walked down the aisle with Tom, all I wanted was a husband who would love me flawlessly and understand me completely! I expected Tom to play the role of God in my life and meet all my needs for love and worth. I forgot that he had feet of clay just like me. So when he failed, I felt hurt, deceived, and trapped in an unhappy, unsatisfying marriage. When he criticized me and I felt that I couldn't please him, I fought back in my pain with the best weapon I had—a cruel, cutting tongue.

But that wasn't what God created my tongue for! This small but powerful member of our body was given to us to communicate the love of God and to speak of the worth of our brothers and sisters as creations of God. How it must grieve the Creator when that piece of muscle in our mouths becomes a sword of destruction, cutting others down, speaking lies, and murdering with our words.

You can see the murderous effects when you compare Genesis chapters 2 and 3. Immediately after Adam and Eve sinned, they covered themselves with fig leaves to cover their nakedness. The total openness they had always enjoyed was gone with the wind.

As God confronts Adam you can almost hear a tonal difference in Adam's words and attitude toward his wife. Before they ate of the tree of the knowledge of good and evil, she was *"Ishshah...bone* of my bones and flesh of my flesh." After the fateful bite, she was "the woman whom You gave to be with me, she gave me from the tree, and I ate."

"The woman"?

What happened to the tenderness? What happened to his desire to protect, honor, and identify with his partner? Something has changed...and remains changed to this day, apart from God's grace and help.

Can't you imagine the awful pain and guilt Eve had to wrestle with because she listened to the wrong voice? The effects must have been all too obvious to her as she continued in her relationship with Adam. Once sin entered the picture, words often became weapons—instruments to wound, demean, and damage rather than to help, build up, and encourage. From that point on, as Proverbs 18:21 tells us, death and life were in the power of the tongue.

But what is it that makes our tongues so destructive? James gives us the answer and, if we can grasp what God is showing us and take it to heart, it could become the very cure for many a troubled marriage.

Counsel from James

Virtually all of the third chapter of James focuses on the way we speak to one another. The apostle begins in verse 2 by saying, "We all stumble in many ways."

How simple and yet how profound.

If only we could remember just this much in our marriages! *We all stumble.* Every one of us. And we do so in a million ways. None of us is perfect. We all make mistakes and fall short, even of our own ideals. So when we're ready to blow our stacks at our mates for doing that awful thing one more time, James would encourage us to remember that we've no doubt committed that other dreadful thing just as often.

"So cut your mate some slack," the apostle might say. Grant him or her a helping or two of the grace we all need every day. Who among us would invite TV cameras and tape recorders to follow us through the course of a day, recording every word and action for later broadcast? No, let's just take refuge in the fact that we *all* stumble in many ways, and we all need grace and covering from God and from one another.

James then says, "If anyone does not stumble in what he says, he is a perfect man, able to bridle the whole body as well" (3:2). In other words: Beloved, if you can keep your tongue under control, then you can keep the rest of your body under control as well (and who has mastered *that?*).

I want to be that disciplined servant of the Lord, don't you? I want every part of me to be under the Spirit's control. This chapter has made me more determined than ever. What a woman I would be! Oh, how God could use me to minister to this bleeding, wounded world. But it won't come without great personal discipline—and major infusions of His transforming power in my life. To point out the difficulty, James continues:

Now if we put the bits into the horses' mouths so that they will obey us, we direct their entire body as well. Look at the ships also, though they are so great and are driven by strong winds, are still directed by a very small rudder wherever the inclination of the pilot desires. So also the tongue is a small part of the body, and yet it boasts of great things. See how great a forest is set aflame by such a small fire! And the tongue is a fire, the very world of iniquity; the tongue is set among our members as that which defiles the entire body, and sets on fire the course of our life, and is set on fire by hell (verses 3-6).

James uses two pictures to illustrate how the tongue packs a wallop far beyond its diminutive size: He compares it to the bit in the mouth of a well-muscled horse and the small rudder of a mighty ship. "Don't misjudge the importance of the tongue just because it's small," James seems to warn us. "It has an impact far beyond what its trifling appearance might suggest!" That impact can be for good, unleashing great potential, productivity, and joy...and it can also be for ill, creating devastation and destruction beyond imagination.

Just as one little match can destroy a whole forest of towering Ponderosa pines, each one many feet thick and soaring over 100 feet into the air, so an uncontrolled tongue can wreak havoc in a marriage. All of us have felt the slicing pain of sharp, cutting words spoken by a restless tongue. Maybe at some vulnerable moment in your life you were told you were stupid or incompetent or ugly. One nasty comment like that can change the whole course of a life!

When someone we love lashes out at us, it cuts to the quick. Even an offhand, sarcastic comment can slice us to the bone and leave a gaping wound, especially if it is said before others. It will be something all too easy to remember through the years...and much too difficult to forget.

Oh, Beloved, we so need to learn how to bridle our tongues! Remember how the mighty oil tanker, the *Exxon Valdez*, ran aground off the pristine waters of Prince Rupert Sound in Alaska? The ship's master had been drinking and became careless at the helm. And that moment of carelessness resulted in one of the greatest ecological disasters of our time. Billions of dollars and untold hours of toil were required to clean up the black, sticky mess that coated the beaches and killed the wildlife for many, many miles of that once unspoiled coastline.

That is a picture of what careless words can do in a marriage. Talk about shipwrecks! Far too many broken hulls already line the rocky coasts of this nation.

It Begins in the Heart

Jesus tells us that man speaks out of the abundance of his heart. In other words, it is the wellspring of our heart that determines what flows from our mouths. Is it sweet and fresh, refreshing and helpful? Or is it polluted and acidic, causing illness and damage? If I keep my heart with all diligence, then what comes out of my mouth will be the wisdom from above, rather than that which is earthly, natural (unspiritual), and demonic (see James 3:13-17).

The key lies in our hearts. And if you are a child of God under the New Covenant, you have a *new* heart, not a heart of stone. Your responsibility is to keep it clean through confessing your sins and keeping short accounts with God, even as David did in Psalm 51:1-10.

Whatever camps in your heart, my friend, is going to be on your tongue.

Bitter heart, bitter words.

Joyful heart, joyful words.

Loving heart, loving words.

If we want to communicate with our mates in ways that honor God and minister to our spouses, the key is keeping a right heart...day by day, hour by hour. In Ephesians 5:4, Paul tells us that there must be "no [none, zero] filthiness and silly talk, or coarse jesting, which are not fitting." Not fitting for a child of God who is instructed to be an imitator of God and walk in love, just as Christ also loved us and gave Himself up for us (see Ephesians 5:2). This means, Beloved, that when we talk to our mates there is to be purity in our speech. It is to be peaceable, not a call to battle. Our words are to be gentle, to be reasonable. Reasonable means "ready to yield"—not always insisting on our own way, our own viewpoint. Reasonable speech is full of kindness and mercy.

Trash Talk?

If you want your marriage to thrive, then you need to learn to speak with gracious words, not rotten ones. In Ephesians 4:29, Paul writes, "Let no unwholesome word proceed from your mouth, but only such a word as is good for edification according to the need of the moment, so that it will give grace to those who hear."

The word translated "unwholesome" in this passage actually means "rotting" or "decaying." I'll never forget when I was 14, and it was my turn to get the garbage can to the curb for the morning pickup. It had been hot weather and the stench was overpowering. But what was worse was what happened when I set the big can down and jarred the lid. It fell off, exposing a white sea of maggots. It was utterly gross. It still makes my skin crawl to think of it. Scripture says that unwholesome words are just like that. Loathsome and repulsive. Disgusting and repugnant. Such things do not belong in the heart or on the tongue of a child of God!

It is popular in sports these days for athletes to "trash talk" each other, and what a habit of life that can become. God's children should never speak in a way that demeans or disrespects; if the words on the tip of our tongues aren't words that build or encourage or heal or bless our Lord, we should swallow them. Our goal should be to build up others, *especially our life partners.*

Paul also tells us that our speech should be "according to the need of the moment." Before you and I speak, we need to take time to think about what is most appropriate. In other words, what does my husband need to hear at this particular time? What words would particularly benefit my wife at this moment? And how should we speak such words? With *grace.* Our words are to "give grace to those who hear." Grace is unearned, unmerited favor or blessing. It is receiving something good and pleasant even when in reality we haven't warranted it. Have you ever met someone who spoke that way—with gracious, kind words that seemed to flow right from the heart? You never forget such a person. There is a fragrance about his or her life. And it is the fragrance of Jesus.

Rose-Colored Glasses

On a recent flight home I read a short *USA Today* article with an intriguing headline: "Sweet Nothings Help Marriage Stick." For ten years, I learned, the University of Washington (UW) has been studying the question, "What makes marriages last?" Their studies have led them to the conclusion that spouses who "see each other through rose-colored glasses" are the ones whose marriages endure. Those who divorce are more inclined to be cynical and negative, "viewing each other through fogged lenses." Such couples seem to be unable to say anything positive about one another. Psychology professor John Gottman found that a key predictor of divorce includes a husband's unwillingness to be influenced by his wife, who is most often the one trying to solve marital problems. Another indicator? A wife's hostility and tendency to start small quarrels that escalate into bigger conflicts.

In James 4:1, the apostle tells us what causes dissension in relationships. "What is the source of quarrels and conflicts among you?" he asks. "Is not the source your pleasures that wage war in your members?" The word translated "pleasures" is the Greek word *hedone*, which means "inner desires." We quarrel and fight, James says, because of the uncontrolled desires raging within us.

Have you ever been hurt because your husband or wife didn't meet your expectations? Did you want something—only to be refused? You wanted to be loved, understood, comforted, encouraged, or held, but your spouse seemed either unwilling or unable to meet your need. You sent out all the right signals, but they weren't received. Did it leave you feeling a little nettled, maybe a little angry?

I understand. I've been there, too. And I've had to consult with myself so I wouldn't lash back in anger. It was as though a war was going on within me, a war I must say my dear husband seemed completely oblivious to. I've struggled and fretted, cried and fumed because I didn't get what I wanted. And *then* what happens? James spells out the awful truth: "You lust and do not have; so you commit murder" (4:2).

You find yourself thinking dark thoughts...terrible thoughts...even murderous thoughts...if you don't hurriedly bring your thoughts captive to the obedience of Jesus Christ. Oh, I don't mean we march to the gun cabinet, load up the shotgun, aim, and fire. I mean we let loose with both barrels filled with hateful, spiteful, angry words. We murder our mates with the buckshot of iron verbs.

From what dark corner of our nature do these savage blasts come? What lies behind such warlike words? It's a mind out from under the control of the Spirit. It's the lust of our flesh. Listen...

> Now the deeds of the flesh are evident, which are: immorality, impurity, sensuality, idolatry, sorcery, enmities, strife, jealousy, outbursts of anger, disputes, dissensions, factions, envying, drunkenness, carousing, and things like these, of which I forewarn you, just as I have forewarned you, that those who practice such things will not inherit the kingdom of God.

> But the fruit of the Spirit is love, joy, peace, patience, kindness, goodness, faithfulness, gentleness, self-control; against such things there is no law. Now those who belong to Christ Jesus have crucified the flesh with its passions and desires. If we live by the Spirit, let us also walk by the Spirit. Let us not become boastful, challenging one another, envying one another (Galatians 5:19-26).

Four Solid Foundation Stones

I want us to look at four essential factors of marriage that must be in place before good communication can happen. If you work at these four essentials, they'll provide a solid basis for positive communication that leads to a strong, healthy marriage.

1. Uphold the priority of your marriage.

The marriage relationship is to have priority over every other human relationship. That's the message of Genesis 2:24: "For this reason a man shall leave his father and his mother, and be joined to his wife." Our marriage partner is to come before any other human being. *Everyone* else falls into the background—including our parents.

Is your mate number one in your life? Or do you allow parents, in-laws, relatives, friends, business associates, or even children take the place intended for your spouse? If the desire of your heart is to establish healthy communication patterns between you and your partner, the place to begin is right here. Make sure you uphold the priority of your marriage. A recent survey stated that 61 percent of married men feel that their wives were a little too focused on the kids. Be careful, women, that you don't neglect your husband—even for your children. Not only will he suffer, but it will set a bad example for the children. If you want to keep your marriage strong (and free from regrets!), the relationship between husband and wife must remain preeminent, second only to a relationship with Christ.

2. Uphold the permanence of your marriage.

The word "join" in Genesis 2:24 means to glue together so that two become one. In other words, marriage is to be permanent, lasting, not to be undone in this life. Jesus Himself commented on this Old Testament teaching in Matthew 19:6 when He said, "What therefore God has joined together, let no man separate." God declares that couples must remain firmly committed to each other until the moment death parts them.

3. Uphold the oneness of your marriage.

Genesis 2:24 also says of the married couple, "And they shall become one flesh." This oneness is not merely physical. Because my body is the house of my soul, marriage is also an *emotional* or soul oneness. And because my body is the home of my spirit, marriage is also a *spirit* oneness. This profound union—physical, emotional, spiritual—is an essential factor in marriage. In God's eyes, you and your spouse are one in every way.

How many of our difficulties in communication would vanish if we stopped to ponder this oneness-of-flesh before we opened our mouths? If we consciously thought of our mates as the other half of ourselves, would we be so quick to criticize? To harangue? To belittle or scold or insult? Wouldn't we automatically give our spouse the benefit of the doubt?

4. Uphold the openness of your marriage.

Before the Fall, Adam and Eve enjoyed complete openness, for they "were both naked and were not ashamed" (Genesis 2:25). They hid nothing from each other. They shared the fullness of their hearts without a thought of concealing the least feeling or desire. We would say they were totally transparent with one another.

But the moment they fell into sin, *everything* changed.

As we have already noted, openness was a thing of the past. Immediately they covered themselves with fig leaves. They put on a protective layering to cover their nakedness, and the total openness they had always enjoyed instantly vanished.

In Christ, we can recover some of the openness that Adam and Eve lost in the Garden. We can learn to speak the truth in love to each other, desiring each other's best, acting for each other's benefit. Transparency between marriage partners is not easy to develop, but it is well worth every effort.

The truth is, each of these four essentials takes a lot of work to uphold. But without this kind of ground-level toil, all the excellent communication principles in the world will do us little good. On the other hand, if we determine to act on these essentials, positive changes will naturally begin to occur in our patterns of communication.

For example, will you allow yourself to talk about separation or divorce? No, because you remember that marriage is a priority relationship. *It's not even an option* because you remember that marriage is a permanent relationship. You won't even entertain such thoughts because you remember that two have become one—physically, emotionally, spiritually. You know that if you were to take that "one flesh" and break it in half, you would wind up with two halves, not two wholes.

Will you allow yourself to clam up and refuse to communicate with your spouse? No, that's not an option, either, because you remember that openness is an essential factor in marriage. To refuse to communicate is to hide from your spouse, and you would be following the same fatal road taken by Adam and Eve so long ago.

Beloved, when you uphold the priority, permanence, oneness, and openness of your marriage, you lay a foundation for godly communication that cannot help but solidify and energize your marriage relationship. You'll find yourself speaking words that build up rather than tear down.

Practical Insights

I've been looking forward to this part of the chapter! I believe with all my heart that some of the practical insights I will share in the next few pages can have an instant impact on the atmosphere in your home. Stick with me!

When you talk to your mate, you need to remember that the individual to whom you are speaking is a composite of many things: personality, character, talents, giftings. Your spouse is a product of his or her upbringing, conditioning, teaching, and training. When you look into the eyes of another individual, you are speaking to a person with a history. Remember that! This is a person with past conflicts, triumphs, failures, and disappointments. The way he or she views a situation may be completely different from the way you see the very same set of circumstances. That difference may baffle you, but remember you are not looking at life through the same set of lenses.

You and I really have very little knowledge of an individual's emotional, mental, or spiritual state at any given moment. Throw fluctuating hormones into that mix and—my goodness!—we need to give each other lots and lots of leeway.

The way you communicate is influenced by who you are; the way your mate hears you is influenced by who he or she is. Your communication attempts are constantly filtered through all manner of extraneous material in both of you! Even the way you sit, stand, or gesture as you talk—and the very words and phrases you use—may trigger memories in the other person of some words or deeds or scenes from long ago. Those memories may be pleasant or they may be terribly hurtful. Do you see how these things might affect the way your words may be received?

Let's see if a diagram might help to explain this process.

The Components of Communication
Between Husband and Wife

Each partner brings these areas into every communication:

Your Consequential History
Knowledge and wisdom
Past experiences
Self-image
Sense of humor

Current State
Emotions
Mood
Current conflicts
- *with others*
- *with each other*
- *with yourself*
- *with God*
- *at work*

The Condition of the Heart
Is it evil or good, heart of stone or flesh?
(See Matthew 12:35; Ezekiel 36:26)
The mouth speaks that which fills the heart.
(See Matthew 12:34)

The Body
Body language
Tone and volume of your voice

In light of all this, is it any wonder communication can be such a chore? This is an issue that is so much larger than mere words. You must also account for the *interpretation* of those words…their coloring and shading, their tone and delivery, their timing and context. Nor can those words be separated from body language and facial expressions. This is why certain phrases, gestures, and expressions can set another person off in a way that takes you completely aback. You never meant anything close to the way those words were received! What happened? Your words triggered a memory. A past hurt. A long-running disappointment. A current of suppressed anger or frustration. And your innocent comment brought it all flooding back.

Oh, Beloved, this is why we need to walk moment by moment in the Spirit of Christ. This is why we always need to be "quick to listen and slow to speak" (James 1:9). We need to be really sure we are hearing what is actually being said, and we need to give grace to the person from whom we are hearing it. We need to take people at their word, rather than relying on our own interpretation of what they've said. Otherwise, our communication may encounter a stone wall and fall uselessly to the ground.

Here is an important proverb to remember when communicating:

> The spirit of a man can endure his sickness,
> But as for a broken spirit who can bear it?
>
> —Proverbs 18:14

Never, never break another person's spirit. *You will lose him! You will lose her!* Don't ever make your mate—or anyone else—the brunt of your jokes. Never ridicule. Never mock. Be very, very careful with barbed humor. Your words, so lightly spoken, may remain in an individual's soul until his or her dying day. Ridicule and mockery is cruel and kills communication. As Solomon wrote, "A brother offended is harder to be won than a strong city" (Proverbs 18:19). If you have offended your mate or another in this way, go and ask forgiveness.

How I love the words of Job: "I could strengthen you with my mouth, and the solace of my lips could lessen your pain" (Job 16:5).

What a ministry we can have to our mates and others just through our carefully chosen, tenderly delivered words. It makes me cry out, as I did last night when I finally turned off my computer and went to bed, to carefully guard my words and use my tongue to minister life, healing, and hope to others. To keep my tongue from evil and my lips from speaking deceit...to do good, seek peace, and pursue it (see Psalm 34:13,14).

Sharpening Your Skills

When a woman's magazine asked married men what was the glue (beyond love) that held their marriage together, the greater majority of them—59 percent—responded "friendship."

One thing you can't help notice about friends is that they talk. This is why we need to constantly evaluate and work on our communication skills, so that we won't slip into some bad habits that may strain the "friendship factor" in our marriages. Here are a few I've been working on.

1. Learn to communicate with your eyes.

Someone has said that the eyes are the window to the soul. When you talk to anyone, especially to a loved one, it is important to look him or her directly in the eyes. If you are a dad, this gesture exudes strength and security. If you are a mom, it conveys concern and warmth. If you are a child, it shows respect and confidence.

And what does it say to your mate? It says: *You have my full attention.* And isn't that what we crave in our relationships? It reassures us of our importance to our spouses.

If someone speaks to you, look directly into his or her eyes. When I do this, I ask God to let His love and acceptance flow from my eyes to the other person. I am amazed at how often people will say to me, "Kay, your eyes are so loving." It wasn't always that way. People used to say, "I wish you could see your face!" I guess it was a "hard" sight to behold.

The change in my countenance has come through much prayer and practice.

Learn to flirt with your mate (but only your mate!) with your eyes. You know what I mean! Wink. Smile. "Light up" when he or she enters the room. In a crowd, watch your mate until he or she looks at you, and then send out a romantic flare of some sort (being careful where you aim it). Develop something special between the two of you…even if you're in your sixties or seventies. (You can't tell what it will do for those "golden years." It might enhance your circulation or keep you from becoming senile. You might be surprised!)

2. Give the gift of your full attention.

You really can't listen to someone while reading the newspaper, watching television, or doing a hundred other things that divert your attention. You may be saying "uh-huh" and "oh really?" but you're not truly engaged. It is condescending to listen with half an ear when a loved one is speaking. Mates and children will eventually "get the idea" and walk away from you, understanding that whatever you may be doing or watching at that moment is more important than they are. My friend, that doesn't communicate value!

In reality, there is nothing more important than sharing our experiences and thoughts and observations with one another. There can be no *real* oneness in marriage without communication. Communication really is the key to the rest of your relationship…including in the bedroom. Communicate well and physical expression will flow from it. Neglect communication and expect a long, cold night.

3. Respond when someone speaks to you.

When a family member tries to talk with you, show him or her that you consider his or her statement worthy of acknowledgement. I once heard Dr. James Dobson relate a story about a mother whose teenage son was awkward at keeping a conversation going. One day she hit on the idea of teaching him to "pick up the ball" in a conversation. She threw a ball to him, he caught it, and threw it back. Then she just held it. When he looked puzzled, she explained that conversations were just like tossing a ball back and forth. You don't simply "catch" a comment and hold it; you respond by tossing it back. That's the way the game is played!

4. Keep a confidence.

Nothing cuts off communication faster than a leak in the confidence barrier. The wall of trust that surrounds the family relationship cannot be broken (or even cracked) if you are going to succeed in heart-to-heart communication with your mate.

5. Avoid pat answers.

One of the most difficult struggles I have had in communicating (although I'm doing better!) is that I tend to dispense advice too quickly. Because of my personality, I am "quick on the trigger" with my opinion, and then I am ready to move on. But like it or not, Beloved, it takes *time* to listen. It may take quite a while for your loved ones to express what is really on their hearts. If you throw out pat answers before you've heard them out, you have cut off a valuable channel of communication.

Learn to relax, to be available, to listen patiently, and to be sure your mate has "said it all" before you jump in to give advice. And even then—don't jump! In reality, your loved one may not need your advice at that point. He or she may simply need a compassionate sounding board from which to bounce a thought or idea. Pause and see if he or she really *wants* your insights or whether your partner simply wants to be *heard*. While you listen, ask God to give you discernment whether to speak…or just listen with both eyes and both ears. One of the wisest responses you can make might be to simply ask, "What do you think about that?" or "What are you going to do?"

6. Allow your mate to open up about his or her fears.

This may be difficult for all of us, but it is particularly difficult for men. Admitting weakness or fear may seem unmanly. Yet many times when a person can discuss his or her fears *without* you quickly trying to dispel them, diminish them, or put a Band-Aid of advice on them, then the tension may ebb away (and with it, perhaps, the fear).

It's also good to help your spouse verbalize the emotion. You might say, "How does that make you feel?" or "If I had been there, I would have felt pretty intimidated. Maybe even scared." Often, once the "fear" word is out on the table, it doesn't seem quite so daunting.

7. Continually look for ways to build your mate's self-esteem.

What a communication builder this is! You won't believe what doors this principle will open.

My sweet husband came into my office just a few minutes ago to tell me how much he admired me for my diligence in writing this book, my putting in so many long hours. (It's been a sacrifice on his part, too, because I haven't given him as much attention as usual.)

What a lift that was for a weary writer! Just to have him walk into the room and say those things—and then pray for me before he left for the office. The encouraging glow continued to fill that room long after he had driven away. These are the little things that so strengthen the marriage bond, and we must not neglect them. How foolish we are if we do!

8. When you talk, don't attack!

Lord, help me practice this. I have been so grieved by my tendency to launch into the attack mode. What wounds this can cause. What bitter memories this can produce. What a foothold this can offer to the enemy of our marriages and our souls.

Let the goal of your discussion be healing, not further destruction. If you become frustrated because you feel that you're not being heard—or perhaps you have *never* been heard—on some issue, just cool it. Cool it quickly. Let your engine idle way down before you open your mouth. And pray. Give that mounting frustration to the Lord. Maybe your mate will hear, will heed, and will change...and maybe he or she won't. Nevertheless, he's still your husband...she's still your wife. You can only do so much, and then if there is no change, just remind yourself that God can use the situation in your own life to make you more Christ-like!

9. Never, never let the sun go down on your wrath.

When you become angry (and there is such a thing as "righteous anger"), don't let that anger control you. If you do, you have sinned. Ephesians 4:26,27 tells us, "Be angry, and yet do not sin; do not let the sun go down on your anger, and do not give the devil an opportunity." In other words, don't allow anger to seethe, simmer, or boil overnight— it burns the pot. Communicate! Make things right—or at least pass-able—before you go to sleep. As Scripture says, Satan will be quick to exploit unresolved anger.

10. The word "divorce" should never be in your vocabulary.

I mentioned this earlier, but I want to emphasize it one more time. Make it a rule, Beloved, that you are never going to use the "D" word. Don't threaten it. Don't discuss it. Don't entertain it. Don't ponder it. Don't even joke about it. Never raise or initiate the subject of divorce or separation. (We'll talk more about this later. And, yes, I realize that there can be extenuating circumstances.) If the subject should ever come up for any reason, don't react. Simply state the fact of your commit-ment—that it will only be severed by death.

Dear friend of mine, how I wish I could go back with you to the beginning of this chapter and say all of this all over again…and again and again until it has a permanent place in your heart. I cannot overem-phasize communication in a marriage relationship. Neither can you overemphasize communication in yours. It is so much more than a skill to be developed. It is a lovely, living tree to be nourished and tenderly cultivated through the years. And once you begin to enjoy its fruit, you will have a marriage to be envied. Remember, O man, and remember, O woman, when you stand before God you want to have a marriage without regrets.

Let's pray.

O Father, we are taking in so much. Help us to remember. We don't want to miss anything that You have to say to us. May we listen…may we hear what You are saying, and may we desire to please You more than life itself.

Thank You for what You're teaching us, Lord. We know these words will only be as good and as effective as they are lived out among Your dear children. May we be not just hearers of the Word, but doers also.

Oh, Father, we stand on tiptoe in anticipation of what You are about to do in our lives and in our marriages. Fix these great truths in our minds and anchor them in our hearts. And may we walk in a manner worthy of the gospel of Jesus Christ—especially in the way we speak to and live with the mates You have given us. And Lord, thank You for so tenderly communicating with us in Your precious Word and through Your precious Son. In His strong name we pray, amen.

CHAPTER

10

SEX...GOD'S WAY

IT WAS AN EVENING I WILL NEVER FORGET.

I was 12 years old, sitting at the kitchen table in my parents' tiny brick house. I was doing my homework while listening with half an ear to a science program on the radio. The show used dramatizations to catch people's attention, and whatever they did that night certainly caught mine. It wasn't long before I abandoned all pretense of doing schoolwork. The radio had my complete attention.

After all these years, I still remember the topic: the Rh factor of human blood. One speaker noted that if a father and mother had an incompatible Rh factor, any baby they produced could face grave problems.

Immediately I was puzzled. My curious mind loved anything medical—I was going to be a nurse when I grew up. What I couldn't figure out as I listened was what on earth the *father's* blood had to do with it. It was the woman who had the baby!

I knew that Mom had worked for a doctor. Surely she would be able to solve this riddle. So I turned around in the chair and asked, "Mother, what does the father's blood have to do with the baby's?"

Her response has remained printed on my memory for over 50 years. She could have said so many things or brushed off my question altogether. But that wasn't what she did. Thinking back now, I wonder if she had been waiting for such an opportunity.

"Oh, Kay," she said, "it's so *beautiful*." And she went on to explain the story of human reproduction.

What, my friend, is your perception of sex?

Is it beautiful or dreadful?

A chore or a delight?

The most precious gift you can give your mate…or a "necessary evil" to be avoided as much as possible?

Is it an uncomfortable, embarrassing part of life…or is it exciting, soothing, rejuvenating?

Is it something to get over with quickly…or a time to luxuriate in the pleasure of one another?

Is it an area of contention between you and your mate…or that which melts you into one?

Is it something you anticipate and dream about…or something you never think of unless you're reminded, "Hey, it goes with the marriage contract"?

Does it? Does it go with the marriage contract? Yes, according to God's own Word, it certainly does. And the Bible isn't shy at all about speaking to this crucial issue of marriage.

This is a very important chapter, Beloved. In many ways, I feel that I am treading on sacred ground. It is my prayer that God might use these next few pages to enlighten, heal, liberate, and bring delight and blessing to your marriage. As a matter of fact, before you read any further will you pause to pray with me?

Father, I ask that in Your sovereignty You will speak so clearly, so specifically, that this dear reader will find answers to the questions he or she seeks. I only dare to ask this because You are God, and You promise to supply all our needs.

Lord, we want to understand Your grand design in marriage— why You created us male and female. We want to understand what pleases You—and what brings You grief—in this intimate aspect of our marriage. As we have said again and again, Lord, we want to have no regrets and no shame when we stand before You at the end of time. We ask that You would bring grace and healing into our lives. Grant us freedom from anxiety, feelings of insufficiency, guilt from the past or present, insatiable lust, perversion, or frigidity.

This is our cry…and we thank You that Your ears are open to the cries of Your children. We ask this in the name of the One who came that we might have life and have it abundantly. Amen.

If your sex life is going to be all that it should be, then you must seek to understand God's mind on the subject. If, at this moment, you're feeling a little uneasy because of what you might discover in this chapter, please relax. God's will is always good, acceptable, and perfect. We can trust Him to show us the best and most bountiful way to travel through life.

Designed for Pleasure

According to Genesis 1:28, God's first instructions to Adam and Eve were to be "fruitful and multiply, and fill the earth." In other words, "I made you male and female, now enjoy one another and have children." Sex was to be the first item on the first couple's agenda—even higher in priority than their oversight of the world.

From the very beginning, God designed us for pleasure. How do I know? I know because God could have made the sexual act a tedious, perfunctory one.

But that wasn't His design, was it?

God designed us in such a way that the greatest excitement the nerve endings of our bodies can ever experience happens in the process of sexual intercourse. He *built* us that way. As the woman receives her husband into herself, they experience a oneness beyond what they will ever know with any other human being. It is the highest, most ecstatic sensation a man or woman can know—if the marriage partners are careful to consider each other's pleasure.

My friend, do you truly believe that God created the whole human body—including the sexual organs—and declared the sum total good? Then why should we shrink to speak of that which the Creator has declared good? Yet I do find myself with this dilemma: I have no desire to shock or offend any of my readers. Yet what's the alternative? That you would miss God's best for your marriage? That you would find this information in some secular source that neither honors God nor respects marriage? How important it is to know some of these basic things if we want to give each other the joy and delight God intended!

When God designed woman, He gave her a clitoris, just above the vagina, the husband's gate to oneness with his wife. This is the most sensitive part of a woman's body. When properly stimulated, there is an onrush of blood to those tissues, causing them to become engorged for the pleasure of both her and her mate. The man's penis is engulfed, locking them together as one. What the clitoris is to the woman, the tip of the penis is to the man. Both were created by God for pleasure of the highest sort. Considering facts like these helps you understand what brings about a woman's orgasm.

You must know and realize that God created you for pleasure, not simply procreation. None of this is disgusting or evil in His sight. He is the Master Designer of human sexuality.

What of the rest of our bodies? Our mouths, hands, arms, legs, loins, breasts? Each one has its own nerves and sensory receptors. Each is part of God's design, meant to be stimulated, enjoyed, and delighted in—but all within the hallowed confines of marriage. God says "marriage is to be held in honor among all, and the marriage bed is to be undefiled."[1] In other words your sexual enjoyment of one another and your union with each other in no way defiles you. In His book of wisdom, Proverbs, God says, "Rejoice in the wife of your youth. As a loving hind and a graceful doe, let her breasts satisfy you at all times; be exhilarated [literally, 'intoxicated'] always with her love."[2]

---

1. Hebrews 13:4.
2. Proverbs 5:18,19.

The sexual union is a moment to drown yourself in the pleasure of one another, to be caught in the whirlpool of ecstasy that takes you deeper and deeper into one another until all is spent and you lie quietly in one another's arms feeling your oneness as never before. This, Beloved, is God's design and intention. Again, it was intended to bring delight…and to ensure the continuance of His creation.

Sometime at your leisure, read the Song of Solomon together in your bedroom. If you have children, send them out (or wear them out and put them to bed!). Then, behind locked doors, surrounded with soft music and candlelight, cast yourself in the role of the husband and his bride. Treat it as a drama. Read God's script and act out your role. Go for an academy award.

I promise you that if you will read the Song of Solomon, even without acting it out, then you will begin to see how very significant sex is to you and to your oneness as husband and wife.

What Women Need to Know

Because men are turned on by the visual, the way you present yourself as a woman is so critical. Yes, his eyes may be momentarily attracted by other beautiful women he may see in the course of a day (he isn't blind!), but it's you—his wife—that he wants. And if you are available and responsive to him, you are *all* he wants. He finds his security, his significance, his acceptance with *you*. And if he is secure with you, dear one, you are all he needs. Isn't it wonderful to know that?

Acknowledging this aspect of a man's sexuality, I urge you to find out what is attractive to your husband. Do all you can to be as physically appealing as possible. Watch the underwear you wear—no elastic hanging from the legs of your panties, no pins at the waist, no holes in the back. Black is sexier than white, especially in panties, and usually makes you look slimmer. Lace can be nice…or maybe he prefers the jockey look. Learn what he likes; because he is your husband, wear it for his sake.

At the same time I say all this, let me also caution you as a woman to be careful how you dress when you leave the bedroom. You don't want to be guilty of awakening lust in another man by the suggestive way you clothe your body. By now you know that men who are turned on by sight are not just dirty old men. This is part of being a man. Short skirts, skin-tight clothing, and low-cut blouses all have one purpose— to advertise a woman's sexuality. When you get dressed, ask the Holy Spirit what He thinks about your outfit before you leave the room. After all, your body is *His* temple.

This visual aspect of a man's sexuality is *so* crucial for a wife to understand. Perhaps what you have traditionally thought of as sexy is not the same as what your husband thinks. In a recent survey, men were asked the question, "What do you notice first in a woman you just met?"

Forty-four percent said, "Her smile."

Thirty-seven percent said, "Her breasts."

Sixteen percent said, "Her legs."

I wonder if wives really understand how inviting their smiles are to their husbands. We may not achieve perfection in our makeup or hairstyle, and we may not have the build of a super-model, but we can always wear a smile—and give our husbands a welcome that makes them want to come home. If we will remember this, it will go a long way in our marriages and in our sexual relationships.

If you find yourself reluctant to have sex because you feel self-conscious about your body, don't let those thoughts rob your marriage of intimacy. You don't have to look like a cover girl or a movie star for your husband to deeply desire you. I can promise you this: Your husband is not going to want to wait to have sex with you until after you lose five pounds! Sex isn't simply a pleasure for men, it is a *need*. And where is he to find the answer to his need with its accompanying pleasures? It is to be in you, and you alone, sweet one.

Strive to make sex as pleasurable as you can by knowing your man, by understanding his ways, and by keeping yourself as attractive as possible. Do all those little feminine things that affirm your womanhood such as bathing in bubbles, shaving with your own razor, and oiling down your body with sweet smelling lotions. Your availability and willingness will keep your husband a contented man. What's more, you will look so much more beautiful in his eyes than the image that looks back at you in the mirror. And it's *his* eyes that are far more important than the world's...or even yours (because we are so hard on ourselves).

But, you say, "I'm filled with disgust and mad at myself over the way I've allowed myself to get. I can't stand to look at myself in a mirror." You're not alone! When we look at ourselves in the mirror it is for the purpose of critiquing what is and has happened to our bodies. Your husband, normally, won't be nearly as critical as you are. You are his...his chosen one.

Let me simply say that if you can do anything to make yourself more attractive to your husband (and do it in a healthy way without harming yourself), then choose your course and start today. You'll feel better about yourself. But don't deny your husband just because you're in the middle of a self-improvement project!

If your heart is filled with discouragement, go to God and ask Him to help you be all that you can be. He loves you and cares more about the details of your life than you could ever begin to imagine.

What Men Need to Know

Now it's the man's turn to listen. And here is Lesson #1!

Women are responders.

You can often tell a great deal about a husband and how well he fulfills his role by looking at his wife. Generally speaking, it is a man's tender touch accompanied by loving words that draws a woman to him. As one man wrote, "The Look and the Touch are especially popular because they can generate a vicious cycle of happiness. Touching my wife makes her smile, which leads to a kiss, which may trigger sexy thoughts that inspire her to wear certain clingy fashion items, which causes me to rejoice and flex energetically and announce, 'I am a man! See my glory! Life is good.'"[3]

If you want to have sex with your wife tonight, start preparing her early in the day. Or, better still, a day in advance. Talk to her in the tender, loving way she likes best. If you honestly can't discern what

---

3. Brian Alexander, "Men in Love," *New Woman,* June 1999.

pleases and delights her as a woman, then ask God for an opportunity to talk to her about it. When that opportunity comes, listen very carefully. Take notes if necessary! She'll be impressed.

Whatever you do, just remember that touch is so important. God put all those delicate nerve endings in our skin, and when it is caressed, so to speak, it releases healthy chemicals into our bodies. Put your arms around your wife, stroke her face, and tell her how much you appreciate her. Massage her neck, tell her that you love her, give her a sweet kiss, pull out her chair at the dinner table, reach over and hold her hand or give it a squeeze. Don't make sexual advances until you know she is ready, or she begins to encourage you. Because woman is a responder, it is so important to set the stage for sex.

Your wife may not want to have sex with you if she feels she's ugly or is being used or neglected. Once again, *she is a responder.* If you can remember that and act accordingly, it will make a huge difference in your relationship.

As women we don't want you to criticize us and then take us to bed. We don't want you to sit in your chair watching the tube all evening while we knock ourselves out cooking, cleaning the kitchen, helping the kids with homework, and folding the laundry—and then expect us to gladly hop into bed with you.

You're a man; you love the pursuit. *Pursue your wife!* Heed the words of Ephesians 5, and love her as you love your own flesh. Cherish her, help her, compliment her, make her feel beautiful, admire and appreciate her, speak to her sweet words, draw her bathwater, tuck the kids into bed, wash her back, and it won't be difficult for her to fall into your arms. And if it still is, then you need to find out what the problem is!

Why Don't We Want Sex?

Why do marriage partners—even men—sometimes lose interest in sex? Personally, I think the main culprit is sheer exhaustion. Tiredness and lack of exercise kill the sex drive. We become so stressed out and bone-tired that all we want is time alone, time for ourselves, and time for blessed sleep. Incessant busyness is the plague of our contemporary lifestyle, and it is greatly damaging to our physical intimacy as husbands and wives.

Of course there may be other reasons, too. These could include misconceptions about sex, past sexual abuse, guilt, anger, and even physical problems. The way we eat, what we eat, and even the medicines we take can diminish our sex drives.

One of the most common reasons that believers may struggle with enjoyment of sex is the sense of guilt that arises from immoral sexual activity in their pasts. That is precisely why our good and loving God gave us His rules and commands for our protection. He understands very well that sex outside the marriage relationship is devastating to our very personhood. In 1 Corinthians 6, Paul writes to a once licentious group of people to remind them that although we are sexual beings, God did not make the body for sex; rather, He made our bodies for Himself. Having said this, Paul then urges the Corinthians to flee sexual immorality. Every other sin that a man commits, Paul tells them, is outside the body. But the immoral man sins against his own body.[4] Unrestrained immorality and deviant sex acts can severely damage our capacity to enjoy sex with a lifelong partner as God intended.

For some people, sex awakens all manner of horrific or sickening memories. As a result, the very thought of someone touching us as others did in their disobedience causes us to want to run, to hide, to curl up in a ball where there will be no edges of our being exposed. If we were promiscuous before marriage—with our future mate or with someone else—we can carry a sense of uncleanness or bitterness into our marriages that shut down our normal responses and desires.

Is there a cure for such problems?

Thank God, there is! The Bible gives us the hope of a clean start, a fresh beginning. Healing and restoration are available to those who seek God's face and obey His precepts. I'll touch on it briefly, but you might want to read my book *Lord, Heal My Hurts* for a more complete discussion.

---

4. 1 Corinthians 6:13-18.

Clean, Restored, and Made New

Did you realize that the Greek word for salvation, *soteria,* speaks of deliverance? When God saves us, He delivers us. And that deliverance is so complete that we are simply no longer what we used to be. In Romans 6:6, we learn that our old self, what we were before we were born again into God's family, is dead.

The old us is gone. We're brand-new in Christ.

In 2 Corinthians 5:16,17, Paul says, "Therefore from now on we recognize no one according to the flesh; even though we have known Christ according to the flesh, yet now we know Him in this way no longer. Therefore, if anyone is in Christ, he is a new creature; the old things passed away; behold, new things have come." The problem comes when we don't know, believe, or live in the light of the total deliverance God has given to us. When I live as if my old, dead-and-gone identity still exists—the one who was abused or the one who wittingly or unwittingly disobeyed God's precepts in the sexual realm—then I am dragging another person into bed along with my spouse. And three's a crowd! You cannot give your mate your full attention when you are preoccupied by past mistakes and illicit sexual experiences.

In Roman times, one of the more gruesome punishments for murder was to strap the dead person's body to that of the murderer so that he dragged the corpse with him wherever he went. This is what so many of us do. We shackle ourselves to our old self, the self who died years ago, and drag that corpse wherever we go.

What a foolish thing to do. Why do we carry the stench of death with us when God tells us that we are brand-new creations in Christ? The old things have passed away! When you really take this to heart, Beloved, and keep the coffin nailed on that old self, your sex life will take on a whole new freedom. Freedom from the past; freedom from guilt!

"But, Kay," you say, "it happened *after* I was saved. We knew the Lord, and we hopped into bed anyway." If that is the case, dear reader, then you both sinned. So what do you do? You do what God says in 1 John 1:9. Name the sin for what it was—that's what the word "confess" means. Then believe God, who "is faithful and righteous to forgive us our sins and cleanse us from all unrighteousness."

Have you done that? If yes, then you *are* clean. Period.

If possible, talk over some of those hurtful matters with your mate. Get them into the open. Discuss them and confess them to God. Receive His forgiveness, *then move on.* Now you are cleansed "by the washing of water with the word" (Ephesians 5:26). What more can God do? What more can He say? He is *for* you, not against you. Now go forward. Every time a memory or a thought of guilt comes to your mind, resist it. It's from the enemy. Keep drawing near to God, and He will draw near to you. Thank Him for the blood of Christ that just keeps on cleansing you over and over and over. Forgiven one, learn from your experience and vow to God and to your mate that, with God's help, you will never break the heart of your Lord or your spouse again.

But What if I Don't *Feel* Like Having Sex?

God has an answer for that, Beloved, in 1 Corinthians 7:1-5:

> Now concerning the things about which you wrote, it is good for a man not to touch a woman. But because of immoralities, each man is to have his own wife, and each woman is to have her own husband. The husband must fulfill his duty to his wife, and likewise also the wife to her husband. The wife does not have authority over her own body, but the husband does; and likewise also the husband does not have authority over his own body, but the wife does. Stop depriving one another, except by agreement for a time, so that you may devote yourselves to prayer, and come together again so that Satan will not tempt you because of your lack of self-control.

When we marry we have a duty before God to meet our mate's sexual needs. These needs should never be met in a way that demeans or devalues our mates. They are to be met pleasantly, submissively. Once I marry, my body is not "mine alone"; it belongs to my mate. The husband has authority over his wife's body and she over his. But notice that even if you abstain it's to be for only a little while to prevent immorality. Your sex drive is a gift from God, and if you cannot control yourself, then you need to get married. That is why Paul goes on to say in verse 9, "But if they do not have self-control, let them marry; for it is better to marry than to burn with passion." The outlet is marriage—sex in marriage.

I wonder how many are aware of these biblical precepts before they enter into the marriage covenant?

Think Before You Say No

There is no reason to refuse one another sexual gratification. Abstinence should only come by mutual agreement, and then only for a reasonable amount of time. The purpose for abstinence should be for extended prayer, *period.* Headaches, backaches, and being tired are not legitimate excuses, although out of love these along with other reasons should be considered. You need to remember, Beloved, that there is nothing wrong with the raw sexual drive. God created us with desires and hormones! Therefore, if you deprive one another of God's means of quenching sexual fire, you put your mate squarely into the path of temptation. And you will answer for that because you have sinned by disobeying God.

Because women are not usually as easily aroused, I can tell you there have been times when I have dearly wanted to say no. (Desire can flare up at the most inopportune times!) And there have been a few rare occasions when I have asked, "Do we really need to?" Which, translated, means, "Can you wait?"

But I can also tell you that in those rare incidents I found it hard to get to sleep afterward. Why? Because I know that I was more concerned about myself than I was about my husband. I know what the Word of God says about dying to self, and I want to be all God wants me to be. So I have simply decided that I will honor this part of the marriage commitment and will keep it without resentment. I will give it my all, even when I "don't feel like it."

Once you say no to your partner, it is easier to say no the next time—and to continue to come up with excuses. It has been proven that the more you put off this intimate oneness, the easier it becomes and the less you desire it. It becomes a sad habit of life, a residual, recurrent infection insidiously draining the marriage of its vitality and strength. It robs us of a depth of intimacy we all need. And it wounds the one who was rejected. He or she can't help feeling, "What's wrong with me?" Sex affirms our masculinity and our femininity at the deepest level.

It's apparent that in marriage, a good sex life increases your happiness. By the same token, happiness—satisfaction with life and with yourself—usually increases libido. It's a cycle we don't want to ignore, and one that we should do all we can to maintain. We need to work at the success of one another as a lover in the bedroom and as a valued person beyond the bedroom. Sometimes the most loving thing a wife can do when her husband is dealing with some sort of blow to his ego or self-worth is to become the aggressor in the bedroom. Sex with your mate can be a very valuable ministry—and that is how you need to see it at times.

Don't Put Your Mate in a Vulnerable Position

Be forewarned, Beloved. When you say no for an illegitimate reason—especially repeatedly—it puts you both in a vulnerable position. Remember, your primary sexual organ is your mind; therefore, when your need is not being met in the marriage bed where God intended, you will find yourself dealing with the attractions of your eyes and thoughts that run toward fantasy. In our society, we must also beware of the unscrupulous aggression of "people on the make," ready to prey on the vulnerable. Or they could simply be people in the same situation as you: married without sex.

(By the way, let me insert just a word of wisdom here. Never share your marital problems with a person of the opposite sex—always counsel with the same sex. Too many tragedies occur in male/female marital counseling situations.)

Unless there is some physical reason (such as impotence or frigidity), it is just plain hard to handle sexual rejection. Sex is an integral part of our design—something we need and long for. Something which defines us at the deepest level. It hurts to be denied. For that reason, when the sexual drive cannot be fulfilled (for whatever reason), you must cling to the cross.

You know, Beloved, the more I think about marriage and about life in general, the more I realize that if we are going to live life God's way, then we live it at the cross. Who said it better than the apostle Paul?

I have been crucified with Christ; and it is no longer I who live, but Christ lives in me; and the life which I now live in the flesh I live by faith in the Son of God, who loved me and gave Himself up for me (Galatians 2:20).

The Kids Keep Getting in the Way!

Our children, the very product of our sexual relationship, can become the greatest hindrance to it if we're not careful. When the little ones appear on the scene and become old enough to be curious about what Mommy and Daddy are doing, our sexual freedom undergoes a drastic change.

What do you do? Many parents allow their children to rob themselves of the most important thing that kids need for their well-being and upbringing—parents who love and care for each other deeply. In a recent interview, 61 percent of the men polled said they felt their wives were "a little too focused on the kids."[5]

I talk to many young couples today who don't seem to have a clue where to begin with raising children. I'll tell you one very good place to begin: loving discipline.

Part of that discipline is to help children fit into the home environment, rather than allowing them to *run* it. As a husband and wife, you need time alone—time to enjoy one another, time to physically delight in and satisfy one another. Whether you have admitted it or not, the strength of your marriage depends on this to a great degree.

With that said, let me share several things that can contribute to a secure marriage with children in the home. First, you need a place that is your sanctuary—a place where the two of you can be alone without being paranoid. Your bedroom should be that place, and if there are two or less bathrooms in the house, you need to have the bedroom with the bath. Both these rooms need locks on the doors.

That's the first place you begin, my friend. Get locks!

5. "The Married Man's Survey," *Redbook*, 1999.

Second, your bed does not need to be the family gathering place. An occasional family gathering there is fun—when my boys were little, we thoroughly enjoyed piling in together, but it has always been by invitation only. Make that rule and stick to it. Teach your children from the very beginning that when a door is closed they don't open it without knocking and being invited in. Model this for your children, and they will learn by instruction and by example.

When you bring your babies home from the hospital, they need to sleep in their own bed, not yours. Don't get them into the habit of sleeping with you because this becomes a hindrance to a free and spontaneous sex life. And believe me, Beloved, if you will work at keeping a regular sex life in your relationship, you will build a strong bond between you. Sex solidifies your oneness. Don't let anything or anyone hinder it! If you had a friend who called and was in desperate need, you would drop everything and do what was necessary to get there and help. This is what you need to do for your mate.

Meet his needs. Take them very, very seriously.

Meet her needs. Make it a priority.

Just closing the door and coming together as husband and wife can create some of the most memorable and treasured experiences of your marriage. These are times you will remember through the passing years, with memories prompted by a wink or a coded word known only to the two of you.

Make time for each other. Plan an evening-out or day-out for mom and dad minus the children. There is a wonderful book by Linda Dillow and Lorraine Pintus called *Intimate Issues,* which offers all sorts of creative suggestions. If you are broke and can't afford a sitter, you probably have friends who are in the same situation. If they are friends who hold the same values that you hold, have the same heavenly Father, and follow the same Lord, then work out an arrangement to swap out babysitting time. Just make sure that you make those times together special—not times to hash over problems, straighten each other out, or discuss what you don't discuss well. Each date ought to include time for laughter, words of love and affirmation, and time to enjoy each other physically as much as you want. This may mean sending the kids to your friend's house while you spend the evening at home with the whole house to yourselves.

Be Faithful to One Another

Above all, dear ones, be faithful to one another. Don't bring God in as your judge. God's will for you is your sanctification, your holiness, which means that you are to abstain from sexual immorality in any and every form. Learn how to possess your own vessel—your body—in sanctification and honor, not in the lustful passion of this world around us that does not know Christ. Don't ever transgress or defraud another person sexually. Remember, the Lord is the avenger if you do.[6] Infidelity will *not* go unjudged by God. The Bible solemnly assures us that "fornicators and adulterers God will judge" (Hebrews 13:4).

The book of Proverbs adds a deeply significant dimension to this discussion. Look again at Proverbs 5. You'll see once more that God is amazingly insistent about keeping sex within the boundaries of marriage. Read verses 15-23:

> Drink water from your own cistern
> And fresh water from your own well.
> Should your springs be dispersed abroad,
> Streams of water in the streets?
> Let them be yours alone,
> And not for strangers with you.
> Let your fountain be blessed,
> And rejoice in the wife of your youth.
> As a loving hind and a graceful doe,
> Let her breasts satisfy you at all times;
> Be exhilarated always with her love.
> For why should you, my son, be exhilarated with an adulteress
> And embrace the bosom of a foreigner?
> For the ways of a man are before the eyes of the LORD,
> And He watches all his paths.

---

6. 1 Thessalonians 4:3-8.

His own iniquities will capture the wicked,
And he will be held with the cords of his sin.
He will die for lack of instruction,
And in the greatness of his folly he will go astray.

God is telling us that sex is to be enjoyed with our mates alone. The exhortation that a man should not "disperse his springs abroad" refers to the man's sperm; he is not to spread it around to strange women. God meant for a man to be fruitful and multiply only with his wife. I'm saddened when I think of the many thousands of illegitimate children born to American soldiers and foreign women as an aftermath of war. So many times, such as in Vietnam, the children of these illicit unions become hated social outcasts. They have no fathers to care for them, and their mothers often hold them at arm's length. This is just one example of the serious, long-term consequences of stepping outside of God's design for sex. Sexual desire may be spent in a matter of minutes, but the consequences and the pain go on and on and on.

You *Can* Bear Sexual Temptation

In our culture so saturated with sexual promiscuity, it can seem almost impossible to retain our sexual purity and stand up against the many temptations we find in our paths. But 1 Corinthians 10:13 assures us that God never ever allows us to be tempted beyond what we can handle: "No temptation has overtaken you but such as is common to man; and God is faithful, who will not allow you to be tempted beyond what you are able, but with the temptation will provide the way of escape also, so that you may be able to endure it."

Every true child of God has the resources to abstain from any unbiblical expression of sex. So let's not be confused. It is possible to control the sex drive with the help of the Holy Spirit! The fruit of the Spirit, remember, includes self-control. A life yielded to the control of God's Spirit has the ability to master the sex drive in a way that honors God.

At our last couple's conference at Precept Ministries International headquarters, I felt impressed by God on Saturday night to take the audience from one passage to another showing them that *habitual sin* in specific areas—including adultery and homosexuality—may be evidence that you have never been born again. We looked at passages like 1 Corinthians 6:9-11 and Ephesians 5:1-8 that warn us not to be deceived. Then God led me to give an invitation. Nine men and one woman looked at me eye to eye to say that they had just received Jesus Christ as their Lord and Savior.

Before I gave that invitation, I spelled out what it meant and what it cost to receive Christ. I emphasized that salvation frequently comes with suffering. That becoming a follower of Jesus Christ means we are to deny ourselves, take up our cross, and follow Him for the rest of our lives.

The next day one of our staff members, David Lawson, received a phone call from one of the men who had received the Lord Saturday evening. The man, who was a pastor, told David that for 20 years he had been involved in random homosexual relationships. He'd simply get in his car, drive to another city, pick up a man, have sex with him, and drive back home. Neither his wife nor his congregation knew a thing about it. He thought this was just "a problem in the area of his sexuality" until God opened his eyes on Saturday night and showed him that he had never been born again. His behavior was incongruous with genuine salvation.

Now he knew there was no way he could pastor his church. He had to resign. He was a brand-new babe in Christ, and new believers are not to hold positions of leadership. This brand-new Christian confessed his sin to his wife, and to his congregation, and then resigned. More than anything else he wanted to be obedient to his new Lord and Master, Jesus Christ. David has nurtured this couple along, and I have had the high privilege of putting my arms around his wife and commending her for her Christlikeness in forgiving as Jesus forgave. What trophies of God's grace they are!

O dear one, as you read this, do you need to experience the same forgiveness and grace? Are you caught in habitual sin? Would you like to be set free, to become a new creation in Christ Jesus? If so, you can know that God placed this book in your hands and brought you to these pages so that He might set you free. God says that whoever commits sin habitually becomes the slave of sin, but if the Son sets you free, you will be free indeed.

What do you have to do?

Simply confess your sin. Tell God you want to be set free, and thank Him that Jesus has broken the power of sin by dying on the cross for you, for becoming sin for you that you might have His righteousness. Tell God that you believe that Jesus, having paid your sins in full, was raised from the dead so that you might receive Him and walk in newness of life. When you finish, thank Him for the gift of eternal life and record today's date somewhere. Why? *Because it's your birthday! You have just been born again, born of His Spirit!* And as I said to those nine men and one woman, "Welcome to the family, Beloved."

Now...How Are You Going to Live?

What my mother told me that night so many years ago made a lasting impression upon me: Sex really is beautiful. Yet the beauty of sex shines all the more brilliantly when seen in the pure light of God's Word. How I wish I had known God's Word and lived by it so that it might have stayed beautiful through all my years.

Remember, Beloved, the secret to real fulfillment and deep contentment in sex is going back to where it all began—to God's perfect plan for marriage. When one man and one woman fully yield themselves to Him, and then commit themselves to each other within the bonds of holy matrimony, they lay the foundation for a lifetime of delightful physical intimacy.

And it doesn't get any more beautiful than that.

RAISING GODLY CHILDREN: WHERE DO YOU BEGIN?

❦

WHY OH WHY DIDN'T WE THINK OF IT?

Why didn't we talk about it?

Why didn't we consider it?

Why didn't we seek counsel?

Why didn't we talk about it in the evenings, and across the breakfast table, and as we drove from place to place? More to the point, why didn't my husband and I discuss this topic before we ever walked the aisle?

What topic could be more important than raising a child who will bring you joy, rather than grief, through the years of his or her life? And yet somehow, unbelievably, the subject hardly ever came up. We just assumed that because we were in love, everything would "come out all right."

But life doesn't work that way, does it, Beloved?

Getting married is the single most important decision of your life, next to deciding to follow the Lord Jesus Christ. The second most important decision you will make is: How are you going to raise your children?

Why is that so important? Because children are your heritage. Your future. Most likely, they will walk this planet for many years after your death. And realize it or not, accept it or not (and I didn't), the way your children turn out can either bring you incomparable joy or unspeakable grief.

Why Didn't I Realize These Things?

I was young, headstrong, independent, confident, and far away from home. Mother wasn't there to give me counsel, nor were aunts, uncles, or extended family. Tom was a naval officer, and like military families everywhere, we were constantly on the move. My only counsel came from my peers—other young women my own age. And we simply had our babies and raised them as best we knew how. We dealt with day-to-day issues rather than long-term ones. And in a very real sense, we "produced after our own kind." We replicated what had been modeled for us.

Thankfully, though I was never taught about good parenting, I at least had good and loving parents who modeled it. Even so, I didn't have a book like the one you hold in your hands right now. I wasn't in a church setting where, as Titus says, "Older women are to...encourage the young women to love their husbands, to love their children, to be sensible, pure, workers at home, kind, being subject to their own husbands, so that the word of God may not be dishonored" (Titus 2:3-5).

Our society has become so mobile, so busy, so stressed out, so *tired* all the time that we can never seem to find the time to sit and learn from those who have "been there and done that" before us. In the days when women gathered to can their fruit, make their quilts, and so on, there was plenty of time to talk and to share not only recipes, but also the concerns of womanhood.

And before the days of television and this hectic lifestyle in which we find ourselves, there was more time to get together with other couples and their children and really talk about life so that we might learn from one another.

Times have changed, Beloved. And there are few these days who are willing to say no to the pressures of work (usually both parents) and to the nonstop lifestyle that keeps us running from activity to activity or from website to website on the Internet. If we're not willing to slow down and govern our lives (rather than being governed by our society), we need to at least take advantage of every opportunity to access good biblical teachings on marriage and parenting through good books, seminars, Christian tapes, and radio programs.

Most of all, we need the Bible itself, with the Holy Spirit as our teacher. In the little book of Proverbs alone, you will learn much about raising children. As a matter of fact, as you read and discuss the proverbs with your spouse, you might want to pick one specific color of highlighter and use it to mark every verse that teaches about fathers, mothers, and children. What a resource that will be to you through the years!

A Solemn Stewardship

Your children will either be a source of joy and satisfaction to you as the years go by or the source of deep heartache. And just as we want to have a marriage without regrets so we need to aim toward parenting without regrets as well. Believe me, no one in their later years wants to deal with the unbelievable guilt associated with foolish or neglectful parenting. It isn't worth it, my friend!

Ultimately, every human being is accountable to our God for his or her decisions and behavior. In Matthew 18, Jesus made a very sobering statement about caring for children. He said that it would be better for someone to have a millstone put around his neck and be cast into the sea rather than to cause a child who believes in Him to stumble (see verses 1-6).

Why would our Lord say something like this? Because, Beloved, He tells us that children are a gift from the Lord.[1] God is the one who brings the sperm and egg together, who causes the child to be conceived in the mother's womb, and who numbers that child's days when as yet there are none of them.[2] He is the one who says, "Let the children alone,

---

1. Psalm 127:3.
2. Psalm 139:13-16.

and do not hinder them from coming to Me; for the kingdom of heaven belongs to such as these" (Matthew 19:14).

Children are a stewardship from the Lord. Apart from the stewardship of our own lives, they are the most important responsibility we will ever have from the hand of God. Although they are born with inherent sin, they are given to us like soft clay to be shaped and molded by us. There is an innocence about them, a trust, until they are trained otherwise. It is in a child's heart to believe what he or she is told or promised. That is why Jesus said "the kingdom of heaven belongs to such as these."

There is no one in all the world more important to children than their mothers and fathers. And if they can't trust their parents, whom can they trust?

Can you understand now, dear one, why there are so many disillusioned, frightened, insecure, hurting children in the world? At the turn of the millennium, over half the children in the United States are living with only one of those two people who were responsible for bringing them into the world. Millions of others have never had a chance at life at all. They were put to death by the consent of one or both of their parents—murdered in the very place where they were conceived and were to be protected until the days of their births.

Does this tell you the value our society places on our children? Doesn't it reveal who is really number one in our lives? If we follow the statistics, it certainly isn't our children. Nor is it our mates. Collectively, it's self, isn't it? *My* happiness. *My* welfare. *My* well-being. *My* fulfillment. *My* development. *My* career. *My* needs. *Me, me, me.*

For the unyielding, immovable centrality of *self*—there is only one solution—and it is death. It is the call to deny ourselves, take up our crosses, and follow Jesus. And that, Beloved, is what raising children is all about.

How I wish I had realized this before I ever gave birth to my sons! But I didn't. And I regret it. So what can I do about it? I can share with you what I wish I had known and done, so that you can learn from what God has taught me, and, perhaps, live your life with fewer regrets.

The Greatest Gifts

In an affluent culture, we parents can be liberal with the money and gifts we give to our children. There are times when we "pull out all the stops" in order to buy things we really can't afford. Sometimes I wonder if we spend money like that as a replacement for the *real* gifts of love we ought to be giving our children every day. Let me suggest several such gifts...the best gifts of all.

The Gift of Parents Who Love Each Other

This is by far the greatest gift you can give your child. Nothing will bring more security, peace, and joy to the heart of your son or daughter than to know that Mom and Dad love each other and intend to stay married to each other *no matter what.*

God hates divorce, and one of the reasons He does is because it makes your children "unclean."[3] In other words, divorce places children in a terribly vulnerable position, in a situation where they don't need to be, where they should *never* be. Just as God created the womb for the security of the unborn, so He created the union of a man and a woman for the security of growing children. Your marriage and the home it creates should be a secure haven where a boy or girl can grow and develop into a healthy individual. This is God's design.

Please hear me, Beloved. This may be the most important statement I make in this whole chapter: *The best and most important and loving thing you can do for your children is to build a strong, stable marriage with your spouse.* Nothing apart from Christ is more important.

Not designer clothing.

Not a large home with nice furniture.

Not a newer, safer car with dual air bags.

Not the newest computer with the zippiest chips.

Not ski vacations in the Rockies.

Not tennis lessons or soccer camp.

Not a college fund.

Not even health insurance!

---

3. Malachi 2:15,16; 1 Corinthians 7:14.

You can have all of those things, and many more besides, yet end up with the most insecure, unhappy, maladjusted children anywhere. Kids need to see Mom and Dad love each other. Kids need to know their parents are together forever. Kids need the security of a home that will ride out any storm.

That's why the other chapters in this book on marriage without regrets are every bit as important as this one. Husbands and wives need to stay together, to "double seal" their commitment and their sacred vows. If you divorce, then you will have to answer to God for not only breaking the marriage covenant, but also for putting your children in a situation God never intended for them to face or have to cope with.

Many of you understand what I am saying because you are a product of a broken home, and (unless there was great abuse) you undoubtedly wanted your parents to stay married. Not only that, you may have taken some of the blame on yourself for the split. If only you had done this or that, said something, tried something, or prayed harder, perhaps your parents would have stayed together. What an intolerable burden of guilt some children take upon themselves for their parents' marital troubles.

Please, don't ever let anyone deceive you with words about how resilient children are and how they can weather a shattered home and bounce right back. Divorce is unbelievably traumatic for children. In the book *Exploring Psychology*, the authors quote the research of Mavis Hetherington and her colleagues, who stated that divorce places "children at increased risk for developing social, psychological, behavioral, and academic problems." These problems vary, say the researchers, according to the intensity of parental conflict, the child's temperament, and whether the child is uprooted from familiar friends and classmates in the process.

> Typically divorce provides children with a double dose of stress. Immediately following their parents' divorce, many children feel angry, resentful, and depressed. Young children may blame themselves. Older children may exhibit heightened aggression and noncompliance. Compared to those who grew up in intact families, children of divorce grow up with a diminished feeling of well-being. As adults they are more likely to divorce and less likely to say

they are "very happy." There is wisdom it seems, to society's ages-old idea that a loving, stable home life offers the best hope for nurturing children.[4]

What is stated in this psychology book has been confirmed over and over. You have seen it in your experiences again and again, just as I have seen it in mine. When you are considering the heart of a developing child, there is *no* substitute for the foundation of a loving, stable relationship between Mom and Dad.

Dr. Armand Nicholi, who served as a psychiatrist at Harvard Medical School, said this at a White House briefing: "It is now known that emotional development in children is directly related to the presence of a warm, nurturing, sustained and continuous interaction with both parents. Anything that interferes with the vital relationship with either parent can have lasting consequences for the child."[5]

Oh, Beloved, how I wish I had known these things! How I wish that the two men I went to for counseling—men who wore clerical collars and claimed to represent the living God—would have told me what God says about divorce and the effect it would have on my sons! I so dearly loved those boys. I had always dreamed of having children. To me, it was an integral part of marriage. So deep down inside me there was not only a desire to be the mother I should be, there was also the ambition. The conflict came with the desire of my flesh: to find a man that I loved and would provide me with the marriage I'd always dreamed about. A Hollywood romance!

I don't even remember talking about the divorce to my boys or asking them how they were doing and what they were feeling. I was too immersed in my own pain. I clung to the belief that if Tommy and Mark had me, that was all that was needed. But it wasn't!

In his report, Dr. Nicholi put to rest any vain hope that children will "get over" their pain and just move on into life. He reported that 37 percent of the children in his studies were even more unhappy and

---

4. *Exploring Psychology*, 2d ed. (New York: Worth Publishers, Inc., 1993), p. 76.

5. White House briefing, 1984.

dissatisfied 5 years after the divorce than they had been at 18 months after. In other words, time had *not* healed their wounds. In his summary, Dr. Nicholi said that divorce brings such intense loneliness to children that its pain is difficult to describe or even contemplate.

I don't know about you, Beloved, but reports like that grieve my heart and kindle a fire within me to help others not jump onto our society's fickle, self-absorbed bandwagon. I want to do all within my power to convince men and women to stop and think about their futures—and the *consequences* of their actions. There is more at stake here than the selfish interests of one or two individuals!

The Gift of Access to Our Time and Attention

Kids need to have Mom and Dad around.

Available.

Reachable.

Touchable.

Accessible!

My friend, this simply isn't happening in many homes today. Not only is the father out and gone, earning a living and climbing the business ladder, but in an alarming majority of homes, so is the mother. Our children are spending more time with "hired help" in one form or another than they are with their mothers. This is a trend that has taken a terrible toll on our culture. Maybe if we understood how we came to this point, we could consider options for how to turn the situation around.

Before the industrial revolution in our nation, 50 percent of the population lived on farms. Mom and Dad were both at home and accessible to their children. Children were taught at home or went to school and then worked at home under the instruction of the parents—usually daughters with mothers and sons with fathers. As a result, children were being mentored for their respective roles as mothers and fathers, homemakers and providers. Often they lived in an extended family situation or a close community where everyone knew everyone else and helped watch over the children and keep them in line.

With the industrial revolution, however, there was a migration into the cities and the factories. This meant father was away from home for longer periods of time, distanced from his children. Communication with dad was diminished as the father became more and more a figurehead rather than a mentor and friend. The approbation and encouragement had to come from mother—while disapproval, criticism and punishment were relegated to dad when it became too much for mom to handle.

Then, because of economic necessities, decreased manpower during the world wars, and better birth control methods, families decreased in size. With our scientific progress women had more household aids giving them more time for other things. Higher education became possible to more and more people, including the daughters. Add to this "the search for identity." Increasingly women stepped out of the home into the marketplace...into careers. Eventually the extra income brought in by mother was deemed essential—especially in the age of "bigger and better and now."[6]

What is the bottom line? Things on the home front have drastically changed. The America so many of our men fought and died to protect through two world wars is losing a cultural war on its own turf. Our families, as well as our morals, are progressively deteriorating. We are being destroyed from within because as a nation we have departed from the precepts of God's Word that were foundational in the forming of this once great nation.

If you are going to raise a family, Beloved, if you are going to bring children into this world, then you need to *parent* them. And your children desperately need and want you to parent them! They need you there for them. And I mean *really* there.

• There to talk to.

• There to wrestle and snuggle and tickle and play and laugh.

---

6. Quoted in *Reader's Digest*, August 1999, "Live Well on One Income," by Andy Draper, from *Shattering the Two-Income Myth* (Wenatchee, WA: Brier Books, 1997).

- There to turn to when the days seem dark and hopeless.

- There to ask questions about God, His Word, and His ways.

- There to test pet theories, wild ideas, and crazy dreams.

- There with enough energy and focus to make each child feel loved, cherished, and special.

- There not only in body, but also in heart and soul.

- There to kiss away hurts, bandage the inevitable cuts and bruises, and speak comfort to the broken hearts.

What should you do?

You may not like my answer. You may not want to hear it or believe it. But here it is: *I believe you should do everything you can to have mother at home when the children are at home.* A woman has no greater career than being a godly wife and mother. Add on another career and it is inevitable that her God-ordained career will suffer. Not only does it put a strain on your marriage simply because she is worn out (and we all have our limits), it puts a strain on the children because *they* are worn out.

Children today lead incredibly hectic lives. Believe it or not, one of the greatest concerns with children today is sleep deprivation. Adequate rest is part of God's design for our bodies. As we sleep, the body recovers, restores, and rebuilds—but it needs an average of eight hours per night for adults to do its job. For children, that requirement is even higher. Anything less, research has found, puts the body into a state of deprivation that greatly affects our waking hours and how we function as a person—especially in the area of decision-making. Sleep is crucial to our physical, emotional, and mental well-being.

Why is so much sleep being lost these days? It's because everything begins earlier and ends later...because Mom has to be out of the house and off to work at the crack of dawn. O, Beloved, don't you see the wisdom of God in ordaining women as the keepers of the home? When she is not allowed to fulfill her calling with undistracted devotion, it affects the whole family unit and the way it functions.

If all this makes sense, may I suggest that you get on your knees and ask God to show you how to make this possible. I'll give you some suggestions in the next chapter as we look at the subject of finances. However, for now, just two cautions.

First, *any time you decide you are going to do things God's way rather than the world's, you're going to experience warfare.* Just count on it! The prince of this world—the devil—does not want you to have a biblically based marriage and family life. He desires to sift you and your family as wheat—so don't, as the Scriptures say, be ignorant of his methods or devices!

Second, *realize that your children would be better off having less possessions and a smaller home than they would be having less of mother—and less of father.*

Yes, Dad, God has high expectations of you as well! I cannot tell you how important it is that fathers give adequate attention to their children. A careful reading of the Scriptures reveals that God addresses fathers much more than mothers when it comes to the raising of children. As the head of the home, the father is the one who is ultimately responsible before God for his family.

Beginning the day with a little wisdom from God's Book, even if only a verse or two, helps bind God's precepts for life as "signs on their hands, frontals on their foreheads"—you are writing God's Word on the doorposts of your house and your gates.[7] In other words, when you send them out into a world that lies under the power of the evil one, they are dressed for success in the armor of God with a two-edged sword in their hands![8]

Let your children hear you pray for them individually at the breakfast table. When they go out the door, when they face situations at school or in after-school activities, when they are tempted to do wrong, when they have to stand alone to do what is right, they will remember your prayers on their behalf. And it is the nature of children deep down

7. Deuteronomy 6:8,9.

8. Ephesians 6:10-17.

inside, even though they are little sinners, to want to please their parents, especially when they know their parents love and care for them.

The Gift of Time—Quantity and Quality

Learn to make the most of your time as parents. Redeem it. Buy it back rather than let it slip through your fingers. This is what God calls us to do in Ephesians 5:15,16: "Therefore be careful how you walk, not as unwise men but as wise, making the most of your time, because the days are evil." He follows this with the command to be filled with the Spirit and gives specific instructions to wives, husbands, children, and fathers.[9]

Time is a priceless commodity. It is the very definition of a nonrenewable resource. How wise we need to be in the way we spend it. The time we invest in raising children God's way will someday reap unbelievable dividends.

My oldest son, Tommy, who was at a critical age when I divorced his father, was my beloved enemy most of his adult years until the age of 37. Never in all my darkest hours of torment over this relationship did I dream what a comfort, joy, and delight he would become to me. His care, his love, his calls, his interest in what I am doing and wanting to hear all about it are such a gift from the Lord. But it's also part of the harvest of the time, prayers, and unconditional love I sowed in his life—especially at times when he needed me the most as an adult.

I don't know how many times I've reminded women that their satisfaction in life will not come from the praise of strangers, as satisfying as that might be. True, irreplaceable satisfaction comes when, as it says in 1 Timothy 2:15, their children "continue in faith and love and sanctity with self-restraint."

After a brief 18 years, your children will probably move away from home. So order your life accordingly, Beloved. Make spending time with them as a family a priority. I say this even if it means Dad must take a lesser-paying job or delay his career advancement. After a while the

---

9. Ephesians 5:22–6:4.

world will cease to applaud your efforts and compensate you for your time, but the love and approbation of your children—or the lack of it—will go with you to your grave…and live on in your children and your children's children.

The Gift of Lavish Love

Touch your children. Caress them. Hold them—even if you weren't brought up this way.[10] Remember, in Titus 2 God tells the older women to teach the younger women how to love their children.[11] So if you have never had this modeled in your life as a woman or a man, ask God to lead you to someone who can teach you. Ask Him to show you the importance of your touch, your presence, your physical care, and your attention. No matter what you do, no matter what you feel you have to do to financially survive, don't detach yourself physically from your child.

It has been proven that children, no matter what culture they come from, develop an intense bond with those who care for them.[12] Watch a child. Observe his eyes when he catches the smile of the one whose face and voice is familiar to him, the one who has talked to him, loved him, fed him, cuddled him. At 8 months of age, stranger anxiety begins to fully emerge, thus they are quick to crawl or turn to mother or father and become greatly distressed when they can't find them or are separated from them. At 12 months, many infants cling tightly to a parent when frightened or expecting separation and, when reunited, shower the parent with smiles and hugs. No social behavior is more striking than this intense infant love called "attachment," a powerful survival impulse that

---

10. The Touch Research Institute at the University of Miami studies the advantages of making physical contact. Among other things, they discovered that it reduces stress, relieves PMS, boosts immunity, and encourages babies to grow. Premature infants who were gently stroked 15 minutes a day for 10 days gained 47 percent more weight than those who weren't. The massage infants were also more responsive and left the hospital six days earlier. The Institute also discovered that it helped people lose the blues. Children hospitalized for depression who were given a 30-minute rubdown daily for 5 days felt less anxious and slept better. Touch also eases pain, gets smokers to quit, and benefited the one administering the touch! In one study senior-citizen volunteers who massaged neglected and abused infants living in a shelter reported that they themselves were less depressed, visited the doctor less often and had higher self-esteem. (Taken from "Mind and Body," McCall's Health, *McCall's* magazine, May 1999, pp. 208-11.)

11. Titus 2:4.

12. *Exploring Psychology*, 2d ed. (New York: Worth Publishers, Inc., 1993), p. 71.

keeps infants close to the care-givers. Among the early social response— love, fear, aggression—the first and greatest is this bond of love.[13]

In an experiment done with infant monkeys, it was proven that attachment is not associated with nourishment but with contact. Separated from their mothers after birth, the little monkeys were placed in a sterile environment with "artificial mothers." One was a wire cylinder with a wooden head and an attached feeding bottle. The other was a cylinder with a wooden head, but covered with foam rubber and wrapped with terrycloth. There was no feeding bottle on this second "mother." Even so, the infants preferred the soft mother to the one with the bottle. In fact when they needed nourishment they still clung to the "soft mother" as they leaned over to drink from the bottle attached to the wire mother. Their greatest need was touch.

This is why you need to hold your baby when you feed her. Draw her to the warmth of your breast…talk to her, caress her little cheek, rub those tiny feet, sing about Jesus, and gently rock your precious gift from God. Of course, the temperaments of your children will differ, and one might need more attention than the other. But whatever the need, you need to *be there* to meet it. The more secure the attachment of your child, the stronger he or she will be in other relationships and in unfamiliar situations. O, Beloved, become a parent who observes your child and stays sensitive to his or her needs. Meeting those needs will pay unbelievable dividends in the future. In fact, there isn't a stock fund or an IRA or any other investment in the world with a payoff like this one!

In the experiments I mentioned earlier, researchers also noted that secure attachment promotes social competence. The study reports that monkeys deprived of a "soft mother" had trouble as adults. When other monkeys their own age were placed in their cage, they either cowered in fright or lashed out in aggression. Upon reaching sexual maturity, most were incapable of mating. Artificially impregnated females were often neglectful, sadistically cruel, or even murderous toward their firstborn offspring. "The unloved," stated the researchers, "had become the unloving."[14]

---

13. Ibid.
14. Ibid., p. 73.

And so it is in the world of men and women and boys and girls! If you study abusive parents, you will often find abuse in their backgrounds. The sins of the fathers, so to speak, reach from one generation to another, until finally one in the long line finds salvation and deliverance in Jesus Christ. Then, with careful teaching and mentoring, that cruel chain may finally be broken.

Another Lesson from Creation

We are living in an unprecedented time of violence in our nation. And violence begets more violence. But sometimes we have to sit back and wonder what has caused such an enormous escalation. Who can remember such a time when children were shooting and wounding other children?

A few years ago, I came across an interesting article about the violent deaths of white rhinos in the Pilanesberg game reserve near Johannesburg, South Africa. Some of the rhinos had gaping wounds in their backs. Others had broken ribs and internal injuries that could only have been inflicted by much larger animals. Elephants were suspect, but everyone knew elephants didn't kill rhinos unless they were defending their little ones. These killings simply didn't fit the picture.

Then, from a helicopter, observers actually spotted elephants attacking white rhinos. At the approach of the helicopter, the attack broke off. But a few days later, three young male elephants—still in their teens—were found loitering in the area. Further investigation turned up this possible scenario. In the 1970s, Pilanesberg pioneered an effort at restocking elephants in the game parks. Instead of killing baby elephants marked for slaughter in other places, the young were taken from their mothers and moved to Pilanesberg. There they were given only two adult female elephants to care for them.

The normal pattern in a male elephant's life is to be raised by his mother until he is about 15, at which time he drifts away and links up with other male elephants led by a patriarch.

However, when these male elephants grew up with two surrogate mothers there was no male patriarch, no adult males for them to follow. Because of this, these young elephants became "juvenile delinquents"—

on their own with no adult supervision, highly aggressive, testing their strength on other animals. Elephants have high memory retention and strong emotional attachments. These "atypical rebellious teen" elephants watched the slaughter of their parents, then were transported from their natural habitat where they competed with 69 other elephants for the attention of their two surrogate mothers.

Interesting, isn't it?

These were simple animals deprived of parents. Doesn't it suggest something to you about the violence in our culture and around the world? If we refuse to listen to the precepts of God's revealed Word, He can even teach us through creation itself! And if young monkeys need soft, nurturing mothers, young elephants need mothers and fathers, how much more do little boys and girls need moms and dads who will love them, touch them, talk to them, and be there for them through the turbulent years of childhood!

Let me say it again, dear one, as I wrap up this chapter. Children are a gift from the Lord, a trust from the God who formed them and knows their needs from the very beginning. In His wisdom and providence, He made you and your spouse their parents. And while you may not have had the parenting you needed or longed for when you were growing up, you can still become a father or mother molded by God's hand, instructed by His Word, and guided by His wonderful Holy Spirit. As a husband and wife, help and remind each other that your children need *your* touch, *your* love, *your* care, *your* presence.

They need it from mother *and* father. (And yes, my brothers, real men *do* change diapers and tuck little ones into bed!)

If you want a child that will bring you joy, not grief, Beloved, this is where you begin. And it's in the very same place where your heavenly Father began...with sacrificial, unconditional love.

CHAPTER 12

RAISING GODLY CHILDREN: OUR HOPE AND RESPONSIBILITY

I HAD JUST FINISHED MY TEACHING SESSION, and Jack and I were walking out of the ship's theater into the soft tropical evening. We were on a Bahamas cruise: three short days where people could not only visit Nassau and Freeport, but could also learn from the Scriptures under a number of well-known Bible teachers.

It wasn't long before a couple about our own age approached us out on the deck. "Kay," the man said, "thank you for sharing about your son. It…it…it…" His lips were trembling and the words came haltingly as he sought to keep his emotions in check. The color of his eyes welling up with tears reminded me of the clear blue waters along the beaches of Nassau about to lose their blueness because of the clouds overhead.

The man paused and tried again. "It gave me—us—hope." And he looked over at his wife, who nodded. With that, Jack and I took a walk with our new friends, bonded immediately by mutual pain, attracted to one another by hope.

I've put my arms around many a grieving parent, "weeping with those who weep." There is simply no other pain in all the world like the pain of a broken relationship with your own child. Children are bone of our bone, flesh of our flesh, the fruit of our lives and our union. And to have them turn against you or walk away from all you have taught and know to be right is to feel overwhelming failure. My heart aches for both parent and child, for there is so very much they are missing! How well I understand the wail, the lament of King David as he cried, "Absalom, oh Absalom my son!"

It was a cry on my own lips for years.

A Promise…or a Proverb?

So often parents will say to Jack and me, "Where is God in all this? Why didn't He keep His promise? Doesn't He say in the Bible, 'train up a child in the way he should go, and when he is old, he will not depart from it'? That's what we did! But it didn't work. Our child is estranged from us and living in horrible sin."

The truth is that the often-quoted "train up a child" verse was never intended to be an iron-clad promise. It is a *proverb*—a maxim of life from God. It is a word of insight and wisdom that in no way overrides human will or the responsibility of an individual to respond properly to his training. Besides that, simply seeing that your child shows up in church or Sunday School or Christian school is not the sum total of "training."

It is a beginning, yes. But *only* a beginning.

We Initiate the Process

Let's take a closer look at the verse I just quoted—a classic passage on the training of children.

> Train up a child in the way he should go, even when he is old he will not depart from it (Proverbs 22:6).

The word translated "train" is the Hebrew term *chanak*, which means "to inaugurate, to initiate."[1] When we train a child, we are the ones who initiate the process. *We* inaugurate the action. We don't merely drive them to where we think it will happen, drop them off, and say, "Okay, you're here. This is it. Go do it, kid."

Training is a day-in, day-out exercise—not a once-a-week event!

It is something you must initiate *and carry through*. To imagine it otherwise, Beloved, is simply self-deception. When you think of raising children, think of a bright orange highway sign marked with the words "Under Construction." Let that thought remind you that if you try to cut corners on the construction or do a halfhearted job, you're going to cheat your children and yourself. Yes, the grace of God will go a long way in helping a young man or woman recover from an undisciplined or godless youth, but how much better and easier it is to simply do it right in the first place!

Be Willing to Explain

In the book of Ephesians, Paul writes: "Fathers, do not provoke your children to anger, but bring them up in the discipline and instruction of the Lord" (6:4).

It's interesting to me that God directs these words specifically to the father. His instruction and discipline, the passage tells us, is to be "of the Lord"—according to *His* precepts, *His* commandments, *His* ways. How important, then, for a father to be a man of God's Word.

I've said it 10,000 times: Christianity is not a "woman thing"! Our culture may slip in and out of that lie of the enemy, but it has no place or foundation in God's Word. Far from it! The man is not only to be the head of his wife, but he is responsible for leadership within the church of Jesus Christ. As the head, he carries a great load: the responsibility of not only loving, protecting, and providing for his wife and children, but also for understanding God's truth and imparting it to his family.

---

1. R. Laird Harris, et al., eds., *Theological Wordbook of the Old Testament* (Chicago: Moody Press, 1980), vol. 1, no. 693, p. 301.

"Well," you might reply, "I'd like to do that, but there just aren't enough hours in the day." Really? Are you sure? The fact is, there usually are enough hours in the day to do what we really *want* to do. Do you read a newspaper or a novel in the evening? Do you work out at a health club or watch sports on TV? So often it isn't a question of "time" as much as it is "priorities."

The Greek word translated "instruction" in Ephesians 6:4 is *nouthesia,* a compound word combining the terms for "mind" and "to put in." The father is responsible to see that his children receive and understand God's precepts. It is training by word—whether encouragement or reproof—and requires constant communication.

It's easy enough to say to our children, "You will do this or believe that *because I said so.*" But what sort of reason is that? What if another authority figure says something different? How can your children discern what is right and what is wrong? They need to know what *God* says, what *God* commands, what *God* expects, desires, hates, and warns us about. Teach your children His precepts and standards of life, my friend, and you will never regret it.[2]

Stop and consider how much time you take to really sit down and talk about the issues of life with your children. How many of us make the effort to really explain, "This is *why* I don't want you doing this or that"? Remember, my friend, asking "why" does not necessarily mean your boy or girl is being rebellious or talking back. Children have every right to know and understand these things. I'm not saying that we always have to explain ourselves, but I believe that far too often we brush away our children's legitimate questions and concerns with a brusque, impatient answer. Let's face it, most of the time we simply don't want to be bothered.

That is not bringing them up in the instruction of the Lord. That is not proper training, in the biblical sense of the word. What's more, that's not how our Lord taught and trained His disciples. He *welcomed*

---

2. We can help you do this through the "Discover 4 Yourself" Inductive Bible studies for children. These studies, which can be purchased from Precept Ministries International (1-800-763-1990) or at Christian bookstores around the nation, are written for any child who can read, up to 12 years of age. They are unique and considered a children's favorite in the home-schooling market!

questions—and asked many Himself! He used such occasions as opportunities to teach, often using object lessons and stories. Think of the hours He spent patiently teaching and explaining as that little band journeyed from place to place. Jesus embodied the truth of Deuteronomy 6:6,7:

> These words, which I am commanding you today, shall be on your heart. You shall teach them diligently to your sons and shall talk of them when you sit in your house and when you walk by the way and when you lie down and when you rise up.

Read through the Gospels and you will see it again and again. If we are going to follow our Lord's model of teaching and training, we need to take our children's questions and concerns seriously. And here's where the rubber meets the road: *We need to make the necessary time in our schedules* to really talk things over. The best way to communicate with your children is not to sit them down for a lecture, but rather to let truth flow from your conversation as you drive, do a project together, sit around the dinner table, play a game, or sit together on the bed at night.

Teach Them to Obey

And what is the first thing we need to teach them?

We need to teach them to obey.

This is a process that begins as soon as their little legs begin to churn around the room and those little hands begin to reach for forbidden treasures.

Ephesians 6:1 says it plainly: "Children, obey your parents in the Lord, for this is right." God says parents are to train their children to obey them. Why? Because it pleases Him—and it is one of the best things you could ever do for your children's future happiness.

When our youngest son, David, was growing up, I remember using materials from the Bible Memory Association. It was teaching that utilized the ABCs through the memorization of appropriate Bible verses:

> A: All we, like sheep, have gone astray, Isaiah 53:6.
> B: But He was wounded for our transgressions, Isaiah 53:5.

We were doing great on "A" and "B," but when we came to "C," we suddenly ran into a brick wall: "Children obey your parents in the Lord, for this is right." It seemed that David just could not learn that verse. We went over it repeatedly, but he kept saying, "I can't remember it."

Greatly puzzled, I went to the Lord and asked Him for insight. The Lord showed me that my son didn't *want* to learn that verse! He didn't want to memorize a passage that required him to obey his parents. Even at that tender age, David knew he was accountable to God.

I can remember so well the moment I confronted him over the situation—it's one of those times that runs like a video clip in the memory. I can remember exactly where he was standing in the old farmhouse on the Precept Ministries' property. (He was so cute!)

"David," I said, stooping down so I could look him in the eyes, "do you know why you have trouble learning that verse? It's because you don't want to *obey* it. And that's not right, David. Remember, this is what *God* says children are to do."

And do you know what? He learned that verse—*snap*—just like that!

One of the things that greatly distresses me is to see children who rule over their parents. Through improper training, they have learned how to manipulate their parents through crying, screaming, and persistent begging or nagging.

Children taken out into public places should know how to behave properly. Jumping on couches, picking up treasures on people's coffee tables, and playing tag in the middle of a church service is unacceptable behavior—and speaks of a lack of discipline on the part of the *parents*.

If you begin training early, Beloved, you will have children that you—and others!—will enjoy having around.

Teach Them to Honor Their Parents

Once again, Paul doesn't mince any words. He is very, very clear. "Honor your father and mother" (Ephesians 6:2).

To honor one's parents is different from simply obeying them. To honor them means to *respect* them, to hold them in high esteem, to grant them the regard due them because of their divinely ordained position as parents. It's a larger concept than mere obedience.

Because God is sovereign over all, even over His choice of parents, children are to honor their parents *regardless of whether or not they deserve such honor.* Listen, Beloved, God can bring good out of even the lousiest home life—if someone in that household seeks to honor His precepts.

My mother is a shining example of this truth. Anyone who has met my mother knows her to be one of the most loving people on earth. Yet she had a very unhappy childhood. There are no two ways about it; her father was just plain mean. Grandma should have never married him on the rebound after losing her first love, but she did—and that choice would grieve her for many years.

Grandpa not only neglected Grandma, he refused to care for his little girl's needs. I always remember hearing from Grandma how he refused to buy my mother shoes as a child. Not surprisingly, I suppose, his morals were as rotten as his temperament. He eventually left them and married another.

Life wasn't easy for my mother. But do you know what? God used her appalling situation to make her into one of the most loving women you could ever meet. I watched my mother honor her father even though he didn't deserve it. And God made her into a woman of excellence. And I watched her honor my grandmother, too, even though Grandma had made some tragic mistakes in her life.

Both my parents had pain-filled, unhappy childhoods, yet both honored their parents and stepparents and cared for them right to the time of their deaths. Can't you imagine what an impression that has made on me? Of course it has! And I intend to follow their example. I am determined to love and care for my mother in my own home, just as she did with her mother until Grandma died.

Exhort—Don't Criticize

How, then, are we to train our children in such a way as to carry out these instructions? How can we teach these lessons in a way that will cause them to stick?

Once again (as is so often the case), the *context* of Scripture comes to our aid. "Fathers," Paul instructs, "do not provoke your children to

anger, but bring them up in the discipline and instruction of the Lord"
(Ephesians 6:4). In other words, exhort, encourage, and edify…don't
criticize. Criticism tears down, while exhortation lifts an individual to
a higher plane.

Exhortation calls our children to the next level and encourages them
even when it must gently rebuke them. It says things like, "Oh, son,
listen to me. That kind of behavior isn't worthy of you. That is beneath
you. You don't need to do that. You don't want to behave that way!" And
then it paints a compelling picture of what our children can become—
and how this will please God in heaven and the two loving parents here
on earth!

Years ago I wrote down something from a child psychologist by the
name of Guno: "If children live with criticism, they do not learn responsibility."[3] It's not hard to see why this should be so. Why should I take
responsibility for something I know I'll be criticized for? Why put
myself out when I know my efforts won't be appreciated?

"You could have cleaned the kitchen a little better."

"You did a terrible job on the garage."

"Can't you ever do anything right the first time?"

If our children receive criticism no matter what they do, they'll soon
give up. *(Who wouldn't?)* They won't learn responsibility; instead, they
will learn to condemn themselves and others. (If you couldn't please
your parents, I'll bet your kids can't please you. Patterns of criticism
often get passed down from generation to generation.)

When children (and even adults!) are subjected to constant criticism,
they learn to doubt. They *thought* the kitchen was clean; they *thought*
they did a good job on the garage. But since you criticized them, what
they thought must be wrong. And they begin to question their own
judgment.

Now, let me pause for a moment on that one and say, "Please don't
think me naïve. I do realize there are times when your sons or daughters do a poor job, know it, and simply hope to get away with it. When

---

3. Source unknown.

this happens, you have to wisely call their hand and not let them go until it is done right. Otherwise you might find yourself training them to do a poor job and get away with it. The key is to remember they are children, not adults—nor are they the perfectionist you probably are. So handle it with grace!

As I share all this, I remember one day when I told David to clean the kitchen. At that time in our family history, it was a solo job for him. As it turned out, David left some things undone, so we needed to review his performance after he pronounced himself finished.

But with David, I had to move carefully.

He needed to be appreciated for what was done, so I told him what he had done well and how much his hard work meant to me. *Then* I told him, "But, son, when you do this, you need to remember such and such." The spoonful of sugar made the medicine go down much easier.

We all need correction, but there's a huge difference between correction and criticism. Correction shows a child how to take what is wrong and make it right; it does not demean the child. Criticism, on the other hand, says destructive things like, "That was stupid!" "How dumb can you be?" "You failed again. Why am I not surprised?" "You never do *anything* right!" Criticism points out the flaws in a child's performance without highlighting the child's personal strengths. It complains rather than shows how to take what was wrong and make it right.

Don't do that, Beloved! It is *so* destructive! You only have to watch a few biographies on television's A&E channel to realize how devastating such comments can be. Don't provoke your children to anger. Watch your words carefully. Talk to them, correct them, instruct them as you would want someone to handle you. Remember, in all that you do you are training your children by example.

Direct—Don't Dictate

Last, we must learn to give direction to our children without becoming dictators. Our task is to mold and shape them into responsible persons who one day (sooner than we think!) can make sound decisions on their own.

Now I know kids are unable to make their own decisions when they're very young. But as we grow, God moves us all from law to grace. The law is made for the unrighteous and for sinners. Since you brought a little sinner into this world, at the beginning you have to give him or her "the law."

Let me share with you two brief insights the Bible teaches about the law that may be helpful for you in raising children, and particularly in dealing with rebellious teens. In 1 Timothy 1:8-10, we see that the law "is good, if one uses it lawfully, realizing the fact that law is not made for a righteous person, but for those who are lawless and rebellious, for the ungodly and sinners, for the unholy and profane, for those who kill their fathers or mothers, for murderers and immoral men and homosexuals and kidnappers and liars and perjurers, and whatever else is contrary to sound teaching."

In Galatians 3:23, we read that "before faith came, we were kept in custody under the law, being shut up to the faith which was later to be revealed." In other words, the law is our protector to keep us from blowing it and messing up our lives until Christ comes. If I had obeyed the law, I would have never divorced my first husband—and what pain it would have saved my children and me!

This, Beloved, ought to show you the importance of parameters for your children, of keeping them in custody under your rules and regulations until they come to the place of maturity where they can make wise and responsible decisions. This loving custody lasts until the young man or young woman becomes accountable for his or her actions and assumes responsibility for the consequences when God's precepts are violated.

Give your children *clear* limits and boundaries, my friend. It is one of the most loving things you can ever do for them. These boundaries will be (and should be) fairly tight and inflexible at the beginning, but relaxing and growing broader with time. *Your goal is to move them from law to grace!* Two of your major goals ought to be to train them to make their own decisions and to discern right from wrong when they don't have the letter of the law to guide them. Teach them how to reason, to think, to see ahead of time the possible consequences of some plan or decision they are considering.

In other words, train them to become responsible adults.
There's nothing more wonderful or rewarding.

Understand Their Bent

When Proverbs 22:6 instructs parents to "train up a child in the way he should go," it's talking about setting a child on God's pathway to life. The word translated "way" is the Hebrew term *derek*, which refers to a road or a course of life. It means to walk along a certain path. The term comes from another word which means "to bend a bow," a picture of a tool bent according to its natural characteristics so that it can fulfill its purpose. The Amplified Bible picks up on this idea: "Train up a child in the way he should go [*and in keeping with his individual bent or gift*]" (emphasis added).

Consider Their Uniqueness

We need to recognize each child as an individual, which is the way God looks at us, with unique gifts and distinct bents. In other words, Beloved, we need to *study* our children. Observe them. Keep in mind each one's personal strengths and weaknesses, abilities and quirks, unique personality, and temperament. We are to provide an *adaptable* kind of parental guidance that shapes and regulates a child's character so that the child learns to walk in the way of the Lord and develops according to his or her God-given bent.

Our three sons are all extroverts—self-confident and capable men who love each other dearly. Yet each is unique. Mark is my sensitive peacemaker. He has his antennas way out there and seems to quickly pick up on how others feel. I tried to take that into mind when I corrected him or attempted to direct his path. David received fewer spankings than did my other two sons; I found I could regulate his behavior better by talking to him than by spanking him.

The point is to study our children, to know them well, so that we can use whatever methods work best to bring each child into Christlikeness as a healthy, well-balanced human being. One of the practical results of this study is the realization that your child is unique. He is not like every other child. She isn't like Suzie down the street, and he isn't like your little brother when you were growing up. This boy or girl is a unique, never-to-be-duplicated masterwork from the hand of an all-wise Creator.

Take time to write down your children's strengths and weaknesses. Watch each child in different situations. Look for the unique gifts and bents of each one, and ponder their special abilities. And, most important, *find out where your child excels—and then encourage him or her in that area! Pour on the affirmation!* It costs you nothing, and yet its value to your child can be incalculable.

One of the gifts I saw in David was leadership. So I deliberately encouraged him in that area. I read biographies of great leaders to him at night. I took him to movies and afterward discussed what we saw.

Mom or Dad, how well do you really know your son or daughter? What are your child's gifts? At what does he excel? Where does she really shine? What does he enjoy, and where does he struggle? How does she relate to people? Is she quiet or outgoing? Look diligently. Pray often. Then wisely begin to shape your training accordingly. God will lead you, Beloved, for this is His child, His special creation that you are raising.

Honor Their Individuality

Be very careful, Beloved, of trying to make your children into what *you* want, rather than into what God has designed for them. Look for ways to honor your child's individuality. Help your children see that their lives have unique worth and value. Help them understand that they were designed by God and created in His image. When they're old enough for a biology lesson, or after the "where do babies come from talk," take them to Psalm 139 and show them that God knew from eternity past which sperm would meet up with which egg. He knew that each of my children would have his own temperament, his own personality, and eventually his own place in God's sovereign plans. I shared with my boys how Jack and I value each one individually…as well as their wives and our grandchildren: Meg, John, Joseph, Ryan,

Daniel, Jesse, Abigail, Annie, and Alexander (according to their birth order). Each is so wondrously unique and special.

Your own children need to see the same thing. And in the process, teach them that they are not their own, that God loved them so much they were bought at a price—the very blood of the Son of God.

Do your children know that you have accepted them? Are they certain beyond the shadow of any doubt that they are special to you? It doesn't matter if your child came into your home through birth or adoption or marriage. In the awesome sovereignty of God, that little boy or that little girl has come to live under your roof as part of your family. And he or she needs to hear again and again that nothing pleases or delights your heart more!

If we will help each of our children to feel totally and completely accepted, then we will be raising young men and women ready to blossom into all God wants them to be.

Give Them a Vision

Part of training our children according to their unique bents is giving them a vision of what they may become. Build a picture in their little minds of the successful adults they can become. Have you noticed how most of us live up to the image others have of us?

God Himself does this very thing. In Jeremiah 29:11 our Lord says, "I know the plans that I have for you…plans for welfare and not for calamity to give you a future and a hope." Our Lord builds a picture of our future that is so bright and beautiful that it becomes a word of hope and comfort to hang onto in the midst of judgment.

Do you remember the biblical account of Gideon? Do you remember where his story began? He was threshing wheat inside a cistern while hiding from marauding Midianites. As he cowered in that hidden place, an angel of the Lord appeared to him with the greeting, "The LORD is with you, O valiant warrior" (Judges 6:12).

"Valiant warrior? Who? Me? What could the angel possibly mean?"

Gideon was hiding from the enemy, but God knew what Gideon could *become!* He was giving him a glimpse into what He planned to do through his life. In a similar way, you can give your kids a glimpse of their futures. Help them to see the great things God can do through them as His workmanship (see Ephesians 2:10).

Encourage your children to imagine how God might use their unique strengths in His service around the world. Paint a picture of the future that's so compelling they will enter adulthood with eagerness and expectation. Give them a bright vision of days to come that convinces them of their worth and inspires them to risk great things for God. Who wouldn't choose an exciting future like that?

Discipline Them

Finally, Beloved, we must deal with the issue of discipline. This is an unpopular subject in our culture these days for more than one reason. And yet it's a subject that needs to be examined in the light of God's wisdom and instruction.

So let's return to Ephesians 6:4, and look at a word I purposely delayed looking at until now: "Do not provoke your children to anger," says Ephesians 6:4, "but bring them up in the discipline and instruction of the Lord." In Greek, the word translated "discipline" is *paidea*, which refers to the sum total of the training of children.

To discipline our children is to regulate their behavior, to show them what is right and wrong, to teach them the importance of setting God-honoring goals. What are they to live for? What really has value? More important than anything else, we're to point them to the eternal.

Regulate Their Behavior

Through discipline, we seek to control the behavior of our children so that they might reap godly character. And how do we do that? By setting and enforcing clear, unmistakable boundaries. And we begin as soon as they are mobile and can understand a yes from no. From their earliest days we teach them how to please God.

Be extremely watchful and careful, my friend, about the company your child keeps. I cannot emphasize this point strongly enough. Paul summarizes this principle in 1 Corinthians 15:33: "Do not be deceived: 'Bad company corrupts good morals.'"

I've seen it happen time and again. A child becomes like those he or she runs with. When your child gets a little older and starts dating someone who shows little respect for you or your faith, you need to put your foot down. Regulate your child's behavior and forbid that relationship from continuing.

"But they'll see each other behind my back," someone objects.

Not if you stay alert and awake, they won't!

Listen, my friend, you need to *know* where your child is. That is one of the major tenets of responsible parenting. Pick up the phone and check things out. Talk to other parents. Hold your child accountable for being at specific places at specific times. Do whatever is necessary to be sure where your child is and what activities he or she is involved in. This is a job God will not allow you to delegate! Never support your children in sin—no matter what age they are!

Set Reasonable and Enforceable Boundaries

Don't say to your child, "Johnny, if you don't mind me, then you're not stepping out of this house for the next six months." That's neither reasonable *nor* enforceable. Don't pronounce a judgment that you can't or won't keep. In other words, stepping over a set boundary should *always* bring the just consequences that were clearly stated and understood.

It begins when they're young. For instance, if you see your young one about to disobey you and pick up your treasured vase, you need to say something like, "Jenny, I'm telling you that you are not to touch that vase. Don't pick it up; don't run your fingers around it; don't put your hands anywhere near it. If you touch it, Mommy's going to take you to the kitchen where you will sit in a chair for one hour so you can think about what you did and how sad it makes me and God when you disobey." Then, dear heart, if Jenny disobeys, you need to follow through and carry out your word.

Never delay in carrying out any promised consequences. Ecclesiastes 8:11 says, "Because the sentence against an evil deed is not executed quickly, therefore the hearts of the sons of men among them are given fully to do evil." Correct your children quickly, while there is still hope (see Proverbs 19:18). If you don't discipline them at the beginning, it's hard to start later on.

You see, one way or another we are training our children. The way we handle their disobedience is the way we train them. If they know they don't have to come into the house until we're screaming our lungs out, they won't come until *then*. They know just exactly how far they can go.

I know of a woman who used to work as a nanny. She served one household in which both parents gave their children "three chances" to obey instructions. Do you know what happened? Those kids never did anything without being told three times—until the nanny showed up. Her first day on the job, this young woman told one of the children to do something. When he ignored her, she immediately applied a previously explained consequence.

The startled child stammered, "B-b-but, Mom and Dad always give us *three* chances."

"Well, I don't," she replied. "When I ask you to do something, I expect you to do it the first time. And if you don't, there'll be consequences." From that day on, after being told just once, the kids obeyed (the nanny—not the parents!).

When you discipline your kids, make sure you do it diligently. Proverbs 13:24 says that he who loves his son "disciplines him diligently."

Sometimes it's just too hard, too inconvenient to get up out of our chairs to discipline unruly children. We don't want to exert ourselves to do what ought to be done. Quite simply, we get lazy—and soon the hard-won lessons of discipline begin to evaporate in the stagnant air of sloth.

Don't let this happen in your home, Beloved! Remember, you are raising a child given to you by God—and the future parent of your grandchildren! Be diligent in your discipline. Work at it, and *keep* working at it. Don't allow laziness to steal what you've already accomplished. In the end, you'll gain a lot more than a few stolen moments in the La-Z-Boy.

Eventually, as your children learn to operate within the boundaries you set, you can begin to widen the boundaries. And over the course of years, you can take those boundaries down altogether because you will have completed the training of your child.

The Legitimacy of Corporal Punishment

As I talk with you about all this, I must in all integrity deal with the place of corporal punishment in discipline because the Bible has a good deal to say on the subject. Proverbs 22:15 says, "Foolishness is bound up in the heart of a child; the rod of discipline will remove it far from him." In some cases, controlled corporal punishment is not only acceptable, but it is required. Little sinners need "the rod." But they need it God's way—and that is the key to effective discipline that brings the blessing of God.

God talks about the rod more than once in Proverbs. Each time He speaks of it, He reminds us that it is for the child's good and our peace. Proverbs 13:24 tells us, "He who spares his rod hates his son, but he who loves him disciplines him diligently."

But please don't miss one very important detail in these Scriptures. We're to use "the rod" and not "the hand." Use your hand to deliver love, to caress your child, to hug him, to provide for her needs. But for discipline, use a neutral object like a rod.

My boys knew very well that there was a "Mother's Helping Hand" hanging up in the kitchen—a wooden board shaped like a hand. When one of them disobeyed, he had to retrieve Mother's Helping Hand and give it to me. Mother would take this fearsome tool and apply it to the posterior of the disobedient. It was my "rod."

Sharing the *reason* for the rod is important to your children so they understand what you are doing. In Proverbs 29:15, God says, "The rod and reproof give wisdom, but a child who gets his own way brings shame to his mother."

And where should we apply this rod? I believe God built a child's bottom for that purpose. There's a lot of padding down there. So use the rod there, where it's safe—never on the back. The rod, properly applied, breaks the child's stubborn, defiant will.

One time when Mark was in junior high, he walked up to me and said, "I'm going to leave. I don't belong here," and then he rattled off a bitter litany of complaints. He told me we didn't appreciate him, that we weren't treating him right, that he had just had it. His tirade came at the end of several weeks in which he had been a bear to live with. I looked into his eyes and said, "My son, I love you so much that I am not going to allow this to continue. I will not have you turning into one of the troubled teenagers I work with; I expect something higher and better from you. I love you so much that I'm going to spank you. Now, you get down on your knees."

My son obeyed, and right beside his bunk bed I paddled him until he was softly crying. When I finished, he turned around, put his arms around me, buried his head in my tummy and loved me. He had become docile. And I had my sweet Mark back again. How wise and true are God's proverbs! "Correct your son, and he will give you comfort; he will also delight your soul" (Proverbs 29:17). Mark is such a delight to my soul!

Now, in carrying all of this out, you have to understand your child's temperament. If you have a child who is not going to cry no matter what, then don't deliver a punishment that will lead only to bitterness. Find something else that works. Discipline your child according to his bent.

Finally, don't let your child threaten you (and they all try). They'll say, "If you do that to me, I'll run away." "If you do that to me, I'll make a scene." But keep your boundaries intact. Stick to your guns.

I used to tell my kids, "I'm responsible to discipline you. I love you so much! But *you* determine how you take this discipline. There's only so much I can do. The way you respond will determine the consequences you face."

The Rewards of Discipline

A woman wrote me a few years ago to describe how godly discipline had changed her daughter's life. Read her words and be encouraged that God's Word still has the answers we so desperately seek.

I received a call from the principal at the junior high my daughter attended. He said he wanted to talk with me. I went in to talk and discovered she was in a group that was smoking pot. I came home crying, but got out my notes from your teaching on child discipline and was ready when she came home.

With the Bible in hand I took her into her room and read all the verses on discipline from Proverbs. Then I spanked her until she cried softly. I loved her and cried with her.

Well, God worked a miracle. From that day on, she became the top student in her class. She graduated as valedictorian in her class. She graduated from college summa cum laude with her picture on the front page of both newspapers. She's finishing her second year at medical school and will, I hope, graduate from there and be a surgeon.

I am only boasting in the Lord because I know that she could have ruined her life if God had not taught me how to discipline her.

This is not an isolated case. I've heard from hundreds of parents whose children have reaped the benefits of appropriate, measured, godly discipline. Proverbs 23:13,14 says, "Do not hold back discipline from the child; although you strike him with the rod, he will not die. You shall strike him with the rod and rescue his soul from Sheol." (*Sheol* was the Hebrew equivalent of hell—the pit, the grave). God says you and I, as parents, are responsible to discipline our children and save them from the devastations of death.

What If They Still Don't Turn Out Right?

Please remember two things, dear parent, as we close this chapter. First, remember that though you might do everything right in raising your son or daughter, that child still has a free will and a responsibility before God to make the right choices. He or she must bear the personal consequences of foolish or sinful actions.

A number of years ago, John White wrote a book entitled *Parents in Pain*. He and his wife, Laurie, had raised a fine family—yet one of their sons nearly destroyed himself through alcohol addiction. Many nights the Whites, who lived in Canada, drove the streets looking for their son, only to find him passed out in the snow.

The Whites had raised this son with the same love, care, and attention they had given their other children. He was there for family devotions when they all gathered around the dinner table and sang and prayed together. The other children loved those times so dearly that they continued to return home for encores. Yet this son chose to wander off on his own. To the day the book was written, he remained in rebellion. He had made his choice, and his father used that painful circumstance to help others understand that Proverbs 22:6 is *not* a promise. It is simply a statement about how life normally turns out when we live in a certain way. Normally it comes true…*but not always.*

Finally, remember that until your child dies, you haven't read "the rest of the story." I can't even count how many letters I have received about rebellious children who have returned to their spiritual roots. They sowed to their flesh and reaped an awful harvest, and yet one day had a head-on collision with the grace of God and experienced His sweet salvation.

So, dear parent, keep on loving, keep on praying…and leave the porch light on.

Trophies of Grace

Raising children is a difficult business, and it can put a great strain on a marriage if you don't agree together to do it God's way and let the Bible be your handbook.

I don't think any of us has perfectly followed God's precepts for rearing kids who honor Him and bless us. But the most wonderful news of all is that even when we blow it, even when we don't always flawlessly follow God's prescription for raising godly children, our Lord is still in control. He can even take our mistakes and transform them into trophies of His grace.

My two oldest children came from a broken home. They went for a long time without a daddy in the home, and it was very hard on them.

Yet you know what? Both those boys determined that they were going to be the very best dads they could be—and they're giving it all they've got! God took the ashes of my destroyed marriage and made something beautiful out of them.

He can do the same in your home, Beloved. He can take your marriage, whatever it is, and make something beautiful out of it. You can live before God in such a way as to have a marriage without regrets.

> *O Father, we thank You so much that You, too, are a parent—and that You understand our hearts, our fears, and our desires when it comes to our children. We know that You are the perfect parent, and yet all Your children are not perfect. Some are in rebellion. In fact, Father, we confess that we have not always done what is pleasing in Your sight.*
>
> *Thank You for continuing to love us. Thank You for Your example, for what You have modeled for us in the pages of Your Word. O Father, teach us that when we have doubts, when we are confused about what to do in our parenting, we can find the answers in Your Word and in prayer before You.*
>
> *Just as we want to have a marriage without regrets, so we want to raise our children in such a way that when we look back on the path we took, the principles we upheld and enforced, and our attitude in it all, we will have no regrets. May this family on earth bring glory to Your family in heaven.*
>
> *For Your name's sake we ask these things, amen.*

CHAPTER

GOD HELP US…
IT'S MONEY AGAIN!

❧

IT WAS 1958, AND WE HAD 20,000 DOLLARS IN THREE BANKS.

I couldn't help but be impressed. For a gal who scrimped, saved, sewed her own clothing, and survived on an allowance of 20 dollars a month while in nursing school, I was stunned that we were so well off. We had a new car, a beautiful English Tudor home, and Tom (I thought) was settling into the routine of a student in seminary.

Everything was cared for and covered. Our second son, not even a year old, had his own little nursery upstairs off the bath. But even with all this financial security, there were two things Tom wanted me to do. First, he wanted me to work outside the home. Second, he wanted me to record on a steno pad every nickel I spent.

I did both.

I found a job as an office nurse to an excellent internist and pinched every penny. During my lunch hour each day, I would comb the antique shops near our office and dream of finding some furniture at good prices to put in our sparsely furnished house. The thing I wanted the most was dining room furniture. Our tiny Formica kitchen set with tubular legs looked so tacky in the beautiful, formal dining room.

So I would walk, shop, and dream. At that time I had "religion" in my life, but no real relationship with God. It never occurred to me to talk to Him about my worries, desires, and longings.

Then one day, I found it. I was ecstatic! It was a buffet, a table, and six chairs—all for 125 dollars! I could hardly wait to tell Tom.

When I finally did, his cold response stopped me in my tracks. I can still see us standing there in the dining room by that cruddy little kitchen set. "I'm sorry," he said, "but we're not going to buy it."

I couldn't believe my ears! What was so unreasonable about spending a hundred bucks and change on a piece of furniture we really needed?

"But, Tom," I said, "why not? It's only 125 dollars. And we really need it. The kitchen table and chairs can go back in the kitchen where they belong. We'd finally be able to entertain friends. This—thing is so out of place in a home like this. Besides…we have 20,000 dollars in our savings account! And I'm working!"

Tom's face hardened. "We're not buying the dining room set. I'm going to school."

Crushed and desperate, I looked Tom straight in the eyes and said "Well, I'm earning the money, so if you won't buy it, then *I'll* buy it with *my* own money." And that's exactly what I did. When our divorce followed several years later, there was no debate about whose dining room set it was.

Tom and I had not made ourselves "one flesh" in the financial area of our marriage. We came from two different perspectives and never discussed or resolved those differences *before* marriage. That mistake fueled the deadly attitudes that eventually led to our divorce.

And that, Beloved, is no way to build a marriage without regrets.

Danger Zone!

Marriage counselors tell us that money is one of the major causes of marital strife. When a husband and wife cannot agree on how to handle their money, their disagreements will eventually spill over into other areas of their relationship—and the fighting all too often ends up in divorce court.

Why are finances such a sore spot for many married couples? I believe it's because so few of us have any idea of what God says about handling and spending money. We don't know His Word; we don't grasp His precepts. We enter marriage with contrary views about finances, and often-times *neither* view lines up with God's! Typically our lessons in handling our finances are learned from parents who may or may not have been good financial planners themselves. And because we so often allow emotions to dictate how we handle our finances, the struggle to control the purse strings often becomes a power struggle. And so the fight is on. And it can drag on for round after bloody round.

We spend money for all sorts of reasons.

- solace for our pain

- to aid us in an identity crisis

- to compensate for some loss or disappointment

- to fill a vacuum in our hearts

- to support a habit

- to "make us happy"

Many times our attitude toward money comes from a childhood experience that has colored our perceptions. This is why money—and how it is handled—can be one of the most significant discussions you should have before you enter into marriage.

In her book *The Nine Steps to Financial Freedom*, Suze Orman tells of watching her father risk his life running into a burning building to rescue a large metal cash box. When he threw the rescued box to the ground, the skin on his arms and chest went with it.

Money had always been tight for them. There never seemed to be enough to pay the bills, and it became a source of great tension in her parents' marriage. That day of the fire, at 13 years of age, Suze learned "that money was obviously more important than life itself."

"From that point on," she wrote, "earning money, lots of money, not only became what drove me professionally, but also became my emotional priority. Money became...my singular goal." According to this secular author, "True financial freedom doesn't depend on how much money you have. Financial freedom is when you have power over your fears and anxieties—instead of the other way around."[1]

That's good counsel, and there are many insightful books on the shelves today that can aid us in this area of life. But before we immerse ourselves in man's wisdom and perspective on money, we need to make sure we have God's view. When we understand what God says about this important part of our lives, then we will have a plumb line for measuring everything else we read in the days and years to come.

If both you and your spouse agree to let *God's* financial principles serve as the guidelines for your home, you'll eventually eliminate most (if not all) of your money squabbles. You'll be working from the same foundation and, in that way, increasing the likelihood for financial harmony and the blessings that will follow.

So let's see what God says about money, and then we'll talk about a few practical ways of managing those God-given resources.

What God Says

The Bible brims with instructions about money. God gives us numerous principles in His Word regarding money and stewardship so that we might protect ourselves from the lingering, heartbreaking problems caused by financial carelessness.

Let's begin with two fundamentals that will hold you through any financial crises.

God is the source of all things

Where do we go for knowledge about these things? Some run to the Internet. Others scan the *Wall Street Journal* or dozens of money

---

1. Suze Orman, *The Nine Steps to Financial Freedom* (New York: Crown Publishers, Inc, 1997), p. 3.

magazines. Still others tune into financial counselors on cable TV or talk radio. But the Bible leaves no doubt about the true source of knowledge in this area: It's Father God.

> The LORD makes poor and rich; He brings low, He also exalts. He raises the poor from the dust, He lifts the needy from the ash heap to make them sit with nobles, and inherit a seat of honor; for the pillars of the earth are the LORD's, and He set the world on them (1 Samuel 2:7,8).

> Every good thing given and every perfect gift is from above, coming down from the Father of lights, with whom there is no variation or shifting shadow (James 1:17).

Everything we have comes from the Lord. The whole world is His—from every karat of gold to every last dust particle. Every single blade of grass and the cattle on a thousand hills that eat it all belong to Him.[2] All that happens is in God's hands; He is sovereign, ruling over *all*. He is able to raise the poor from the dust and lift the needy from the ash heap over all. And that is why we can say God is the source of all good things. So whatever you have, Beloved, whether it seems much or little in your sight, remember that it came from His hand. To acknowledge this with thanksgiving, to humble yourself before Him in trust and praise, this is the beginning of financial wisdom.

God is the provider of all things

When God placed Adam, Eve, and all the other creatures in the Garden of Eden, He gave them everything they needed. From the very beginning, He took loving care of His creation. Even when Adam and Eve sinned and tried to cover themselves with fig leaves, God provided animal skins. *(Much classier, don't you think?)*

All through the Old Testament we read account after account, story after story of God's faithful provision. King David wrote, "I have been

---

2. See Psalm 50:10.

young and now I am old, yet I have not seen the righteous forsaken or his descendants begging bread" (Psalm 37:25). God takes care of His own!

Jesus, the Son of God clothed in human flesh, affirmed these things in person. Listen to His words from a glorious, green, flower-strewn mount overlooking the Sea of Galilee. Catch the intonation of His words as you look across the water rippling in the afternoon sun.

> And who of you by being worried can add a single hour to his life? And why are you worried about clothing? Observe how the lilies of the field grow; they do not toil nor do they spin, yet I say to you that not even Solomon in all his glory clothed himself like one of these. But if God so clothes the grass of the field, which is alive today and tomorrow is thrown into the furnace, will He not much more clothe you? You of little faith!
>
> Do not worry then, saying "What will we eat?" or "What will we drink?" or "What will we wear for clothing?" For the Gentiles eagerly seek all these things; for your heavenly Father knows that you need all these things. But seek first His kingdom and His righteousness, and all these things will be added to you (Matthew 6:27-33).

There it is—the promise of the Father's provision for His children…with only one condition attached: that men and women would give Him His rightful place in their lives—*first place*. That is why the following warning preceded His promise, words as relevant today as they were 2000 years ago:

> Do not store up for yourselves treasures on earth, where moth and rust destroy, and where thieves break in and steal. But store up for yourselves treasures in heaven, where neither moth nor rust destroys, and where thieves do not break in or steal; for where your treasure is, there your heart will be also.…No one can serve two masters; for either he will hate the one and love the other, or he will be devoted to one and despise the other. You cannot serve God and wealth (Matthew 6:19-21,24).

Jesus knows all too well our fleshly inclination to accumulate things. If you don't have enough room for all the stuff in your house just rent a storage shed! When I was young, people kept *cars* inside the garage; nowadays, half the garages you see overflow with possessions. And the car sits in the driveway!

God tells us the problem with storing up treasures on earth. Eventually they decay, fall apart, get lost, or are stolen. And even if you manage to hold on to your earthly goods for 80 or 90 years, you can't take them with you! *(Who would want that stuff in heaven anyway, when you're a joint-heir with the Son of God?)*

Build your nest egg in heaven. Treasures there are secure for eternity. You don't have to scan the newspapers every day to see if heaven's riches are rising and falling like the stock market. They will *never* fall!

Jesus insists you can't accumulate earthly and heavenly treasures simultaneously. Don't miss that! Your heart is going to be either in one place or the other, not both. "You cannot serve God and wealth," said Jesus.

When I married Jack and we headed for the mission field, we put an ad in the paper announcing what we were doing and declaring all that we possessed for sale. If we couldn't take it with us in our 28-foot travel trailer (with two boys and a dog!) it was for sale. I didn't want to put my heart in storage.

So where's your heart? Where do you spend your time, energy, and money? Either you've made God the focal point of your life or your affections are set upon the things of this earth. Both cannot be true at the same time.

"But if I don't concern myself about earthly needs," someone may say, "my family will starve. Surely God doesn't want that." You're right, He doesn't want that. But He does want to make one important distinction.

God Provides...but *You* Work

Does knowing that God is our Source and Provider mean we can stretch out in our hammocks and say, "I don't need to work. God will take care of me"? The apostle Paul didn't even do that. He made tents so as not to be a burden to anyone. One of the ways God provides for you is to give you the intelligence and strength you need to earn a living.

Our Lord expects us to labor diligently. We are to work and earn an income that will help us obtain what we need. Proverbs 10:4,5 speaks to us about such diligence: "Poor is he who works with a negligent hand, but the hand of the diligent makes rich. He who gathers in summer is a son who acts wisely, but he who sleeps in harvest is a son who acts shamefully."

Even a single season of laziness can land you in poverty. The apostle Paul sharply rebuked some slothful people in the church at Thessalonica: "Some among you are leading an undisciplined life, doing no work at all, but acting like busybodies," he wrote. "Now such persons we command and exhort in the Lord Jesus Christ to work in quiet fashion and eat their own bread" (2 Thessalonians 3:11,12). Paul's order was: "If anyone is not willing to work, then he is not to eat, either."[3]

Our Lord's normal provision for our needs will be through the ability He has given us to work with our own two hands. If we need anything beyond what we can earn, He has many ways of supplying it!

I remember a time on the mission field when I became very ill. We needed 35 dollars for medicine, but where would that come from? We simply had no money, not even for a few Christmas presents for the kids. No one except Jack and I knew about those urgent needs. Anxious and desperate for a word from God, I went into the bathroom, the only private place in the house, and cried out to Him. There, with my Bible open, He led me to Psalm 34...and eventually verse 10: "The young lions do lack and suffer hunger; but they who seek the LORD shall not be in want of any good thing."

I came out of the bathroom rejoicing. All fear was gone. I didn't know *how* and I didn't know *when,* but I knew that the provision was on its way.

As it turned out, it came by telegram. A couple in Chattanooga with limited means had sold one of their registered puppies for 50 dollars—and God told them to send it to us! We had enough for medicine and some for presents for the children.

What did God say? "Seek first His kingdom and His righteousness, and all these things will be added to you" (Matthew 6:33). Do you think He means it?

---

3. 2 Thessalonians 3:10.

Now then, Beloved, with those assurances (and please know you are going to find many more as you read through His precious Word), let's turn to some practicalities of handling finances.

Who Handles the Finances?

Some would say without thinking, "The man, of course. He's the head!" Yes, but does that mean he's to do everything? Of course not! As we have already noted earlier, headship does not negate *partnership*. Marriage takes two and makes them one, combining strengths and compensating for weaknesses. And the simple fact is, it may be the wife who is most qualified in this area by virtue of gifting or experience.

Peter tells husbands to grant their wives "honor as a fellow heir of the grace of life" (1 Peter 3:7). A major way to grant her the honor she deserves is to include her in financial decision-making. Many a man could be saved from a bad business deal by consulting his wife and trusting God to move them jointly toward a wise decision.

Do you realize the liberty, order, and strength understanding this one principle can bring to a marriage?

A Place to Start

The book of Proverbs tells us that there may be wisdom in seeking "many counselors." Just a word of caution: Don't let anyone take over your finances. God has entrusted you with those resources, and He will hold you accountable for the way they are handled.

So do some research and study. Take some time to think these things through as a couple. If you don't know where to start, I can heartily recommend the books, tapes, and seminars of financial specialist Larry Burkett.

"But, Kay," you answer, "what if we can't agree about the way money is being spent?" Good question. That is why every couple should have a plan for handling their money.

A budget is a plan that keeps you on track financially and enables you to live within your means and provide for your future. Everyone, whether wealthy or poor, should know where his or her money is being spent. (In fact, that is the way many poor people *become* rich!) Whether you have little or much, God expects you to handle it responsibly. First Corinthians 4:2 reminds us that "it is required of stewards that one be found trustworthy." Everything you have came from God's hand, and He wants you to handle those resources with the wisdom He provides.

Your budget should be mutually planned and mutually agreed upon. This is where prayer, good communication skills, and a meeting of the minds is necessary. Talk about your values and your goals. Where do you want to be 10, 20, 40 years from now? What do you want for retirement? For your children? What do you want to do for the kingdom? What will it take to get there?

You may not have any money now, but it is good to know where you want to go and what you want to achieve should God bless you in this area of life. Write down your ideas and dreams together. I saw my second son and his wife do this not long ago. It served as a parameter in their marriage, providing them with direction, mutual goals, and wise boundaries. And it has worked because in it all they honored each other, their children, and their Lord.

Get on your knees before the Lord before you ever touch a pencil to paper. Being on your knees reminds you that you are utterly dependent on Him for everything! As a couple, talk to God out loud about your situation. Ask Him to show you where you *(both of you!)* can cut back. Thank Him for the opportunity to learn and to trust Him and for what He has given you, no matter how little it is. Tell Him you want to be the best steward you can be—faithful in little things so someday you can prove yourself faithful in greater things.

After committing your way unto God, begin to work on the specifics. (Larry Burkett can give you wonderful, detailed guidance on how to do this.) Since we can't go into detail in one chapter on this subject, I offer this one crucial bit of counsel and warning: Buying on credit is one of the biggest, most dangerous traps you will face in your marriage. Be very, very careful. *Don't charge anything on a credit card that you can't pay off at the end of the month.* The debt will put you in bondage, and the interest rates will hold you hostage.

Expectations Reasonable?

One of the problems young couples face today is the expectation that they should be living at the same standard of living as their parents—forgetting the years that these older adults have labored and the disciplines it required to bring them to where they are. In spite of the incident with the dining room set I described in the beginning of this chapter, some of my happiest memories as a new bride were the times we scrimped, saved, and "made do" in creative ways. It was a good feeling—and something I cherished in an otherwise painful marriage to an emotionally distraught man.

One of the ways I made it as a single mom was to take the money I had to spend every two weeks and divide it up, putting it into envelopes marked groceries, gas, school lunches, and so on. In this way, we could see exactly how much we had. And when the envelope was empty…it was empty!

Budget Your Savings

Here is a discipline that will benefit you through all the days of your life. Save something each month—no matter how little it is. If it means you can't go to a movie, don't go. Rent one instead. Pop your own corn. Ideally you should be saving *at least* five to ten percent of every paycheck brought home (five percent if two paychecks are coming in, ten percent if only one). That's minimum, my friend!

A good and safe way to save is by compounding interest over time. Dean O. Webb, a consultant and assistant to Larry Burkett, showed what simply investing $2,000 per year on an IRA beginning at the age of 25 until you are 65 would profit you. At the end of the first year your investment (at 8 percent interest) would grow to $2,160, but at the age of 65 it would bring you $606,487. (If you invested at ten percent interest it would be $1,073,274!)

If you started that same IRA at 35—waiting 10 additional years—at age 65 it would bring you $266,427 ($340,060 less!). Can you see how important it is to begin investing early? The secret is to start now, invest consistently, and reap consistent returns.[4]

---

4. "Money Matters," Christian Financial Concepts, October 1999.

How Can We Live on One Income?

An article I read recently stated that 34 percent of all American families rely on two incomes, compared with 13 percent back in 1970.[5] The author relates the story of Thomas and Kathryn Henchen, a childless couple living in the Midwest. The Henchens kept a monthly tally of the time and money it took to earn their income. They noted the time spent preparing for work, commuting, working, and decompressing from their jobs. Then they calculated the money they spent on commuting, work clothes, dining out, taxes, and hiring others to maintain their home. "To earn a combined income of $60,000, they logged 108 hours weekly, spending nearly $30,000 annually on work-related expenses (including taxes). In other words, they spent $2 to earn $3 and cleared $16,000. Their hourly wage? A dismal $2.96. They are not alone."

The article points out that "the average dual-career family needs to earn about 35 percent more than a single-income family to meet the same standard of living."[6]

If you are a two-income family with children at home, may I suggest you carefully think through your whole situation. I love the author's conclusion in the article I just mentioned: "Your life can become less stressful, happier, more directed and fuller by embracing one simple idea, one that runs contrary to what we expect as Americans: You can't have it all. The good news is that you can have enough."

Talk to God, Beloved, about staying at home, living on less, making your money go further, and trusting Him to meet your needs as you get your marital and parental priorities in line with the Word of God.

Let me share a letter I received from a dear woman who left her 50,000-dollar job in order to stay home and care for her family. Her first child was born after eight long years of trying to become pregnant. Because of the Medical Leave Act, she was able to spend three months at home with her precious newborn. "When I went back to work," she

---

5. *Reader's Digest*, August 1999, pp. 134-39.

6. Ibid.

wrote to me, "I was heartsick. I wanted to stay home with my baby and really felt that was where my place was. But my husband and I just couldn't figure out how we would make ends meet. We were badly in debt, and my income was triple that of my husband's income."

Because of the demands of her job and commuting time, she was spending only about three hours a day with her baby.

"Seventeen months later," the letter went on, "we learned that I was pregnant again! I just knew that I would not be able to be a good mother to two children when I was barely getting time with one child. My husband wanted me to stay home, and so did I."

But how could they do it? How could they pay their bills? How could they provide for their children? It was difficult for this couple to get by such questions. Finally they came to this conclusion: "We had been praying that I would be able to stay home, but we weren't trusting the Lord to show us how we could do it. When we turned it over to the Lord, He made the way. We got out of debt, and we made plans for me to quit working when the baby was born!"

She wrapped up her letter with this strongly worded conviction: "Kay, I believe that a mother should stay home and raise her children herself, if at all possible. Titus 2:5 says that women should be 'workers at home.' In the year that I have been home, I have seen my husband a much happier man, and our children are growing up in an environment of love where Mommy is always close by. I have grown in the Lord as I have sought His will in my life, and He has blessed me abundantly. Money is often tight but the Lord always sees us through for the things we need. Our family is richer now than ever before, and I give God all the glory and the honor and praise."

Don't Pursue Wealth

King Solomon, the wisest man who ever lived (and also one of the wealthiest), made a remarkable statement about people and money in Ecclesiastes 5:10: "He who loves money will not be satisfied with money, nor he who loves abundance with its income."

That is so true! How often have we said we would be satisfied when we get that next pay raise...but two seconds after we grab the check, we're already wishing we had more. We crave more money even when our financial situation improves. We never seem to have enough. The moment we buy one toy that catches our fancy, our eyes lock onto something new. The cycle never ends. We're never satisfied, no matter how much we accumulate.

But how about those who live from paycheck to paycheck? There's no harm in them wishing for more money, is there? If they won a million dollars, couldn't they give a lot of it to the Lord? But that misses the real question. The question is not what someone would do with a million dollars, but what he or she is doing right now with the 25 dollars sitting in her purse or his wallet.

The problem arises when we allow our money to become a snare to us. First Timothy 6:9,10 says, "Those who want to get rich fall into temptation and a snare....For the love of money is a root of all sorts of evil, and some by longing for it have wandered away from the faith and pierced themselves with many griefs."

I know people who have said, "I'll pursue wealth first, and once I've taken care of myself financially, I'll start serving God."

But guess what? That day never dawns!

Once a person sets out to pursue earthly treasures, he takes himself off the path of pursuing God. As Solomon said, such a person will never be satisfied. He always wants more...and more...and more. It just doesn't make sense to put off serving God in order to take care of all your financial needs. Didn't God say He would be our Source? Didn't God say He would be our Provider?

He will take care of you no matter what your financial circumstances may be. When you pursue earthly wealth, you are saying, in essence, "God, I can take better care of myself than You can." One of my favorite Bible verses about money says, "Give me neither poverty nor riches; feed me with the food that is my portion, that I not be full and deny You...or that I not be in want and steal" (Proverbs 30:8,9).

The writer asked that his needs be met, nothing more. He did not want riches for fear that he might become self-dependent. He asked

God to protect him from poverty so that he wouldn't be compelled to steal and thus cease to rely upon God for his daily sustenance. He wisely asked for what was best: "Feed me with the food that is my portion." In effect, he was saying, "Lord, enable me to take care of my needs."

Not a bad request to bring before the Lord each day!

Giving to the Lord

The Bible mentions several specific obligations we have in regard to spending and giving our money. Before we do anything else with our finances, we need to take care of these obligations.

Giving to the Lord is very much a part of our worship. When we worship someone we honor them accordingly—we look at their "worth ship." Obedience is part of worship. Therefore we need to understand what God expects in our giving.

The Old Testament pattern

God commanded the ancient Israelites to tithe, to give ten percent of their income to the Lord. Many churches instruct their members to tithe based on this Old Testament pattern, but did you know the Israelites actually had *three* different tithes? In reality, they gave to the Lord almost 25 percent of their income—and sometimes even more. So when someone tells you that ten percent is the Old Testament pattern, don't believe it.

What, then, is the pattern for today? Should we be tithing a minimum of 25 percent of our gross income to the Lord? Not at all. You see, this Old Testament system was designed specifically for ancient Israel; it doesn't make sense to apply it to the church age. That's why we don't see tithing commanded in the New Testament.

The New Testament pattern

What kind of guidelines for giving does the New Testament suggest? The apostle Paul spoke at length about giving in 2 Corinthians 8–9. He reported that the desperately poor Macedonians gave a generous financial gift to their suffering brethren in Jerusalem. In fact, they gave "beyond their ability." Most important of all, they "first gave themselves to the Lord."

They gave more than money; they gave *themselves*.

Beloved, our money means nothing to God if we don't first give ourselves to Him! Paul gives us some additional principles:

- If you have more, you're expected to give more (2 Corinthians 8:12).

- If possible, have a financial cushion on hand in case an emergency arises (verse 15).

- If you give generously, you will reap generously; but if you give sparingly, you will reap sparingly (2 Corinthians 9:6).

At the heart of the New Testament's pattern for giving is 2 Corinthians 9:7: "Each one must do just as he has purposed in his heart, not grudgingly or under compulsion, for God loves a cheerful giver."

We are to give cheerfully, as we have purposed in our hearts. God specifies no amount or percentage here. He directs us only to give generously and willingly. And the result? An awesome promise!

> God is able to make all grace abound to you, so that always having all sufficiency in everything, you may have an abundance for every good deed; as it is written, "He scattered abroad, He gave to the poor, His righteousness endures forever." Now He who supplies seed to the sower and bread for food will supply and multiply your seed for sowing and increase the harvest of your righteousness; you will be enriched in everything for all liberality, which through us is producing thanksgiving to God (2 Corinthians 9:8-11).

When you give, you can be sure that God will provide for you. Don't worry that at a time of great need you might be abandoned. If you have been faithful in sharing with others, God will take care of you through others. That's the way the body of Christ is supposed to work. We are to watch out for and take care of one another.

In general, the New Testament pattern for giving is giving generously and cheerfully to support God's work and His people. The Lord has entrusted us with His riches so that we might use them for His kingdom. Beyond that, the New Testament suggests several other ways we should give.

Give regularly. In 1 Corinthians 16:2, Paul wrote, "On the first day of every week each one of you is to put aside and save, as he may prosper." (Put it in your budget envelope!) Our giving shouldn't be sporadic or occasional. God wants us to get into the disciplined habit of each week setting aside for Him a portion of our finances. When you give regularly, you develop the virtues of consistency and faithfulness. And as your giving becomes habitual, you'll become more sensitive to special needs. You'll be more inclined to respond to God's promptings to give—whether it be to a family in need, or a visiting missionary, or a single mother without supplies for a new baby.

Some people who are paid monthly still find benefit in dividing up their offerings into weekly gifts, so that they can participate in giving with God's people as an act of worship and devotion to the Lord.

Give to those who minister to you. In 1 Corinthians 9:9-11, Paul wrote:

> It is written in the Law of Moses, "You shall not muzzle *the* ox while he is threshing." God is not concerned about oxen, is He? Or is He speaking altogether for our sake? Yes, for our sake it was written, because the plowman ought to plow in hope, and the thresher to thresh in hope of sharing the crops. If we sowed spiritual things in you, is it too much if we reap material things from you?

Those who sow spiritual truth—pastors, teachers, missionaries, radio teachers—can rightfully hope that those who benefit from their teaching will provide material support. To muzzle the ox while he is threshing means to withhold provision from one who works hard on your behalf. You don't starve a hardworking ox that's treading the grain you expect to eat. And likewise you shouldn't ignore the physical needs of those who take care of your spiritual needs. In Galatians 6:6, we read, "The one who is taught the word is to share all good things with the one who teaches him." God encourages us to share our material blessings with those who enrich us through spiritual blessings.

Give to widows and the poor. First Timothy 5:3 tells us to "honor widows who are widows indeed." And Proverbs 28:27 says, "He who gives to the poor will never want, but he who shuts his eyes will have many curses."

God desires that His children commit themselves to taking care of widows and the poor. What better way to demonstrate to the world God's gracious nature than to give graciously to those in need? Through such giving, we not only meet people's urgent needs, but we also put God's character on display. For a Christian to withhold provision from those in need would be to contradict the character of God.

Give what is due to the government. During Jesus' earthly ministry the nation Israel sat under Roman domination and were obliged to pay taxes to Rome. The Israelites deeply resented giving their hard-earned money to a foreign government that promoted idol worship. They believed their money belonged to God alone and that it was wrong to have to pay taxes. But when Jesus was approached about the matter, He said, "Render to Caesar the things that are Caesar's; and to God the things that are God's" (Matthew 22:21).

Jesus didn't condemn the Roman taxes. He recognized that although the conquerors oppressed the Israelites, the latter still benefited from Roman government and thus should obey the Roman law. (Paul underlined the same principle in Romans 13:6,7.)

We are to pay our taxes; Scripture leaves no room for dishonesty. If we cheat on our taxes, then we are disobeying God, for it is God who ordained the government that rules us: "There is no authority except from God....Therefore whoever resists authority has opposed the ordinance of God" (Romans 13:1,2).

You might not agree with how the government spends your money, but Scripture makes no exceptions for that. We are to pay our taxes, period. It might help to remember that conditions between Rome and Israel were far worse than they are today between Christians and the

American government. Yet both Jesus and Paul directed the citizens of Israel to pay their taxes. That mandate still applies to us today.

Seek First His Kingdom

Aren't you amazed at how much the Bible has to say about money? God knew how much we would need His principles because our finances are inextricably entwined with day-to-day living. He knows we must deal with the reality of money, but He doesn't want it to worry us. Instead, He calls us to "seek first His kingdom and His righteousness" (Matthew 6:33). When we do so, He has promised to take care of our needs.

There's nothing wrong with having nice clothes, a spacious home, a fun hobby, or taking special vacations. But make sure you are living within the means God has provided and that you are a wise steward of those resources. If you find yourself going into debt or if your pursuits are becoming an obsession, then it's time to make some adjustments. Go back to square one and make sure Matthew 6:33 is true in your life. It simply doesn't work any other way.

In the end, it all comes down to this, my friend: Where is your heart? Are you earnestly pursuing God and a clearer understanding of His Word? Are you passionate about putting His Word to work in your life? What is the focus of your prayers—your own wants or the genuine needs of others? Take a look at your checkbook. Does it reflect the priority of God? Or are your monetary concerns distracting you from such a focus?

Are you building up treasures in heaven or on earth? Are you content with what you have, or do you long for more, in effect telling God that He's not doing a competent job of taking care of you?

Are you giving generously, trusting that God will always meet your needs or do you give grudgingly? Through giving, are you reflecting God's gracious character to others or are you portraying an altogether different picture?

Beloved, we have a God who keeps His promises. He moved heaven and earth to secure our salvation and make possible for us a life of eternal bliss in heaven.

Because He is *omniscient*, He knows all your needs—every single one.

Because He is *omnipotent*, He can do whatever it takes to meet your needs.

Because He is *omnipresent*, He can take care of you wherever you go.

With those kinds of credentials, my friend, who could be more qualified to take care of you? If He has already secured your future in heaven, don't you think He can take care of you in the here and now?

Why is all this so important, Beloved? Because when God truly owns all we possess, when we are fully obedient in this area of our lives, chances are that everything else in life will begin to fall into line. When as husbands and wives we finally acknowledge that *God* owns our pocketbooks, *God* owns our checking accounts, and *God* owns our financial portfolios, then we will begin to live in obedience to His Word, depending on Him to meet our every need. Obedience to the Word and dependence on the living Christ. I can think of no better plan to set a man and woman on the road toward a marriage without regrets.

> *Father, it is You who made us one—husband and wife—and we want to learn to move as one in the area of our finances. Help us, we pray.*
>
> *Sometimes finances are tight, and that makes us anxious. But we thank You for the example of the apostle Paul. Though he faced many trials and heartaches and often wondered if he would live to see the next day, he learned the secret of true contentment. And even in such extraordinarily difficult circumstances, he was able to say with absolute confidence, "My God will supply all your needs according to His riches in glory in Christ Jesus."*
>
> *May it be the same for us, Father. May we never forget that You are the Source of all things, our Jehovah Jireh, our Provider. May we live accordingly, seeking first Your kingdom and Your righteousness.*
>
> *We ask this in the name of the One through whom You promised to supply all our needs, Christ Jesus our Lord. Amen.*

CHAPTER 14

WHAT GOD HAS
JOINED TOGETHER

❧

I WAS SIGNING BOOKS, AND THE LINE WAS LONG. But bless her heart, she had waited patiently to see me. I'm so very glad she did. I wouldn't want to have missed what she had for me.

There was no book in her hand—only an envelope. She smiled as she handed it to me and said half apologetically, "It's probably too late, but here it is." At that point, after a full day of nonstop teaching, I had trouble remembering who she was—or what she might have put into an envelope. But I was delighted just to look up at her, with her short, perky haircut and those pretty eyes that would never need makeup. I knew I had seen her before…but where?

When the day was finally over and I collapsed into my seat on the plane, I remembered that envelope and took it out of my bag. I began reading the contents of the note tucked inside.

> You probably don't remember me, Kay. We met at a one-day seminar in New Jersey. I came up to you after your teaching and told

235

you about how your Precept courses had helped me. You asked me to write you a letter because you were writing a book about just what I had experienced....

Finally, I remembered. (I'll call her Rachel.) Two weeks into our "Marriage Without Regrets" Precept Course, Rachel's husband had told her he wanted a divorce. He gave no reason except to say he just didn't love her anymore. Although it had been painful for her to stay in the course, Rachel stuck with it. She wrote:

> I kept going because I trust God is in control and He had a reason why I was studying this course at this time.

Although her husband agreed to go to counseling, he had frankly told both her and the counselor that he was only "doing it for show," so that his parents and friends would think he had at least tried. Nothing, it seems, was going to change his mind. He wanted his freedom. For four months Rachel endured the agony, as her family and friends prayed.

> My minister was very wise and told me not to make it easy for Bruce to get a fast, no-fault divorce. I kept telling him that there must be a catalyst because to me it seemed like we had a wonderful marriage. We didn't fight, and I thought we had a great relationship that was bonded in our deep belief in God and our Lord and Savior, Jesus Christ.

The grief of those four months was horrendous. Even worse, she felt, than if Bruce had died. But she took it one day at a time, leaning on God all the way until...

> My husband did not move out physically but emotionally he was gone. I asked if I could have some of the tapes of your lectures. My minister allowed me to bring them home. Bruce and I actually watched them together. At first he was hostile. Then slowly, he started changing. All the prayers were working. We started to grow closer. God was doing a real miracle in His life! Your tapes helped!

> Then I found out something that was unbelievable. For five years, my husband had been having an affair with one of my best friends. I was in shock, but it all made sense! He was telling me he played

golf once or twice a week but he had been with her those nights. I was devastated!

Since watching the teaching tapes together, Rachel could see the changes in her husband's attitudes. Their counseling sessions began to bear fruit.

> Prayer and your course had turned my husband around, and he was actually trying to work at keeping our marriage together. This was when your class really helped me know what I should do. Forgiveness was so hard! My Christian counselor was very hard on me. He told me, "For months all you have wanted is to have your marriage reconciled, now it is up to you. Do you want to work on it?"

> Kay, I know God had me go through your course to prepare me for my future. It was very hard! I was so very hurt. But I knew God would help me heal, forgive, and do His will. Had I not been in God's Word, I might have listened to what friends were telling me: "Leave him! He's a jerk!"

> I know he made a huge mistake....He had gotten out of God's will for his life, and he now says he was miserable doing things he knew God didn't want him to do....

Isn't this story a wonderful reminder that God can heal the brokenness in our marriages? Divorce is *not* the only option we have when we're enduring painful relationships. It's terribly important that you and I take the time to understand what the Bible teaches about divorce.

O beloved reader, this is the passion of my heart as I write this final chapter—that you will know God's Word (not mine) on this subject. When you stand as a Christian before the judgment seat of Christ you won't be able to point a finger at anyone else to use him or her as your excuse. Each of us will be held accountable for our own obedience or disobedience.

How Does God Feel About Divorce?

Why was Rachel's husband so miserable through those five long years? He said it was because he was doing things he *knew* God didn't want him to do. You and I know from what we've already covered that "marriage is honorable in all and the bed undefiled, but fornicators and adulterers, God will judge." But what does God say about this man's plans to divorce his wife? Let's look at it together.

God's feelings are expressed very clearly in the book of Malachi. But before we consider those words, let me put the book of Malachi into context for you since Scripture should always be interpreted in the light of its context.

When you read Malachi, it is evident that God is not pleased with His people. Not only are they making false statements about Him (the phrase "You say" is used 11 times in the book), their lives in no way lined up with their words. They were:

- calling Him Father but not honoring Him (1:6)
- calling Him Master but not respecting Him (1:6)
- despising His name (1:6)
- bringing offerings but not what He required (1:8-11)
- Saying "it is tiresome" to serve the Lord (1:12,13)

And what were the priests of the people doing? They were:

- turning aside from the way (2:8)
- giving wrong instruction to others (2:8,9)
- dealing treacherously against their brothers and against God (2:10-12)
- divorcing their wives (2:14-16)
- whitewashing sin (2:17).

These people had departed from God, although they professed to worship and serve Him.

Does any of that sound familiar? The days of Malachi (435 to 415 B.C.) bear a strange similarity to our own era. Many who profess to worship and serve the Lord don't really have a heart for Him. They're only going through the motions. We endure some of the same trials the people in Malachi's era endured—and it's all because we don't listen, trust, and obey!

Marriages were in deep trouble in those days, causing untold grief and weeping. Even the priests, the spiritual leaders of the community, were divorcing their wives. Family troubles were breaking hearts in those days—just as they do today. Let's read Malachi 2:13-16:

This is another thing you do: you cover the altar of the LORD with tears, with weeping and with groaning, because He no longer regards the offering or accepts it with favor from your hand. Yet you say, "For what reason?" Because the LORD has been a witness between you and the wife of your youth, against whom you have dealt treacherously, though she is your companion and your wife by covenant. [The marriage agreement is a covenant—a solemn, binding agreement. It's the most solemn promise that can be made between two people.] But not one has done so who has a remnant of the Spirit. And what did that one do while he was seeking a godly offspring? Take heed then to your spirit, and let no one deal treacherously against the wife of your youth. For I hate divorce… and him who covers his garment with wrong.

Breaking the Covenant

We don't have to wonder how God feels about divorce, do we? He *hates* it. The Hebrew word for marriage is *kiddushin,* which means "consecration, sanctification, set apart unto God." The Hebrew concept of marriage, then, is being set apart unto one another. God is angered by those who say there's nothing wrong with divorce. He made marriage a permanent covenant for the sake of protecting the family and bringing up godly offspring.

God is the sovereign administrator of all covenants, which means that when a covenant is made and then broken, God must act as the judge. God reminds the priests that their wives are their *companions—* wives by covenant. In covenant, two become one.

(Please allow me a little aside here, friend. If you are afraid of what I might be teaching about divorce in this chapter and are tempted to shut this book and read no further, I appeal to you to stay with me. Remember, these pages are written by a woman who was divorced and is now living at peace and being used of God because she knows what God has to say on the subject. I've done my homework!)

Covenants weren't to be broken, upon penalty of death. In Leviticus 18 and 20, for example, God says that fornication and adultery are capital offenses. Both incurred the death penalty. Whether we recognize it or not, in God's eyes marriage is a solemn covenant, and He is responsible to deal with those who break it. The problem in today's world is that we want to write our own rules. We start looking for back doors to our commitments and are quick to excuse ourselves for our evil behaviors.

That plan might work...if there were no God.

But there is a God and He rules! He is a righteous judge. His eyes miss nothing. And He hates divorce with a passion!

"But Kay," you might protest, "that's *Old* Testament teaching. We're *New* Testament people." Beloved, if you were to make such a statement, it would be obvious that you simply don't understand the whole counsel of God. I say that kindly, not arrogantly, because I realize that many haven't studied the Word of God for themselves. Let's move into the pages of the New Testament and compare Scripture with Scripture.

Divorce in the Days of Jesus

By the time Jesus walked this earth, the divorce rate had skyrocketed. Among the Romans, divorce was common, perhaps even expected. Some women remembered the year by the husband they divorced. Jerome, a writer in ancient times, told of a woman who married her twenty-third husband. (She was his twenty-first wife!)

Among the Jews of that day, controversy raged. Two highly respected rabbis held opposite views on the subject of divorce, and the debate surged back and forth for decades. Rabbi Hillel, who died 20 years before Jesus began His public ministry, interpreted God's Word to say that a man could divorce his wife for any reason. The other rabbi, Shammai, insisted: "No divorce for any reason, not even adultery."

Shammai's more strict interpretation of God's law won few fans, for it prohibited men and women from fulfilling their lusts. Nevertheless, his viewpoint gained a small but loyal following.

Into this volatile mix walked Jesus...the author of marriage!

Matthew 19 tells how the Pharisees, a group of religious leaders who hated Jesus, decided to use the divorce controversy against Him. Frustrated by the Lord's growing popularity, they tried to trap Him into saying something that would land Him in hot theological water. Their plan was diabolically clever. If they could trap Jesus into favoring Hillel, they could denounce Him as an immoral person and a rebel against the law of Moses. On the other hand, if they could maneuver Him into supporting Shammai, Jesus would lose favor with the multitudes who liked this ancient version of no-fault divorce. If Jesus went on record against divorce, He might offend Herod, who had illegally married the wife of his brother Philip. John the Baptist had denounced that marriage and lost his head as a result![1] To the wily Pharisees, it seemed an airtight trap. They would condemn Jesus no matter what He said.

> Some Pharisees came to Jesus, testing Him, and asking, "Is it lawful for a man to divorce his wife for any reason at all?" And He answered and said, "Have you not read that He who created them from the beginning made them male and female, and said, 'for this reason a man shall leave his father and mother, and be joined to his wife, and the two shall become one flesh'? So they are no longer two, but one flesh. What therefore God has joined together, let no man separate."

What a scene! At a moment when Jesus was surrounded by a crowd of onlookers and followers, the Pharisees sprung their verbal trap. Confident in their evil strategy, they asked the Master, in essence, "What is your opinion on divorce?"

Without hesitating, Jesus replied, "What does God's Word say?"

What an answer! We should learn from this reply, Beloved. Our Lord doesn't try to battle with these deceptive enemies on the basis of opinion or man's reasoning. He goes straight to the Scriptures…and so should we.

Jesus turned the focus right where it should be, on the will of His Father in heaven. He quoted Scripture then proclaimed, "What therefore God has joined together, let no man separate."

The Pharisees must have been incredulous. How could He have walked through their trap without implicating Himself? But they weren't quite ready to throw in the towel. After recovering, they hit him with an objection: "Why then did Moses command to give her a certificate of divorce and send her away?" Jesus had already dealt with this

---

1. Matthew 14:1-12.

issue in His sermon on the mount. Had any of those Pharisees heard His words that day?

> It was said, "Whoever sends his wife away, let him give her a certificate of divorce," but I say to you that everyone who divorces his wife, except for the reason of unchastity [Greek, *porneia*—covers any kind of sexual immorality], makes her commit adultery; and whoever marries a divorced woman commits adultery (Matthew 5:31,32).

None of the Pharisees questioning Jesus in Matthew 19 were prepared for the Lord's answer. They wanted a law, a rule, a commandment etched in stone. What they received was a glimpse into the very heart of God. Jesus said,

> Because of your hardness of heart Moses permitted you to divorce your wives; but from the beginning it has not been this way. And I say to you, whoever divorces his wife, except for immorality, and marries another woman commits adultery (Matthew 19:8,9).

Jesus made it plain to His disciples in His sermon on the mount and to these religious men that there is only one legitimate cause for divorce: adultery. In Moses' day adultery was punished by death, which obviously broke the marriage union. Adulterers are not executed in today's world, but their actions still break the marriage covenant.

"Except for Immorality"

Let's take a moment and look at the exception clause in Matthew 5:32 and 19:9: "except for immorality." Some debate the meaning of this, and say it is only referring to immorality on the part of the woman that occurred *before* she was married. This, they reason, gives the betrothed husband the right to break the marriage contract, just as Joseph planned to do with Mary before the angel confronted him in a dream. In *Alford's Greek New Testament* we read that fornication must be taken to mean sexual sin not only *before*, but *during* and *after* marriage. The *Arndt and Gingrich Lexicon* says that *porneia* refers to prostitution, unchastity of all kinds, and the unfaithfulness of a married woman. Several other respected sources agree that fornication certainly includes adultery.

According to Jesus, then, adultery is legitimate grounds for divorce. Does that mean that divorce ought to happen automatically after adultery? Certainly not. Remember the letter I shared with you at the beginning of this chapter? Did Rachel have grounds for divorce, according to Jesus? Yes. But did she divorce? No, she chose to forgive, instead. Which course of action do you think was most pleasing to God?

As I see it, we are not to use adultery as an automatic exit out of a difficult marriage. That was never God's intent. God *allowed* divorce in adulterous situations mainly so the innocent party would not have to bear the punishment of a broken marriage all of his or her life. The innocent person would be free to remarry.

By pointing to the sacred text of God's Word, Jesus frustrated the Pharisees in their hope to trap Him in His words. And what of the Lord's disciples? They heard His statement, too, and it alarmed them! Jesus was clearly confirming the permanence of the marriage covenant. So they asked him:

> "If the relationship of the man with his wife is like this, it is better not to marry." But [Jesus] said to them, "Not all men can accept this statement, but only those to whom it has been given. For there are eunuchs who were born that way from their mother's womb; and there are eunuchs who were made eunuchs by men; and there are also eunuchs who made themselves eunuchs for the sake of the kingdom of heaven. He who is able to accept this, let him accept it" (Matthew 19:10-12).

Please realize that Jesus is not denigrating marriage and lauding singleness in this passage. He is simply reminding us that those who marry must honor the union as an unbreakable bond.

What Was a Certificate of Divorce?

Right in the middle of Jesus' answer to the Pharisees, they retorted "Why then did Moses command to give her a certificate of divorce and send her away?" By this time, Jews were divorcing their wives for all sorts of reasons. All they had to say was "I divorce you" three times and it was done!

What was this "certificate of divorce" the Pharisees spoke of? Did Moses really *command* this? This is a very key issue on the subject of divorce and remarriage. The Scripture they referred to was Deuteronomy 24:1-4:

> When a man takes a wife and marries her, and it happens that she finds no favor in his eyes because he has found some indecency in her, and he writes her a certificate of divorce and puts it in her hand and sends her out from his house, and she leaves his house and goes and becomes another man's wife, and if the latter husband turns against her and writes her a certificate of divorce and puts it in her hand and sends her out of his house, or if the latter husband dies who took her to be his wife, then her former husband who sent her away is not allowed to take her again to be his wife, since she has been defiled; for that is an abomination before the LORD, and you shall not bring sin on the land which the LORD your God gives you as an inheritance.

If you read these verses carefully, it is easy to see that Moses was not giving a command to divorce the wife and send her away. Rather, this was a "case law" regarding remarriage not divorce—a condition and a consequence. The passage opens up citing a situation, "the condition." This is followed by a "judgment." This is a word given by God to protect the woman sent away by her husband for some other reason than adultery. The certificate of divorce absolved her of any adultery charge. She was not a woman of shame; she could remarry.

As Jesus said to the Pharisees, Moses permitted the sending away of their wives because of the hardness of their hearts. The Greek word translated "divorce" in Matthew 19:9 and 19:7 is *apolelumenen,* which means "send her away." The Jews were lightly divorcing their wives and not recognizing themselves as adulterers all because they had a certificate of divorce!

Should I Go Back to My First Spouse?

Before we leave Deuteronomy 24, I believe we need to consider one more important principle. I believe this passage contains the answer to a question I am often asked: "I divorced my spouse and remarried. But now I want to go back to my original mate. Can I do that?"

This question gets asked for several reasons. One reason is plain old *guilt*. The guilty party realizes he should have never divorced his first partner and that it was displeasing to God. To soothe a troubled conscience, he considers going back to his first spouse. Or it may be that he simply misses his first mate. This is especially true when he discovers the second mate to be harder to live with than the first. (It gets to be a tangled mess, doesn't it?)

From my study of Deuteronomy 24:4, I would have to say that the answer is no. You cannot go back. Once a woman or a man is joined to another mate, that's it. There is no returning, not even if the second mate dies. Why? Because God says it is an abomination. It brings sin on the land. If it was an abomination then, does it cease to be one now? No, for our God doesn't change.

"But isn't there *grace?*" you ask. Yes, there is grace. There has always been grace. No human being from Adam on has ever been saved by anything but grace. But grace is not licentiousness according to Jude, which means that grace doesn't allow you to live by your desires. According to Romans 8, the indwelling Spirit of God enables us to fulfill the law, not break it!

This is what I believe and counsel. You may not agree, and then I would simply reply that you need to search the Scripture for yourself.

Is Adultery the Only Grounds for Divorce?

No. According to 1 Corinthians 7, adultery is not the only grounds for divorce. Let's consider that passage together.

Paul's first letter to the Corinthians was written to a society much like ours—one torn by immorality and marital strife. Remember, divorce was rampant in the Roman world. As you might expect, the new believers in Corinth had lots and lots of questions. And just as in today's world, questions about marriage and morality seemed to top their list.

Undoubtedly some who had come to know the Lord found themselves "unequally yoked" to nonbelievers. What should they do? Should they leave their unbelieving mates? It is here within Paul's answer that we find the only other biblical reason for divorce that allows the offended person to remarry. Let's read the passage and then examine it together.

> 10 But to the married I give instructions, not I, but the Lord, that the wife should not leave her husband
>
> 11 (but if she does leave, she must remain unmarried, or else be reconciled to her husband), and that the husband should not divorce his wife.
>
> 12 But to the rest I say, not the Lord, that if any brother has a wife who is an unbeliever, and she consents to live with him, he must not divorce her.
>
> 13 And a woman who has an unbelieving husband, and he consents to live with her, she must not send her husband away.
>
> 14 For the unbelieving husband is sanctified through his wife, and the unbelieving wife is sanctified through her believing husband; for otherwise your children are unclean, but now they are holy.
>
> 15 Yet if the unbelieving one leaves, let him leave; the brother or the sister is not under bondage in such cases but God has called us to peace.

Paul's answer is so clear. First, the believer is not to send the unbeliever away if the unbeliever wants to stay. In fact, the unbeliever is better off—and so are the children—if he or she stays in the family. Did you notice verse 14? "For the unbelieving husband is sanctified through his wife, and the unbelieving wife is sanctified through her believing husband; for otherwise your children are unclean, but now they are holy."

When the text says the unbeliever is "sanctified," it is not saying he or she is *saved*. The passage is saying that the unbeliever is set apart—consecrated in a sense—and reaps blessings belonging to the believing partner. The children, too, are protected and "set apart" by having even one believing parent. (Divorce is so incredibly hard and stressful on children. Children of broken homes are more likely to grow up with a diminished feeling of well-being.)

God's instruction to the believer is not to leave the unbeliever. But if he or she *does* leave, there is to be no remarriage. Let's not miss it. Verses 10,11 say, "But to the married I give instructions, not I, but the Lord, that the wife should not leave her husband (but if she does leave, she must remain unmarried, or else be reconciled to her husband), and that the husband should not divorce his wife."

The word "leave" in verse 10 and 11 is *chorizo,* and is one of three words used for divorce. The word for "divorce" is *aphiemi.* Verse 12 reads: "If any brother has a wife who is an unbeliever, and she consents to live with him, he must not divorce her." The term "divorce" in this passage is a present imperative. In other words "don't be attempting to divorce her." We are not to drive away the unbeliever—and that is a command.

What If the Unbelieving Mate Wants a Divorce?

If the unbeliever wants a divorce, Scripture allows it. The believer in that case is free to remarry—but only to another believer. According to verse 16 of 1 Corinthians 7, hanging onto a partner who doesn't want to stay won't necessarily lead to that person's salvation. First Corinthians 7:15 says, "Yet if the unbelieving one leaves, let him leave; the brother or the sister is not under bondage in such cases, but God has called us to peace."

The phrase "not under bondage" is in the perfect tense in the Greek, which means "a past completed action with a present result." In other words, you are free and remain free from that marriage covenant because you did not break it. It was broken by your mate; you were the unwilling victim, the innocent party. Marvin Vincent, a Greek scholar, says that the phrase "under bondage" is "a strong word indicating that Christianity has not made marriage a state of slavery to believers." He also states, "The meaning is clearly that willful desertion on the part of the unbelieving husband or wife sets the other party free."

And if you are set free, Beloved, then you are set free to remarry.

What If I Was Divorced Before I Was Saved? Can I Marry?

After I became a Christian I fell in love with a man by the name of
Dave Pantzer, who is now deceased. I was a new babe in Christ, just a
couple of months old, and I wanted to marry this godly man so badly.
I was so taken with him! I had never met a man who knew the Word.
And Dave was attracted enough to me to go to his pastor for coun-
seling. (This was before my first husband committed suicide.) When
Dave told me that his pastor said no because of my divorce, I was
absolutely crushed.

I remember thinking to myself, "Oh great! God has forgiven me every
sin but this one! What am I doing even dating if I can never get married?"

I didn't know the Word of God at that time. I didn't even know how
to study. As a result, I missed one crucial phrase that I'm about to share
with you. If you mark key repeated words in the Bible text as you study,
you've probably noticed that in 1 Corinthians 7:17-27 the word "called"
is used eight times. It's a word that Paul also opens his epistle with when
he refers to the fact that the Corinthians are saved, they are called of
God. In this passage Paul wants them to understand that it would be
good for them to remain in whatever condition they were in when they
came to the Lord. Were they uncircumcised? Then they shouldn't be cir-
cumcised. Were they slaves? Then they shouldn't seek release—unless
the master deliberately sets them free.

In verses 27,28, we come to God's liberating words about remarriage.
"Are you bound to a wife? Do not seek to be released. Are you released
from a wife? Do not seek a wife. But if you marry, you have not sinned."

Did you see the "but"?

Don't miss it! I missed it for years because I didn't slow down enough
to really look at the text. And, oh, what I missed! "Bound" refers to the
marriage bond. The word "released," used for divorced, is in the perfect
tense—past completed action with a present result. In other words: Are
you divorced? If so, it would be good for you to remain single, *but* if you
don't, you haven't sinned.

"But, Kay," you might ask, *"aren't there any other exceptions?"*

So often people want to know if God allows divorce or remarriage under any circumstances other than death, divorce, or desertion. I know this sounds hard, my friend, but *I know of no other biblical reasons.* Quite frankly, it all comes down to a matter of obedience to the clear teaching of God's Word—and the desire to please God above all else.

Marriage will always be a permanent covenant, and God will always hate divorce. But you are never left powerless, Beloved! Within our hands, within our hearts, we have the most powerful weapon known to man—the power of prayer.

Is Remarriage the Best Way to Go?

Our teaching team at Precept Ministries concurs that the best course is to give the mate who left you time to come to his or her senses, to repent, to find Christ, and to return. There's nothing better than being married to one person only. That is God's design—and it is so much better for the children as well.

I have talked with far too many people who grieve over their remarriage and the impact it had on their children. So many jump from the proverbial frying pan into the fire, making their situations far, far worse rather than better. Your ultimate happiness and identity are *not* found in marriage. They are realized in Jesus Christ. His peace will enhance *all* your relationships, and His perseverance will enable you to endure any situation.

As we have seen from the Scriptures, God takes a very negative attitude toward divorce. Why is it that God is so concerned about the breaking of the marriage covenant?

Beloved, it is because He loves us and He knows that the pain and hurt caused by divorce strikes us at the deepest part of our hearts. And the husband and wife are not the only victims—divorce also causes great pain for the poor children whose homes and lives are torn apart when their parents split.

Let me share with you a story that broke my heart when I first heard it. Perhaps some of my readers who have been through a divorce themselves will be able to identify with elements of this story. Perhaps it will also serve as a testimony to the faithfulness of God in even the most difficult times in our lives.

Mary (as we will refer to her) had been married 21 years when her husband, John, announced that he no longer wanted to be a husband and father. By the time he made his announcement, he had already had the separation papers drawn up and had made all the arrangements to leave. All he needed was Mary's signature on the papers. She was devastated.

The marriage had been rocky for some time due to John's consistent emotional and verbal abuse, along with occasional instances of physical abuse. Once, he had even thrown her to the ground and started to beat her head against the sidewalk while the children watched in terror. She remembers praying, "Lord, please don't let them see my brains splattered on this sidewalk." When the children jumped on him, he finally stopped.

Mary knew that God hated divorce and believed that He could change the situation. She knew that her job was to be the best wife she could be. "As I look back," Mary wrote to me, "I see there were many, many times I failed. Obviously, all the criticism and abuse I had suffered left me with little or no self-esteem. I couldn't even look in the mirror without hating how I looked."

Mary and John had three children: two in grade school, one a junior in high school. When John sat them down on a Saturday morning to tell them he was leaving, they all responded in different ways. The high school age son tried to reason with his father, tried to make him see that this was a huge mistake. Their daughter cried and begged for him to change his mind. The youngest child had the worst reaction. He ran through the house screaming at the top of his lungs. His panicked scream was blood curdling.

John's response was simple and heartless: "I know you don't like this, but you'd better get used to it because its what I'm going to do." And then he was gone. He moved to Illinois and left Mary and the children with $10 in cash and a car that didn't run.

Financially desperate, the divorce forced Mary into the workplace, just like it does so many precious women who instead long to be at home with their children. This was very hard for her to take. "Now," she wrote, "not only had the children lost their father, they had lost out on having time with their mother. I would get home between 6:15 and 7:30 every evening completely exhausted. Then I would start cooking dinner, doing laundry, and somehow try to squeeze in the necessary shopping. I had little energy left to be the mother I wanted to be for my kids. It seemed it took all my strength just to keep the house in order. The children were a great help, but there are so many things only a mother can do. And the money was unbelievably tight. One week we only had a carton of eggs to share between the four of us. My daughter passed out at Youth Group one night due to hunger. At one point we only had one light bulb in the house and would take it from room to room, depending on where we needed to be. But we did not whine or complain, knowing that our precious Lord has 'sifted this situation through His fingers of love.'"

That last phrase came from a book I wrote called *Lord, Heal My Hurts*, which Mary happened to be reading at the time at the time John made his marriage-ending announcement. The book had helped her understand that everything in her life had happened for a reason and that God was using all the pain of her past and present to draw her closer to Jesus. Once John announced his intention to leave, Mary knew that she would have to trust in God in a deeper way than she ever had before.

"I had a choice to make," she wrote to me, "I was either going to hold on to the hand of God as tight as I could and not let go—or I was going to let this destroy me, along with my family. And God was whispering in my heart through His Word, 'I am with you.'"

It was not always an easy road. When John left she made out a budget and found that after all the necessary expenses she only had $13 left for food, gas, medicine, clothes, etc. to last an entire month. This was one of her worst moments. It just seemed so hopeless. "But then I realized that I had taken my eyes off God and was looking straight into an impossible set of circumstances. I put away my budget and kept my eyes fixed on Jesus. He knew our circumstances and He was a faithful provider." He provided a bag of groceries here and a cash gift there so that they never starved or completely went without what they needed.

Then Mary began to pray about the thing that weighed so heavily on her heart—that she had so little time to be with the children. She thought maybe the answer would be a job that ended at 4:30pm. Instead, she was in a car accident that disabled her. But she came to see even this as an answer to prayer, for it allowed time for her to be with her children.

I wish I could share with you all the things that happened in this woman's life. It shows so clearly the kind of pain that divorce can cause. But her story is also filled with precious touches of the Lord's provision. This woman came to see that her husband and provider was God Himself. Though she has experienced such pain and heartbreak, her future is not dim because her eyes are on Him, the One who promised to never leave or forsake her.

Precious one, He will be the same to you.

Is There Any Hope Other Than Divorce?

Just last month a woman named Becky sent me a letter sharing her story of answered prayer. I thought it would be a good note to end this chapter on.

Becky was devastated when she first discovered her husband's infidelity. It simply broke her heart. She found that her husband of 16 years had been involved in multiple affairs and the use of illegal drugs. Not only had he had many one-night stands, but he also had two long-term affairs. It felt to Becky as if her marriage was over, damaged beyond repair. In her despair, she simply stopped praying.

But she was convinced that divorce was not God's will for her, so when she read my book *Lord, Is It Warfare?* Becky found the strength to pray God's Word over her marriage. A passage of Scripture from Isaiah provided the hope she needed to go on: "He saw that there was no man, and was astonished that there was no one to intercede" (Isaiah 59:16). Reading this Scripture, she found new hope that God would intervene in her marriage. She made the hard choice to work at healing her relationship with her husband. Becky writes:

> I started daily to pray Scriptures....I inserted my name, my husband's name, the other woman's name, or anyone that was against my marriage or had bought into Satan's lies of ending our marriage. Right before my eyes God pulled the bitter roots that were causing trouble in both of us....I spent time daily in the Scriptures, praying fervently.

Beloved, God is so faithful. Becky's husband soon became a different man, with renewed love for his wife. Becky testifies that God saved their marriage. "We have now been married 23 years," she says, "and have grandchildren." She discovered the truth that the words of God are His gift and can be used as prayers to mend, heal, and save us. Not every story of marital woe has such a happy ending, but Becky's story is a reminder that we must be faithful to God's Word and walk in trust and obedience. Divorce is not the only option.

> *O Father, You know the face and the situation of the precious ones who have read this chapter. You know their pain, their guilt, their hopes, their decisions, their dreams—their desperation.*
>
> *You know the action they want to take—the escape they long to find, the conflicts without, the fears within.*
>
> *O Father, keep them from moving in any way that is not Your way. Keep them from the deception of fleshly wisdom and ungodly counsel. Speak so clearly that they will know from Your Word that this is Your way and they are to walk in it.*
>
> *Heal wounds, protect the children, turn our hearts toward you, and bring a new purity into our lives and the peace that comes with it.*
>
> *In Your name we pray, amen.*

A FINAL WORD

Now then, give me this hill country about which the LORD spoke on that day, for you heard on that day that Anakim were there, with great fortified cities; perhaps the LORD will be with me, and I will drive them out as the LORD has spoken.

So Joshua blessed him and gave Hebron to Caleb the son of Jephunneh for an inheritance. Therefore, Hebron became the inheritance of Caleb...because he followed the LORD God of Israel fully (Joshua 14:12-14).

WE'VE COVERED A LOT OF GROUND IN THIS BOOK, haven't we, Beloved?

- The role of the man and the role of the woman
- Communication between husband and wife
- The sexual relationship, with all its potential for blessing and heartache
- God's thoughts regarding divorce and remarriage
- Raising godly children in a corrupt society
- Handling finances according to God's eternal precepts

Each one of these subjects has entire books devoted to them in the Christian marketplace. In fact, there are thousands of them!

What we have done in these few pages has simply been to survey the land. More importantly, we have opened the pages of God's eternal Word together and have seen how He speaks to each one of these critical areas in marriage. He has not left us in the dark! He has not set us down without map or compass in some strange, hostile land and said, "Now find your way home. Good luck."

God has left clear instructions for us: precepts to cling to, a road to follow, specific directions that apply to every situation of life. And more than that, He has given us His own indwelling Holy Spirit as guide, counselor, and encourager through all of life. Praise His name!

As we have considered all of these priorities, however, you may have found yourself feeling overwhelmed, perhaps even discouraged. There is *so much* to know, *so much* to remember, *so many things* to learn and practice, *so many changes* that need to be made. And all the while the world around us pushes and pulls us, trying to lure us away from the path of obedience.

Joshua might have felt that way, too, as he prepared to lead Israel into the land of Canaan. It was a land of fearsome giants, wild animals, walled cities, and a population utterly hostile to God's Word and ways. But remember the verse we looked at in the introduction? The Lord told Joshua, "Just as I have been with Moses, I will be with you; I will not fail you or forsake you. Be strong and courageous....Do not tremble or be dismayed, for the LORD your God is with you wherever you go" (Joshua 1:5,6,9).

In other words, "Don't be overwhelmed, Joshua. Don't let these commands and responsibilities blow your circuits and cause you to freeze up with fear or dread. Don't be intimated by the height of the walls or the strength of the enemy. You're going to take that land little by little, day by day, mile by mile, foot by foot, and I will be with you every step of the way."

It's the same with you and me as we seek to build godly homes in a culture that is hostile to every value we hold dear. We can't change the world overnight. We can't change our marriages overnight. We can't even change ourselves overnight! But we can make a beginning, leaning on the strong arm of our Lord all the way.

A little later in the book of Joshua (and this is one of my favorite parts), we get to listen in on a conversation between Joshua and his old friend, Caleb. At the age of 85, Caleb asks Joshua's permission to conquer and settle the hill country around the village of Hebron. Never mind that a race of giants—the Anakim—were there, living in "great fortified cities." Caleb knew that he wouldn't be depending on his own strength to get the job done. "Perhaps the Lord will be with me," he told Joshua, "and I will drive them out as the Lord has spoken" (Joshua 14:12).

And that's just what he did. With the Lord's help, that 85-year-old man who cried out, "Give me this mountain!" went into the hills and carved out an inheritance for his family that would endure for generations.

That's what you and I need, Beloved. The spirit of Caleb!

Perhaps as you've read these words you've found yourself saying, "I have made so many mistakes. I have wasted so many opportunities. I've become sidetracked so many times by the things of this world. I haven't always been strong and courageous."

It isn't too late!

Whatever your situation—single, married, or divorced—you can begin today, *this very moment,* to follow the precepts of God. You may be in your first marriage or you may be in your sixth. It may look like that mountain is too hard to climb and the cliffs are too steep to scale. The challenges you face may be great and the odds against you may seem overpowering. The enemy may have strongholds dug deep into your soul, behind great, intimidating walls of stone.

But if you will just cry out, "God, give me this mountain," and begin to climb in faith, you will feel your Lord's wind at your back.

In the book of Philippians, Paul reminds us to forget what lies behind and to press forward. This is good counsel. You cannot climb a mountain while looking behind you.

My prayers are with you, precious one, as you begin your journey of faith today. Someday, in heaven, we will look back on this time—this turning point, this day of decision—and praise God that He gave us the courage and wisdom to place our marriages and our very lives back into His capable hands.

There's no other way to live…if you want a marriage without regrets.